2018
SUN SIGN
BOOK

Forecasts by
Kim Rogers-Gallagher

Cover Design by Kevin R. Brown
Editing by Andrea Neff
Interior illustration on page 19 by the Llewellyn Art Department
Shutterstock.com/54764008/© mart
Shutterstock.com/110290835/© Libellule
Shutterstock.com/122127973/© style_TTT

Copyright 2017 Llewellyn Publications
ISBN: 978-0-7387-3777-5
A Division of Llewellyn Worldwide Ltd., www.llewellyn.com
Llewellyn is a registered trademark of Llewellyn Worldwide Ltd.
2143 Wooddale Drive, Woodbury, MN 55125
Printed in the USA

Contents

2017

SEPTEMBER
S	M	T	W	T	F	S
					1	2
3	4	5	6	7	8	9
10	11	12	13	14	15	16
17	18	19	20	21	22	23
24	25	26	27	28	29	30

OCTOBER
S	M	T	W	T	F	S
1	2	3	4	5	6	7
8	9	10	11	12	13	14
15	16	17	18	19	20	21
22	23	24	25	26	27	28
29	30	31				

NOVEMBER
S	M	T	W	T	F	S
			1	2	3	4
5	6	7	8	9	10	11
12	13	14	15	16	17	18
19	20	21	22	23	24	25
26	27	28	29	30		

DECEMBER
S	M	T	W	T	F	S
					1	2
3	4	5	6	7	8	9
10	11	12	13	14	15	16
17	18	19	20	21	22	23
24	25	26	27	28	29	30
31						

2018

JANUARY
S	M	T	W	T	F	S
	1	2	3	4	5	6
7	8	9	10	11	12	13
14	15	16	17	18	19	20
21	22	23	24	25	26	27
28	29	30	31			

FEBRUARY
S	M	T	W	T	F	S
				1	2	3
4	5	6	7	8	9	10
11	12	13	14	15	16	17
18	19	20	21	22	23	24
25	26	27	28			

MARCH
S	M	T	W	T	F	S
				1	2	3
4	5	6	7	8	9	10
11	12	13	14	15	16	17
18	19	20	21	22	23	24
25	26	27	28	29	30	31

APRIL
S	M	T	W	T	F	S
1	2	3	4	5	6	7
8	9	10	11	12	13	14
15	16	17	18	19	20	21
22	23	24	25	26	27	28
29	30					

MAY
S	M	T	W	T	F	S
		1	2	3	4	5
6	7	8	9	10	11	12
13	14	15	16	17	18	19
20	21	22	23	24	25	26
27	28	29	30	31		

JUNE
S	M	T	W	T	F	S
					1	2
3	4	5	6	7	8	9
10	11	12	13	14	15	16
17	18	19	20	21	22	23
24	25	26	27	28	29	30

JULY
S	M	T	W	T	F	S
1	2	3	4	5	6	7
8	9	10	11	12	13	14
15	16	17	18	19	20	21
22	23	24	25	26	27	28
29	30	31				

AUGUST
S	M	T	W	T	F	S
			1	2	3	4
5	6	7	8	9	10	11
12	13	14	15	16	17	18
19	20	21	22	23	24	25
26	27	28	29	30	31	

SEPTEMBER
S	M	T	W	T	F	S
						1
2	3	4	5	6	7	8
9	10	11	12	13	14	15
16	17	18	19	20	21	22
23	24	25	26	27	28	29
30						

OCTOBER
S	M	T	W	T	F	S
	1	2	3	4	5	6
7	8	9	10	11	12	13
14	15	16	17	18	19	20
21	22	23	24	25	26	27
28	29	30	31			

NOVEMBER
S	M	T	W	T	F	S
				1	2	3
4	5	6	7	8	9	10
11	12	13	14	15	16	17
18	19	20	21	22	23	24
25	26	27	28	29	30	

DECEMBER
S	M	T	W	T	F	S
						1
2	3	4	5	6	7	8
9	10	11	12	13	14	15
16	17	18	19	20	21	22
23	24	25	26	27	28	29
30	31					

2019

JANUARY
S	M	T	W	T	F	S
		1	2	3	4	5
6	7	8	9	10	11	12
13	14	15	16	17	18	19
20	21	22	23	24	25	26
27	28	29	30	31		

FEBRUARY
S	M	T	W	T	F	S
					1	2
3	4	5	6	7	8	9
10	11	12	13	14	15	16
17	18	19	20	21	22	23
24	25	26	27	28		

MARCH
S	M	T	W	T	F	S
					1	2
3	4	5	6	7	8	9
10	11	12	13	14	15	16
17	18	19	20	21	22	23
24	25	26	27	28	29	30
31						

APRIL
S	M	T	W	T	F	S
	1	2	3	4	5	6
7	8	9	10	11	12	13
14	15	16	17	18	19	20
21	22	23	24	25	26	27
28	29	30				

MAY
S	M	T	W	T	F	S
			1	2	3	4
5	6	7	8	9	10	11
12	13	14	15	16	17	18
19	20	21	22	23	24	25
26	27	28	29	30	31	

JUNE
S	M	T	W	T	F	S
						1
2	3	4	5	6	7	8
9	10	11	12	13	14	15
16	17	18	19	20	21	22
23	24	25	26	27	28	29
30						

JULY
S	M	T	W	T	F	S
	1	2	3	4	5	6
7	8	9	10	11	12	13
14	15	16	17	18	19	20
21	22	23	24	25	26	27
28	29	30	31			

AUGUST
S	M	T	W	T	F	S
				1	2	3
4	5	6	7	8	9	10
11	12	13	14	15	16	17
18	19	20	21	22	23	24
25	26	27	28	29	30	31

Meet Kim Rogers-Gallagher

Kim fell in love with astrology in grade school and began her formal education close to thirty years ago. She's written hundreds of articles and columns for magazines and online publications, contributed to several astrological anthologies, and has two books of her own to her credit, *Astrology for the Light Side of the Brain* and *Astrology for the Light Side of the Future*, both available from ACS/Starcrafts Publishing. Kim is the author of daily e-mail horoscopes for astrology.com, and her work appears in the introductory sections of *Llewellyn's Astrology Calendar*, *Llewellyn's Witches' Datebook*, and *Llewellyn's Witches' Calendar*.

At the moment, Kim is having great fun on her Facebook page, facebook.com/KRGFenix, where she turns daily transits into fun celestial adventures. She's a well-known speaker who's been part of the UAC (United Astrology Conference) faculty since 1996 and has lectured at many other international conferences.

An avid animal lover, Kim occasionally receives permission from her seriously spoiled fur-kids (and her computer) to leave home for a while and indulge her ninth-house Sagg Sun by traveling for "work"—that is, talking to groups about astrology (which really isn't work at all). In typical Sagg style, Kim loves to laugh, but she also loves to chat, which comes in handy when she does private phone consultations.

She is a twenty-year "citizen" of Pennsic, an annual medieval event, where she gets to dress up in funny clothes, live in a tent, and pretend she's back in the 1300s for two weeks every year—which, oddly enough, is her idea of a good time.

Kim can be contacted at KRGPhoenix313@yahoo.com for fees regarding readings, classes, and lectures.

How to Use This Book

Hi there! Welcome to the 2018 edition of *Llewellyn's Sun Sign Book*. This book centers on Sun sign astrology—that is, the set of general attributes and characteristics that those of us born under each of the twelve particular Sun signs share. You'll find descriptions of your sign's qualities tucked into your sign's chapter, along with the type of behavior you tend to exhibit in different life situations—with regard to relationships, work situations, and the handling of money and possessions, for example. Oh, and there's a section that's dedicated to good old-fashioned fun, too, including what will bring you joy and how to make it happen.

There's a lot to be said for Sun sign astrology. First off, the Sun's sign at the time of your birth describes the qualities, talents, and traits you're here to study this time around. If you believe in reincarnation, think of it as declaring a celestial major for this lifetime. Sure, you'll learn other things along the way, but you've announced to one and all that you're primarily interested in mastering this one particular sign. Then, too, on a day when fiery, impulsive energies are making astrological headlines, if you're a fiery and/or impulsive sign yourself—like Aries or Aquarius, for example—it's easy to imagine how you'll take to the astrological weather a lot more easily than a practical, steady-handed sign like Taurus or Virgo.

Obviously, astrology comes in handy, for a variety of reasons. Getting to know your "natal" Sun sign (the sign the Sun was in when you were born) can most certainly give you the edge you need to ace the final and move on to the next celestial course level—or basically to succeed in life, and maybe even earn a few bonus points toward next semester. Using astrology on a daily basis nicely accelerates the process.

Now, there are eight other planets and one lovely Moon in our neck of the celestial woods, all of which also play into our personalities. The sign that was on the eastern horizon at the moment of your birth—otherwise known as your *Ascendant*, or *rising sign*—is another indicator of your personality traits. Honestly, there are all kinds of cosmic factors, so if it's an in-depth, personal analysis you're after, a professional astrologer is the only way to go—especially if you're curious about relationships, past lives, future trends, or even the right time to schedule an important life event. Professional astrologers calculate your birth chart—again, the "natal" chart—based on the date, place, and exact time of your birth—which allows for a far more personal and specific reading. In the meantime, however, in addition to reading up on your Sun sign, you can use the tables on pages 8 and 9 to find the sign of your Ascendant. (These tables, however, are approximate and tailored to those of us born in North America, so if the traits of your Ascendant don't sound familiar, check out the sign directly before or after.)

There are three sections to each sign chapter in this book. As I already mentioned, the first section describes personality traits, and while it's fun to read your own, don't forget to check out the other Sun signs. (Oh, and do feel free to mention any rather striking behavioral similarities to skeptics. It's great fun to watch a Scorpio's reaction when you tell them they're astrologically known as "the sexy sign," or a Gemini when you thank them for creating the concept of multitasking.)

The second section is entitled "The Year Ahead" for each sign. Through considering the movements of the outer planets (Uranus, Neptune, and Pluto), the eclipses, and any other outstanding celestial movements, this segment will provide you with the big picture of the year—or basically the broad strokes of what to expect, no matter who you are or where you are, collectively speaking.

The third section includes monthly forecasts, along with rewarding days and challenging days, basically a heads-up designed to alert you to potentially easy times as well as potentially tricky times.

At the end of every chapter you'll find an Action Table, providing general information about the best time to indulge in certain activities. Please note that these are only suggestions. Don't hold yourself back or rush into anything your intuition doesn't wholeheartedly agree with—and again, when in doubt, find yourself a professional.

Well, that's it. I hope that you enjoy this book, and that being aware of the astrological energies of 2018 helps you create a year full of fabulous memories!

Ascendant Table

Your Sun Sign	Your Time of Birth						
	6–8 am	8–10 am	10 am–Noon	Noon–2 pm	2–4 pm	4–6 pm
Aries	Taurus	Gemini	Cancer	Leo	Virgo	Libra
Taurus	Gemini	Cancer	Leo	Virgo	Libra	Scorpio
Gemini	Cancer	Leo	Virgo	Libra	Scorpio	Sagittarius
Cancer	Leo	Virgo	Libra	Scorpio	Sagittarius	Capricorn
Leo	Virgo	Libra	Scorpio	Sagittarius	Capricorn	Aquarius
Virgo	Libra	Scorpio	Sagittarius	Capricorn	Aquarius	Pisces
Libra	Scorpio	Sagittarius	Capricorn	Aquarius	Pisces	Aries
Scorpio	Sagittarius	Capricorn	Aquarius	Pisces	Aries	Taurus
Sagittarius	Capricorn	Aquarius	Pisces	Aries	Taurus	Gemini
Capricorn	Aquarius	Pisces	Aries	Taurus	Gemini	Cancer
Aquarius	Pisces	Aries	Taurus	Gemini	Cancer	Leo
Pisces	Aries	Taurus	Gemini	Cancer	Leo	Virgo

Your Sun Sign	Your Time of Birth					
	6–8 pm	8–10 pm	10 pm–Midnight	Midnight–2 am	2–4 am	4–6 am
Aries	Scorpio	Sagittarius	Capricorn	Aquarius	Pisces	Aries
Taurus	Sagittarius	Capricorn	Aquarius	Pisces	Aries	Taurus
Gemini	Capricorn	Aquarius	Pisces	Aries	Taurus	Gemini
Cancer	Aquarius	Pisces	Aries	Taurus	Gemini	Cancer
Leo	Pisces	Aries	Taurus	Gemini	Cancer	Leo
Virgo	Aries	Taurus	Gemini	Cancer	Leo	Virgo
Libra	Taurus	Gemini	Cancer	Leo	Virgo	Libra
Scorpio	Gemini	Cancer	Leo	Virgo	Libra	Scorpio
Sagittarius	Cancer	Leo	Virgo	Libra	Scorpio	Sagittarius
Capricorn	Leo	Virgo	Libra	Scorpio	Sagittarius	Capricorn
Aquarius	Virgo	Libra	Scorpio	Sagittarius	Capricorn	Aquarius
Pisces	Libra	Scorpio	Sagittarius	Capricorn	Aquarius	Pisces

How to use this table: 1. Find your Sun sign in the left column.

2. Find your approximate birth time in a vertical column.

3. Line up your Sun sign and birth time to find your Ascendant.

This table will give you an approximation of your Ascendant. If you feel that the sign listed as your Ascendant is incorrect, try the one either before or after the listed sign. It is difficult to determine your exact Ascendant without a complete natal chart.

Astrology Basics

Natal astrology is done by freeze-framing the solar system at the moment of your birth, from the perspective of your birth place. This creates a circular map that looks like a pie sliced into twelve pieces. It shows where every heavenly body we're capable of seeing was located when you arrived. Basically, it's your astrological tool kit, and it can't be replicated more than once in thousands of years. This is why we astrologers are so darn insistent about the need for you to either dig your birth certificate out of that box of ancient paperwork in the back of your closet or get a copy of it from the county clerk's office where you were born. Natal astrology, as interpreted by a professional astrologer, is done exactly and precisely for you and no one else. It shows your inherent traits, talents, and challenges. Comparing the planets' current positions to their positions in your birth chart allows astrologers to help you understand the celestial trends at work in your life—and most importantly, how you can put each astrological energy to a positive, productive use.

Let's take a look at the four main components of every astrology chart.

Planets

The planets represent the needs or urges we all experience once we hop off the Evolutionary Express and take up residence inside a human body. For example, the Sun is your urge to shine and be creative, the Moon is your need to express emotions, Mercury is in charge of how you communicate and navigate, and Venus is all about who and what you love—and more importantly, how you love.

Signs

The sign a planet occupies is like a costume or uniform. It describes how you'll go about acting on your needs and urges. If you have Venus in fiery, impulsive Aries, for example, and you're attracted to a complete stranger across the room, you won't wait for them to come to you. You'll walk over and introduce yourself the second the urge strikes you. Venus in intense, sexy Scorpio, however? Well, that's a different story. In this case, you'll keep looking at a prospective beloved until they finally give in, cross the room, and beg you to explain why you've been staring at them for the past couple of hours.

Houses

The houses represent the different sides of our personalities that emerge in different life situations. For example, think of how very different you act when you're with an authority figure as opposed to how you act with a lover or when you're with your BFF.

Aspects

The aspects describe the distance from one planet to another in a geometric angle. If you were born when Mercury was 90 degrees from Jupiter, for example, this aspect is called a square. Each unique angular relationship causes the planets involved to interact differently.

Meet the Planets

The planets represent energy sources. The Sun is our source of creativity, the Moon is our emotional warehouse, and Venus describes who and what we love and are attracted to—not to mention why and how we go about getting it and keeping it.

Sun

The Sun is the head honcho in your chart. It represents your life's mission—what will give you joy, keep you young, and never fail to arouse your curiosity. Oddly enough, you weren't born knowing the qualities of the sign the Sun was in when you were born. You're here to learn the traits, talents, and characteristics of the sign you chose—and rest assured, each of the twelve is its own marvelous adventure! Since the Sun is The Big Boss, all of the other planets, including the Moon, are the Sun's staff, all there to help the boss by helping you master your particular area of expertise. Back in the day, the words from a song in a recruitment commercial struck me as a perfect way to describe our Sun's quest: "Be all that you can be. Keep on reaching. Keep on growing. Find your future." The accompanying music was energizing, robust, and exciting, full of anticipation and eagerness. When you feel enthused, motivated, and stimulated, that's your Sun letting you know you're on the right path.

Moon

If you want to understand this lovely silver orb, go outside when the Moon is nice and full, find yourself a comfy perch, sit still, and have a nice, long look at her. The Moon inspires us to dream, wish, and sigh, to reminisce, ruminate, and remember. She's the Queen of Emotions, the astrological purveyor of feelings and reactions. In your natal chart, the condition of the Moon—that is, the sign and house she's in and the connections she makes with your other planets—shows how you'll deal with whatever life tosses your way—how you'll respond, how you'll cope, and how you'll pull it all together to move on after a crisis. She's where your instincts and hunches come from, and the source of every gut feeling and premonition. The Moon describes your childhood home, your relationship with your mother, your attitude toward childbearing and children in general, and what you're looking for in a home. She shows what makes you feel safe, warm, comfy, and loved. On a daily basis, the Moon describes the collective mood.

Mercury

Next time you pass by a flower shop, take a look at the FTD logo by the door. That fellow with the wings on his head and his feet is Mercury, the ancient Messenger of the Gods. He's always been a very busy guy. Back in the day, his job was to shuttle messages back and forth between the gods and goddesses and we mere mortals—obviously, no easy feat. Nowadays, however, Mercury is even busier. With computers, cell phones, social media, and perhaps even the occasional human-to-human interaction to keep track of—well, he must be just exhausted. In a nutshell, he's the astrological energy in charge of communication, navigation, and travel, so he's still nicely represented by that winged image. He's also the guy in charge of the five senses, so no matter what you're aware of right now, be it taste, touch, sound, smell, or sight—well, that's because Mercury is bringing it to you, live. At any rate, you'll hear about him most when someone mentions that Mercury is retrograde, but even though these periods have come to be blamed for all sorts of problems, there's really no cause for alarm. Mercury turns retrograde (or, basically, appears to move backwards from our perspective here on Earth) every three months for three weeks, giving us all a chance for a do-over—and who among us has never needed one of those?

Venus

So, if it's Mercury that makes you aware of your environment, who allows you to experience all kinds of sensory sensations via the five senses? Who's in charge of your preferences in each department? That delightful task falls under the jurisdiction of the lovely lady Venus, who describes the physical experiences that are the absolute best—in your book, anyway. That goes for the music and art you find most pleasing, the food and beverages you can't get enough of, and the scents you consider the sweetest of all—including the collar of the shirt your loved one recently wore. Touch, of course, is also a sense that can be quite delightful to experience. Think of how happy your fingers are when you're stroking your pet's fur, or the delicious feel of cool bed sheets when you slip between them after an especially tough day. Venus brings all those sensations together in one wonderful package, working her magic through love of the romantic kind, most memorably experienced through intimate physical interaction with an "other." Still, your preferences in any relationship also fall under Venus's job description.

Mars

Mars turns up the heat, amps up the energy, and gets your show on the road. Whenever you hear yourself grunt, growl, or grumble—or just make any old "rrrrr" sound in general—your natal Mars has just made an appearance. Adrenaline is his business and passion is his specialty. He's the ancient God of War—a hot-headed guy who's famous for having at it with his sword first and asking questions later. In the extreme, Mars is often in the neighborhood when violent events occur, and accidents, too. He's in charge of self-assertion, aggression, and pursuit, and one glance at his heavenly appearance explains why. He's The Red Planet, after all—and just think of all the expressions about anger and passion that include references to the color red or the element of fire: "Grrr!" "Seeing red." "Hot under the collar." "All fired up." "Hot and heavy." You get the idea. Mars is your own personal warrior. He describes how you'll react when you're threatened, excited, or angry.

Jupiter

Santa Claus. Luciano Pavarotti with a great big smile on his face as he belts out an amazing aria. Your favorite uncle who drinks too much, eats too much, and laughs far too loud—yet never fails to go well above and beyond the call of duty for you when you need him. They're all perfect examples of Jupiter, the King of the Gods, the giver of all things good, and the source of extravagance, generosity, excess, and benevolence in our little corner of the Universe. He and Venus are the heavens' two most popular planets—for obvious reasons. Venus makes us feel good. Jupiter makes us feel absolutely over-the-top excellent. In Jupiter's book, if one is good, it only stands to reason that two would be better, and following that logic, ten would be just outstanding. His favorite words are "too," "many," and "much." Expansions, increases, and enlargements—or basically, just the whole concept of growth—are all his doing. Now, unbeknownst to this merry old fellow, there really is such a thing as too much of a good thing—but let's not pop his goodhearted bubble. Wherever Jupiter is in your chart, you'll be prone to go overboard, take it to the limit, and push the envelope as far as you possibly can. Sure, you might get a bit out of control every now and then, but if envelopes weren't ever pushed, we'd never know the joys of optimism, generosity, or sudden, contagious bursts of laughter.

Saturn

Jupiter expands. Saturn contracts. Jupiter encourages growth. Saturn, on the other hand, uses those rings he's so famous for to restrict growth. His favorite word is "no," but he's also very fond of "wait," "stop," and "don't even think about it." He's ultra-realistic and quite pessimistic, a cautious, careful curmudgeon who guards and protects you by not allowing you to move too quickly or act too recklessly. He insists on preparation and doesn't take kindly when we blow off responsibilities and duties. As you can imagine, Saturn is not nearly as popular as Venus and Jupiter, mainly because none of us like to be told we can't do what we want to do when we want to do it. Still, without someone who acted out his part when you were too young to know better, you might have dashed across the street without stopping to check for traffic first, and—well, you get the point. Saturn encourages frugality, moderation, thoughtfulness, and self-restraint, all necessary habits to learn if you want to play nice with the other grown-ups. He's also quite fond of building things, which necessarily starts with solid foundations and structures that are built to last.

Uranus

Say hello to Mr. Unpredictable himself, the heavens' wild card—to say the very least. He's the kind of guy who claims responsibility for lightning strikes, be they literal or symbolic. Winning the lottery, love at first sight, accidents, and anything seemingly coincidental that strikes you as oddly well-timed are all examples of Uranus's handiwork. He's a rebellious, headstrong energy, so wherever he is in your chart, you'll be defiant, headstrong, and quite unwilling to play by the rules, which he thinks of as merely annoying suggestions that far too many humans adhere to. Uranus is here to inspire you to be yourself—exactly as you are, with no explanations and no apologies whatsoever. He motivates you to develop qualities such as independence, ingenuity, and individuality—and with this guy in the neighborhood, if anyone or anything gets in the way, you'll 86 them. Period. Buh-bye now. The good news is that when you allow this freedom-loving energy to guide you, you discover something new and exciting about yourself on a daily basis—at least. The tough but entirely doable part is keeping him reined in tightly enough to earn your daily bread and form lasting relationships with like-minded others.

Neptune

Neptune is the uncontested Mistress of Disguise and Illusion in the solar system, beautifully evidenced by the fact that this ultra-feminine energy has been masquerading as a male god for as long as gods and goddesses have been around. Just take a look at the qualities she bestows: compassion, spirituality, intuition, wistfulness, and nostalgia. Basically, whenever your subconscious whispers, it's in Neptune's voice. She activates your antennae and sends you subtle, invisible, and yet highly powerful messages about everyone you cross paths with, no matter how fleeting the encounter. I often picture her as Glinda the Good Witch from *The Wizard of Oz*, who rode around in a pink bubble, singing happy little songs and casting wonderful, helpful spells. Think "enchantment"—oh, and "glamour," too, which, by the way, was the old-time term for a magical spell cast upon someone to change their appearance. Nowadays, glamour is often thought of as a rather idealized and often artificial type of beauty brought about by cosmetics and airbrushing, but Neptune is still in charge, and her magic still works. When this energy is wrongfully used, deceptions, delusions and fraud can result—and since she's so fond of ditching reality, it's easy to become a bit too fond of escape hatches like drugs and alcohol. Still, Neptune inspires romance, nostalgia, and sentimentality, and she's quite fond of dreams and fantasies, too—and what would life be like without all of that?

Pluto

Picture all the gods and goddesses in the heavens above us living happily in a huge mansion in the clouds. Then imagine that Pluto's place is at the bottom of the cellar stairs, and on the cellar door (which is in the kitchen, of course) a sign reads "Keep out. Working on Darwin Awards." That's where Pluto would live—and that's the attitude he'd have. He's in charge of unseen cycles—life, death, and rebirth. Obviously, he's not an emotional kind of guy. Whatever Pluto initiates really has to happen. He's dark, deep, and mysterious—and inevitable. So yes, Darth Vader does come to mind, if for no other reason than because of James Earl Jones's amazing, compelling voice. Still, this intense, penetrating, and oh-so-thorough energy has a lot more to offer. Pluto's in charge of all those categories we humans aren't fond of—like death and decay, for example—but on the less drastic side, he also inspires recycling, repurposing, and reusing. In your chart, Pluto represents a place where you'll be ready to go big or go home, where investing all or nothing is a given. When a crisis comes up—when you need to be totally committed and totally authentic to who you really are to get through it—that's when you'll meet your Pluto. Power struggles and mind games, however—well, you can also expect those pesky types of things wherever Pluto is located.

A Word about Retrogrades

"Retrograde" sounds like a bad thing, but I'm here to tell you that it isn't. In a nutshell, retrograde means that from our perspective here on Earth, a planet appears to be moving in reverse. Of course, planets don't ever actually back up, but the energy of retrograde planets is often held back, delayed, or hindered in some way. For example, when Mercury—the ruler of communication and navigation—appears to be retrograde, it's tough to get from point A to point B without a snafu, and it's equally hard to get a straight answer. Things just don't seem to go as planned. But it only makes sense. Since Mercury is the planet in charge of conversation and movement, when he's moving backward—well, imagine driving a car that only had reverse. Yep. It wouldn't be easy. Still, if that's all you had to work with, you'd eventually find a way to get where you wanted to go. That's how all retrograde energies work. If you have retrograde planets in your natal chart, don't rush them. These energies may need a bit more time to function well for you than other natal planets, but if you're patient, talk about having an edge! You'll know these planets inside and out. On a collective basis, think of the time when a planet moves retrograde as a chance for a celestial do-over.

Signs of the Zodiac

The sign a planet is "wearing" really says it all. It's the costume an actor wears that helps them act out the role they're playing. It's the style, manner, or approach you'll use in each life department—whether you're being creative on a canvas, gushing over a new lover, or applying for a management position. Each of the signs belongs to an element, a quality, and a gender, as follows.

Elements

The four elements—fire, earth, air, and water—describe a sign's aims. Fire signs are spiritual, impulsive energies. Earth signs are tightly connected to the material plane. Air signs are cerebral, intellectual creatures, and water signs rule the emotional side of life.

Qualities

The three qualities—cardinal, fixed, and mutable—describe a sign's energy. Cardinal signs are tailor-made for beginnings. Fixed energies are solid, just as they sound, and are quite determined to finish what they start. Mutable energies are flexible and accommodating but can also be scattered or unstable.

Genders

The genders—masculine and feminine—describe whether the energy attracts (feminine) or pursues (masculine) what it wants.

The Twelve Signs

Here's a quick rundown of the twelve zodiac signs.

Aries

Aries planets are hotheads. They're built from go-getter cardinal energy and fast-acting fire. Needless to say, Aries energy is impatient, energetic, and oh-so-willing to try anything once.

Taurus

Taurus planets are aptly represented by the symbol of the bull. They're earth creatures, very tightly connected to the material plane, and fixed—which means they're pretty much immovable when they don't want to act.

Sequence	Sign	Glyph	Ruling Planet	Symbol
1	Aries	♈	Mars	Ram
2	Taurus	♉	Venus	Bull
3	Gemini	♊	Mercury	Twins
4	Cancer	♋	Moon	Crab
5	Leo	♌	Sun	Lion
6	Virgo	♍	Mercury	Virgin
7	Libra	♎	Venus	Scales
8	Scorpio	♏	Pluto	Scorpion
9	Sagittarius	♐	Jupiter	Archer
10	Capricorn	♑	Saturn	Goat
11	Aquarius	♒	Uranus	Water Bearer
12	Pisces	♓	Neptune	Fish

Gemini

As an intellectual air sign that's mutable and interested in anything new, Gemini energy is eternally curious—and quite easily distracted. Gemini planets live in the moment and are expert multitaskers.

Cancer

Cancer is a water sign that runs on its emotions, and since it's also part of the cardinal family, it's packed with the kind of start-up energy that's perfect for raising a family and building a home.

Leo

This determined, fixed sign is part of the fire family. As fires go, think of Leo planets as bonfires of energy—and just try to tear your eyes away. Leo's symbol is the lion, and it's no accident. Leo planets care very much about their familial pride—and about their personal pride.

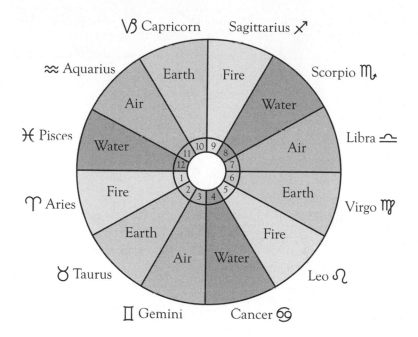

Virgo

Virgo is mutable and therefore easily able to switch channels when necessary. It's part of the earth family and connected to the material world (like Taurus). Virgo energy loves to work, organize, and sort, but most of all, to fix what's broken.

Libra

This communicative air sign runs on high. It's cardinal, so when it comes to making connections, Libra is second to none. Libra planets are people pleasers and the honorary cruise directors of the zodiac, and are as charming and accommodating as the day is long.

Scorpio

Scorpio is of the water element and a highly emotional creature. Scorpio energy is fixed, too, so feelings are tough to shake and obsessions are easy to come by. Planets in this sign are devoted and determined and can be absolutely relentless.

Sagittarius

Sagittarius has all the fire of Aries and Leo but, due to its mutable nature, tends to be distracted, spreading its energy among projects and interests. Think of Sagittarius energy as a series of red-hot brushfires, firing up and dying down and firing up again in a new location.

Capricorn

As the third earth sign, Capricorn is concerned with reality and practicality, complete with all the rules and regulations it takes to build and maintain a life here on Planet Number Three. Capricorn energy takes charge and assumes responsibility quite easily.

Aquarius

The last of the three communicative air signs, Aquarius prefers mingling and interacting with a group via friendships. Freedom-loving Aquarius energy won't be restricted—not for long, anyway—and is willing to return the favor, in any and all relationships.

Pisces

Watery Pisces runs on its emotions—and even more so on its intuition, which is second to none. This mutable, flexible sign is aptly represented by the constant fluctuating movements of its symbol, the two fish.

Aspects

Astrological aspects describe the relationships between planets and important points in a horoscope chart. Basically, they're the mathematical angles that measure the distance between two or more planets. Planets in square aspect are 90 degrees apart, planets in opposition are 180 degrees apart, and so forth. Each of these aspect relationships seems to link energies in a very different way. For example, if two planets are in square aspect, think of what you know about "squaring off," and you'll understand exactly how they're interacting. Think of aspects as a way of describing the type of conversation going on between celestial bodies.

Here's a brief description of the five major aspects.

Conjunction

When two planets are within a few degrees of each other, they're joined at the hip. The conjunction is often called the aspect of "fusion," since the energies involved always act together.

Sextile

Planets in sextile are linked by a 60-degree angle, creating an exciting, stimulating astrological "conversation." These planets encourage, arouse, and excite each other.

Square

The square aspect is created by linking energies in a 90-degree angle—which tends to be testy and sometimes irritating but always action-oriented.

Trine

The trine is the "lazy" aspect. When planets are in this 120-degree angle, they get along so well that they often aren't motivated to do much. Trines make things easy—too easy, at times—but they're also known for being quite lucky.

Opposition

Oppositions exist between planets that are literally opposite one another. Think about seesaws and playing tug-of-war, and you'll understand how these energies get along. Sure, it can be a power struggle at times, but balance is the key.

2018 at a Glance

First of all, consider this: both Pluto and Saturn will spend the year in Saturn's sign, Capricorn—the sign that's most concerned with rules, regulations, and consequences. What a team! These two are plenty potent on their own, but working in tandem, they'll be positively unbeatable. Look at it this way: Sure, Pluto is the Lord of the Underworld, but he doesn't just bury things—he digs them up, too, and enjoys that even more. His new partner, Saturn, just loves to deal with reality, so no matter what Pluto unearths, Saturn will find a way to make an official announcement about it. Saturn is all about responsibility, respectability, and following the rules. So it's not much of a stretch to imagine this team unearthing and exposing all kinds of scandals and conspiracy theories—some of which, as per their joint fondness for the truth and nothing but the truth, will be proven accurate. On the other hand, with these two on what amounts to an astrological fact-finding mission, anything that's unsavory, illegal, or dishonest will emerge, via yet more official announcements, most likely accompanied by much pomp and ceremony—and rest assured that many feet will be held to the fire. Expect ongoing legal battles in social and political arenas on a grand scale, and for long-standing laws to be challenged and changed.

Interestingly, Saturn set off for Capricorn about a week before 2018 began, marking the end of two and half years in Sagittarius, a sign that inspires an appreciation for differing cultures and ethnicities. At its best, Sagittarius moves us to recognize how our societal and philosophical differences can make us all so interesting to one another. Saturn, however, is the ringed planet, so he's quite fond of security—hence all this talk about building "the Wall." Since Sagittarius is so fond of accents and the "foreigners" who own them, however, it's also no surprise that we are collectively dealing with a mass human migration that will change the face of our planet's population concentration—via the Syrian refugee crisis. Once Saturn is settled comfortably in Capricorn and on secure home turf, however, it may be easier for the world in general to feel secure enough to allow new lines to be drawn.

And then there's Neptune—who's also on home turf, aka Pisces—and also operating quite powerfully. Neptune rules fluids and gases, like water and oil, but she's also in charge of invisibility. She set off for Pisces back in 2011, after years in electronic Aquarius, helping to break down the boundaries that electronically separated us. What emerged was wireless technology, via cordless phones and computers. Neptune's most amazing accomplishment to date is "the cloud," which is basically an imaginary place where all manner of data is stored—and accessible. And then there's the emergence of "fake news" and "alternative facts," both of which have Neptune's stamp all over them. Oddly enough, clouds are illusions made from raindrops, so it's only natural that Neptune would be in charge of creating them—and given that "leaks" of information are also such a hot topic, it's interesting to note that clouds have no boundaries. The issues of water and oil will also continue to be on our collective minds, well past the time the Dakota Pipeline defenders fade from our memories.

Here in the USA, the really big news will be the Solar Eclipse on February 15 at 27 degrees Aquarius, which is very close to the US Moon used in many US charts. Eclipses are sudden-acting lunations that activate the minds and hearts of the citizens of a country. This time around, a sudden event could actually mobilize us to come together—which, of course, is what every country needs.

2018 SUN SIGN BOOK

Forecasts by

Kim Rogers-Gallagher

Aries

The Ram
March 21 to April 20

♈

Element: Fire	Glyph: Ram's head
Quality: Cardinal	Anatomy: Head, face, throat
Polarity: Yang/masculine	Colors: Red, white
Planetary Ruler: Mars	Animal: Ram
Meditation: I build on my strengths	Myths/Legends: Artemis, Jason and the Golden Fleece
Gemstone: Diamond	House: First
Power Stones: Bloodstone, carnelian, ruby	Opposite Sign: Libra
	Flower: Geranium
Key Phrase: I am	Keyword: Initiative

The Aries Personality

Your Strengths, Gifts, and Challenges

Your sign is ruled by Mars, once the ancient Roman God of War, now known as the Red Planet. Obviously, he's a hot-blooded kind of guy, so it's no surprise that you're pretty darn fiery yourself. You're famously spontaneous—okay, and extremely impatient, too. You want what you want, and you want it yesterday. Failing yesterday, now will do, but it has to be right now. You love to act on impulse—sometimes just to see what will happen—and you adore challenges and competitions. In a nutshell, kids, you're adrenaline junkies.

Your astrological mission is to show us what passion looks like—in all its forms. Assertion. Aggression. Anger. That may often mean demonstrating what can happen when a slightly heated exchange of words turns into an argument—in rapid-fire fashion. When you're angry, those who know you will simply step aside, duck for cover, and let you vent. Fortunately, that usually doesn't take very long. You're a red-hot heat-seeking missile that moves from point A to point B far too quickly to ever miss a target—and you don't even recognize obstacles, much less allow them to get in your way. Once that's been accomplished, you're good to go.

Of course, passion can also be quite lovely, especially when it happens unpredictably—say, for example, when you meet someone you're sure is the love of your life at the produce stand around the corner and adamantly refuse to let them leave without getting their number. The good news is that you're far too impatient to play games with others, so while you can be a tad intimidating at times, your particular brand of straightforward and sometimes brutal honesty only makes you more endearing. As you get a few years under your belt, you'll learn to control your temper by doling it out carefully and only when it's truly warranted. In the meantime, if your temper turns volatile or physical—well, you'll have to put a leash on it. Remember, discretion is the better part of valor.

Romance and Other Relationships

Talk about a fabulous playmate, Aries! You're game for just about any adventure at just about any time and equally eager to try anything once. The thing is, adventures aren't nearly as much fun if you're adventuring alone. This means that until you find the perfect partner or friend, you'll constantly search for others who aren't afraid to accept a dare, have a healthy debate, or indulge in physically challenging activities. Keep all that in mind if you're partner-shopping right now, and interview new prospects carefully. Be aware of the fact that you're not just looking for a lover. You're also out to find someone who'll take your dare and raise you one more. You're after someone who'll compete with you—or at least try to keep up.

Once you find the right person, you can be quite loyal, sometimes to a fault. And while you may have a roving eye, you usually don't act on it if your needs are already being met. Until you're happily attached, however, you'll think of dating as either a challenge or a hunt. Keep an eye out for charming Librans, your opposite sign, astrologically famous for all-out devotion to their significant others. The other fire signs—fun-loving Sagittarius and ultra-playful Leo—make fabulous playmates and passionate lovers, with an added bonus: they're kindred spirits, so they'll "get" you, even when you're being argumentative. You often tend to be drawn to sexy, intense Scorpios because they're not famous for shying away from a challenge and their passion rivals your own. But be warned—when you two do battle, forgiving and forgetting won't come easily.

Career and Work

You guys are truly amazing, Aries. You're the warriors of the zodiac, never afraid to run straight toward whatever it is that others are fleeing, and, never, ever afraid to stand your ground against an adversary. Obviously, you're natural-born enforcers, set and ready to jump to the defense—and even more so, to the offense—at a moment's notice. It's the adrenaline thing. All this makes you the perfect candidates for occupations that involve wearing uniforms—say, firefighters, EMT workers, police, or security. Basically, any career that involves fire, assertion, courage during urgent situations, or intense physical exercise will suit you just fine. But since your ruling planet, Mars, has everything to do with cutting tools—blades of any kind, that is—you're also often found working in the medical/surgical fields, professions that allow you to wield weapons while wearing a white coat and/or scrubs—a uniform, that is. Since you have a bit of a temper, you do tend to storm off occasionally or even quit your job at a moment's notice. That said, always have plan B ready to go.

Money and Possessions

Money is an odd subject for you, Aries. On the one hand, in keeping with your spontaneous nature, you may be a salesperson's dream come true—over-the-top impulsive, that is, and always willing to pull out your plastic, even if you're perfectly aware that finding a way to pay the bill next month will be stressful. On the other hand, you may be a penny pincher, determined to stick out the whole shopping venture until you find exactly what you want for the price you're willing to pay. Either way, you'll treat shopping as if it were a hunt, and regardless of how quickly or slowly it happens, you won't buy unless and until you know you'll be going home with a proper trophy.

Your Lighter Side

What's fun for you? Well, for starters, as per the personal preferences of action-oriented Mars—your ultra-competitive ruling planet—anything that involves contests or competition is most definitely fun for you. These pastimes don't necessarily have to be physical, as long as they amp up your blood pressure, but winning a board game isn't quite as exciting as bungee jumping. It all depends on what you're in the mood for. If you're feeling the need to vent, incorporating activities that tire you out into your leisure time isn't a bad idea. It seems that paintball is quite popular with many members of your tribe, as are shoot-'em-up cyber-games. Skydiving? Yep. Riding your motorcycle en route to skydive while standing on the seat? On one foot? Wouldn't surprise me at all. Kindly do keep in mind that there are others who love you, though, and think of them before you try anything risky without a proper safety net.

Aries Celebrities

Feisty? Oh my, yes! Fiery? Yep. Unabashedly confrontational, too. If you don't already identify with those descriptions, check out this list of living examples—the "who's who" in Aries Land: Lucy Lawless ("Zena"), Russell Crowe, Steven Seagal, and real-life warrior General Colin Powell. Then there's Bette Davis, whose most cherished possession was reported to be an embroidered pillow that read "No guts, no glory," and who did battle constantly with her famous also-Aries adversary Joan Crawford. But then, there's Maya Angelou and Billie Holiday, two shining examples of how to be yourself, with no apologies—a very Aries trait. And speaking of confrontational, how about Piers Morgan, Alec Baldwin, and Rosie

O'Donnell, none of whom will buckle or cave when an opponent arrives. Add Mariah Carey, Lady Gaga, Aretha Franklin, and Eddie Murphy to that list. Oh, and talk about uniforms! Captain James T. Kirk (William Shatner) and Mr. Spock (Leonard Nimoy) are both card-carrying Aries.

The Year Ahead for Aries

First off, Aries, let's talk about the upcoming adventures of your astrological ruler—Mars himself. This fiery fellow will make major planetary headlines this year due to the fact that he's scheduled to spend no less than five full months storming through just one sign. He ordinarily races through a sign in just two months, so this is most definitely a big deal, celestially speaking. But you're Mars's child, already hot-headed and impulsive, and since the sign Mars will be activating is none other than startling, rebellious, and oh-so-impulsive Aquarius, you should probably fasten your seat belt, and warn those you love to do the same.

Please do make note of the following dates: May 16 through August 12, and September 10 through November 15. Let it be known that during these times, kids, you'll be a lot harder to tame—yes, even in polite company. No, especially in polite company—and most especially if that polite company happens to be a group of people you're pretty much over and very much in the mood to shock, astound, and ditch, once and for all. If they've been holding you back from becoming who you want to be, don't even think twice, and have some fun making your exit, too. If you opt to stay with a current peer circle, it will most likely be because they've asked you to take over the controls. You can still expect some serious fireworks, but at least you'll be steering through them. Above all else, keep in mind that there is a lot of truth to the old adage that we are the company we keep. Feeling like you no longer fit isn't a bad thing. It means you've grown, and it's time to either find a new tribe or help guide the one you already belong to.

That sentiment will be backed up by Jupiter, who'll move through uber-intense Scorpio and your solar eighth house this year, urging you, in no uncertain terms, to take charge—of everything. Sure, it sounds a bit overwhelming, and the amount of responsibility tossed your way may feel pretty darn overwhelming, too, but you'll be astrologically well equipped to deal with the situation(s) in a civil, businesslike way, so not to worry. Keep your cool, keep your nose to the grindstone, and all will be well. Besides, as of November 19, Jupiter will be in Sagittarius and your solar ninth house, helping you to expand your horizons and to experience life during 2019. Sounds like fun, doesn't it? So what's a little hard work in the meantime?

Saturn

Saturn is set to spend the year in hardworking Capricorn and your solar tenth house of higher-ups and authority figures. If you've been out to impress an elder or superior, you won't have to work much harder or much longer to accomplish that aim. In fact, you may discover that the person you're trying to make an impression on has already noticed you—big time. If your antennae have already told you that you're under surveillance—for positive reasons—you're probably already on your best behavior. In that case, carry on, accept all challenges presented to you, and make it your mission to force the powers that be to take notice of your diligence as well as the quality of your work. This planet just loves to present us with dilemmas to be solved and hoops to be jumped through en route to proving ourselves worthy of rewards. Your mission now is to work hard, pay your dues, and surround yourself with others who recognize your potential and are willing to help you along the career path you've chosen. Telling you to be patient is futile, but if you can keep yourself busy and productive for just a bit longer, those much-awaited rewards will come along far more quickly.

Uranus

On May 16, Aries, after seven years in your sign, unpredictable Uranus will move into stubborn, hard-headed, and famously dependable Taurus. What a mix, huh? This transit will put this extremely disruptive energy in an extremely stable sign—in your solar second house of finances, no less. Oh, and this will continue for the next seven years, by the way. Obviously, if you haven't already prepared yourself for the possibility of sudden, unseen, and possibly severe financial changes, better get on that right now. One never knows what Uranus will bring along when he visits, but the unexpected will most certainly be on the agenda. The good news is that over the past seven years that Uranus has spent in your sign, you've become accustomed to dealing with all manner of last-minute turn-arounds and surprising announcements—so, if nothing else, you've most certainly learned the art of flexibility. That will come in handy over the next seven years, as your main challenge becomes adapting to sudden and unexpected changes with regard to possessions and money matters. The good news is that you'll have until May 16 to put a financial safety net in place—so what are you waiting for?

Neptune

Just as she has since April of 2011, Neptune will spend all of her time in 2018 in your solar twelfth house of downtime, privacy, and secrets, Aries, so expect something or someone from the past to emerge—or should I say reemerge—for better or worse. The tricky news is that you've probably already buried this situation or relationship, so being faced with it once again won't be fun. The thing is, you may be forced to make a move—to bring an immediate, obvious end to a relationship you may have been hoping to "ghost" away. The good news is that the more you do what comes naturally—that is, let your anger, passion, and frustration fly—the quicker the whole thing will be resolved. If there's anyone on the planet who just won't tolerate being delayed or held back, it's you, Aries. Don't let misplaced loyalty get between you and your freedom. Let the truth be known to all, settle the matter, and move on. There are brand-new dreams and fantasies out there. Look to the future, not the past. That goes double for those of you born from March 30 through April 7, since Neptune will also form a semisextile aspect to your Sun. Pay attention to your intuition, and when reality becomes a bit too harsh, take some time alone to recharge your batteries.

Pluto

Pluto has been in your solar tenth house of career matters and dealings with authority figures for a decade now, Aries, and over the course of that time, you've learned one lesson very well: if you want to be at the top of your chosen field, you need to make yourself indispensable. That said, now that Saturn—the King of Career Matters—has joined Pluto in this house, if you've worked hard and done business honestly, you can expect to see some serious results in this department over the next two and a half years. Of course, since Pluto will also be forming a testy square to your Sun sign—and to your Sun directly, if you were born between the 6th and the 13th—there may be some challenges to deal with en route to accomplishing your goals. Fortunately, you've never been the type to allow obstacles to get in your way—in fact, you tend to be inspired by them. On the other hand, it's easy to become obsessed when Pluto is in the neighborhood. If your personal life is in turmoil due to the amount of time and energy you're investing in your work, it might be time to consider a more realistic and less stressful schedule.

How Will This Year's Eclipses Affect You?

Think of eclipses as celestial exclamation points. They amp up the volume on ordinary life for us all when they occur, but the signs and houses they occupy show where the possibility exists for sudden, intense, and often quite surprising events. Eclipses occur in pairs, six months apart. Solar Eclipses are supercharged New Moons, bringing the Sun and Moon together and marking peak times for planting seeds in any department of life. Lunar Eclipses are high-energy Full Moons, times of dramatic culmination, fulfillment, and often new beginnings as well, provided the slate has been wiped clean.

There will be five eclipses during 2018, marking an extremely unpredictable year for one and all.

On January 31, a Lunar Eclipse will occur in Leo and your solar fifth house of playmates, fun times, and creative ventures. If you've been working on an artistic project, craft, or hobby, you may finally feel that you've mastered it—so much so that you're ready to take your show on the road and turn it into at least a part-time financial venture. With Jupiter in your solar eighth house of shared resources, you might want to consider taking on a partner—provided they're just as committed to success, that is. Don't start anything up just yet, though. The Solar Eclipse of August 11 is a far better time for a full-scale launch. You have a bit over six months to do your homework on the business end of things, find the right collaborator, and pull it all together. Get busy.

On February 15, a Solar Eclipse will bring the Sun and Moon together in Aquarius and your solar eleventh house of friendships and group affiliations. If you've been uncomfortable within your current peer circle and you have the feeling it's time to make a change, don't hesitate. Go online and find local groups whose goals are more in tune with how you've envisioned your future.

Your solar fourth house of home and family matters will receive a Solar Eclipse in Cancer on July 12, a meeting of astrological minds that could be quite disruptive to your domestic life. The good news is that you won't be afraid to make any necessary changes that have been put off for far too long now. The tough part will be releasing people and situations that are no longer beneficial to the health of your family situation—not to mention yourself. Not to worry, though. Now that you're ready for a change, the Universe will be more than happy to send you a whole new agenda.

On July 27, a Lunar Eclipse will arrive in startling Aquarius. Take a moment to think about what you ended—and, more importantly, what you put into motion—back in February. If you got off to a good start but still haven't seen any returns on your investment, it's time to reassess the situation. What else can you do to bring about success? Why not ask those who've already achieved your aims for advice, support, and maybe even financial help?

The last Solar Eclipse of the year will occur on August 11, once again in Leo and your solar fifth house. This time around, you'll be better equipped to make a case for taking time away from your work schedule to push forward with creative, business-oriented objectives. An appearance on *Shark Tank* isn't out of the question. No matter whom you're trying to sell to, however, or what you're trying to sell them, be sure you know the answers to all their questions before they ask—and be honorable and honest.

Aries | January

Relaxation and Recreation

On the 10th, Mercury will make his way into Capricorn and your solar tenth house—and suddenly, you'll be able to confidently express everything you've ever wanted to say to an authority figure you've previously thought of as unapproachable. It might be an elder family member, or maybe a higher-up you were sure hadn't noticed your hard work. Prepare to have an honest, open, and highly productive conversation.

Lovers and Friends

Around the 8th or 9th, no less than four planets will get together in Capricorn, a sign that's not famous for setting up prime conditions to induce love at first sight. The thing is, as practical and realistic as this sign is, if you meet someone and it feels right to your earthy antennae, it might not be all that tough to make it work. To convince yourself, plan a Netflix-and-chill kind of evening. Soon.

Money and Success

On the 13th, Venus—the keeper of the planetary purse strings—will get into an edgy square with startling Uranus, who loves nothing more than sending along the last thing we could or would have ever expected. That said, no matter how secure you felt about your current financial position, one small ripple in the water now may be enough to cause a hurricane down the road. Pay attention. If you have doubts, then formulate a "just in case" plan.

Tricky Transits

The Lunar Eclipse on the 31st will send a shock wave through your solar fifth house of lovers and playmates, Aries. Whether you're single or happily attached, expect someone quite surprising to unexpectedly storm through your world—with a message. Whether they're providing you with the answers you've been seeking or rousing you to figure things out yourself, you'll be amazed at the truth—or truths—that emerge.

Rewarding Days

2, 6, 8, 9, 10, 15

Challenging Days

12, 13, 17, 24, 27, 31

Aries | February

Relaxation and Recreation

Whatever you're up to on the 3rd, Aries, you'll be doing it up—big time—especially if you've been waiting for a moment like this to let go and have some serious fun. Don't you dare feel guilty, either. Yes, your drug of choice is stress, but every now and then it's good to allow yourself to chill out.

Lovers and Friends

Going back to the 3rd, Aries, let's just say that while you're convincing yourself to relax—perhaps at a local coffee shop—you might run into someone you've never met but feel as if you've known for a million years. If the connection is immediate, don't question it. Your instincts will be running on high. Why question them, especially when this feels so good?

Money and Success

Don't be afraid to take a chance on a lottery ticket or raffle around the 6th, Aries—but don't get crazy. Remember, it takes only one to win, so if it's your turn, it will happen. Also, while we're on the subject of winning, if you're feeling lucky in the department of finances and you need an infusion to make a dream come true, go for it. Just be sure you have a solid, feasible plan to present to the powers that be.

Tricky Transits

The Solar Eclipse on the 15th will set off an emotional earthquake in your solar eleventh house of friendships, group affiliations, and goals for the future, Aries. If you haven't already cleaned house and eliminated anyone who's holding you back from your future, you'll most definitely be ready to bid them a not-so-fond farewell now. Don't feel guilty. It's time to think and plan ahead.

Rewarding Days

2, 3, 6, 18, 19

Challenging Days

10, 11, 12, 17, 25, 28

Aries | March

Relaxation and Recreation

With half of the heavens' inhabitants making their way through fire signs this month, fiery little you will be sorely tempted to do what you do best—to forget about anything even remotely resembling restraint and just do what comes naturally. In some departments, that's the best plan—relationships, for example. In others, however, not so much. Say what's on your mind with your nearest and dearest, but hold your tongue with higher-ups you're out to impress.

Lovers and Friends

On the 6th, loving Venus will set off for your sign—and as magnetic as she is, you can expect to be attracting new admirers (okay, and lovers from the past, too) without even trying. That said, if you're happily attached, you can make your situation even happier by doing just one thoughtful little thing that will bring you two even closer. You're wonderfully creative. Start imagining what that one little thing might be.

Money and Success

Your solar eighth house will play host to a major astrological event on the 8th, Aries. Jupiter, Mr. Wealth and Prosperity himself, will stop in his tracks to give you a second shot at the title in the department of loans, investments, and joint financial dealings. It may take a while, but if you're determined to find financing for something you believe in, get busy. It will happen. Maybe not just yet, but it will happen.

Tricky Transits

Mercury will turn retrograde in your sign on the 22nd, Aries. Now, he's the god of communication and navigations, so you can most definitely expect car, traffic, or travel problems to create a hitch in your plans. As impatient as you are, do yourself a favor and troubleshoot—big time—before you go anywhere, no matter how many times you've made the trip. Think Murphy's Law.

Rewarding Days

1, 2, 4, 14, 15, 19

Challenging Days

11, 12, 13, 17, 22, 23, 24, 29

Aries | April

Relaxation and Recreation

Three planets—including startling Uranus—will pass through your assertive, impatient sign and your solar first house of personality during April, Aries. So if someone accuses you of rushing them or intimidating them, don't get mad—at least, not until you consider the fact that you might well be doing just that. What to do? Well, first off, figure out why you're angry.

Lovers and Friends

The New Moon on the 15th will occur in your sign, just as Mercury stops to turn direct—also in your sign. This will be a very big day for you, most likely with regard to relationships. Should you charge forward and act on your feelings or sit tight and wait a few days? Honestly, not taking action will be tough for you—tougher than usual, that is—but give it a shot.

Money and Success

On the 7th, Venus—in your solar second house of money matters, by the way—will form an easy trine aspect with responsible, respectable Saturn. This marks a terrific time for you to initiate or finalize a financial agreement, especially if your intuition—not just your accountant or advisor—prompts you to do so. Trust your gut, first and foremost.

Tricky Transits

Serious Saturn will collide with your ruler—aggressive Mars—on the 2nd, Aries, which might put you in a bit of a position. Faced with roadblocks or delays due to red tape or a higher-up who's deliberately dragging their heels, what should you do? Put up or shut up? Only you can make that choice—but please do take your time making it. This decision can't be rushed.

Rewarding Days
6, 7, 12, 13, 23, 29

Challenging Days
1, 2, 4, 5, 10, 25, 26

Aries | May

Relaxation and Recreation

The Full Moon on the 29th will occur in your solar ninth house of adventure, education, and exploration, Aries, all done up in fiery, curious Sagittarius. If you don't already have plans to travel, take classes, or expand your horizons in some way, get busy. You'll be craving a break from routine through something—or someone—new and exciting. Best if you make it happen before it happens to you.

Lovers and Friends

On the 29th, Mercury will set off for your solar third house of short trips, block parties, and hanging out with your siblings, which certainly does indicate a whole lot of communicating and socializing. That said, if a neighbor or sibling invites you over to meet someone they think might be interesting to you, don't refuse—no matter what happened last time. One never knows.

Money and Success

Shocking Uranus will set off for your solar second house of finances on the 15th, Aries—where he'll stay for the next seven years. Expect your monetary situation to change many times over the duration. If you don't already have a plan B ready to go in the department of finances, it's high time you put one in place. Consult a knowledgeable friend or a trusted professional the moment you feel the need.

Tricky Transits

If you're asked to speak your mind around the 7th, resistance will pretty much be futile—but be careful. Sure, be honest, but keep in mind that with Mercury square to Pluto, your words will be remembered forever—which will make it pretty much impossible to take back anything you might regret. Be careful what you say—and what you message, text, and tweet, too!

Rewarding Days

6, 11, 18, 19, 23

Challenging Days

7, 8, 12, 16, 26

Aries | June

Relaxation and Recreation
Bright and early on the 1st, three benevolent astro-teams will conspire to help you create a wonderfully peaceful yet somehow also exciting weekend—one you won't forget. That said, if you feel there's an apology that needs to be expressed or accepted, this would be the perfect time to let the spirit of forgiveness move you. Don't delay any longer.

Lovers and Friends
If you're single and you run into someone who seems just perfect for you around the 6th, breathe deep and count to ten. Yes, you may have actually met your soulmate, but if that's the case, they're not going anywhere. So why rush? Take your time. Enjoy the "getting to know you" period of your relationship. Think of it as a special spring that only you two can enjoy, and savor it.

Money and Success
After the 13th, when Venus passes into your solar fifth house, Aries, you'll be tempted to impress prospective lovers with extravagant gestures and possibly lavish gifts you really can't afford. Don't do that. No one's saying you can't pull out all the stops to make sure they notice you. Just don't bankrupt yourself in the process. There's a lot to be said for simple thoughtfulness.

Tricky Transits
If you've been trying to gain the attention of a higher-up, elder, or superior, resist the urge to do anything reckless around the 23rd, Aries. Contrary to popular opinion, bad press—especially when you're out to impress someone—isn't better than no press. Keep your nose to the grindstone, summon up some patience, and earn their interest. Trust me on this one.

Rewarding Days
1, 2, 19, 20, 25

Challenging Days
4, 5, 14, 15, 30

Aries | July

Relaxation and Recreation

With your ruling planet, Mars, currently moving retrograde through your solar eleventh house of friendships, it's not hard to imagine you making contact with an old friend—and maybe even an old flame. That said, if you're happily attached, better invite your partner along. Oh, and don't be surprised if a person you got into trouble with in the past—your "partner in crime"—suddenly resurfaces.

Lovers and Friends

On the 22nd, Venus and Jupiter—the heavens' most benevolent pairing—will get together in a stimulating sextile aspect. Now, these two have been known to be in the neighborhood when love at first sight occurs. Keep an ear out for someone with an interesting and unusual accent, and don't be afraid of approaching them. If just looking at them makes you smile immediately, all bodes well.

Money and Success

Jupiter will stop in his tracks on the 10th, and he's chosen your solar eighth house of shared resources, loans, and inheritances for his station. Obviously, preparing for stalls, delays, and roadblocks in these departments wouldn't be a bad idea. The good news is that if you can wait a while, you'll have everything you were after and more. Can you muster up some patience?

Tricky Transits

On the 5th, the Sun and Jupiter will form an easy trine, just as Mercury opposes energetic Mars. It's best to use this combination of astrological energies by expending some serious physical energy—the nature of which, of course, is up to you. If you're involved and in love, some quality time alone wouldn't be a bad idea. If not, some serious flirting may be in order.

Rewarding Days
5, 11, 22

Challenging Days
1, 2, 4, 16, 31

Aries | August

Relaxation and Recreation
If you set out to impress a loved one around the 5th or 6th, be careful, because your first reaction will be to take unnecessary chances and risk more than you should. Of course, those activities do stir up adrenaline—your drug of choice—so if you're physically safe, you might consider those risks well worth the effort, but still, stay safe. After all, what do you really have to prove?

Lovers and Friends
On the 9th, a testy Venus-Saturn square will make it extremely easy for you to have an argument with your sweetie over how much time you've been spending at work lately. If you must indulge in this non-productive sport, fine—just be sure that you don't say or do anything that will alienate them permanently. Jobs come with expiration dates, but really good relationships don't. If you have one, do what you can to keep it together.

Money and Success
That same Venus-Saturn square will also make it extremely hard for you to negotiate finances—peaceably, at least—with higher-ups. The good news is that if you absolutely must reach an agreement now after a long, hard battle, know that compromise is possible. No, you probably won't get everything you want, but neither will your opponent. Finding the middle ground is the only solution.

Tricky Transits
Mercury will turn direct on the 18th in your solar fifth house of lovers and playmates, Aries, a clear indication that those among you who are single should stop thinking about the past—even if the one who got away has been begging you for a second chance. It's time to look forward. Let the past lie where it will and move on.

Rewarding Days
7, 19, 25

Challenging Days
8, 9, 10, 11, 12, 26, 27

Aries | September

Relaxation and Recreation

On the 7th, Mercury will form a Grand Earth Trine with conservative Saturn and rebellious Uranus, a most unusual meeting of astrological minds that just might inspire you to try something new. This time around, however, if you're in the mood to take a chance, you'll be moved to do it only with a proper safety net in place, rather than relying on a wing and a prayer.

Lovers and Friends

A square aspect between loving Venus and assertive Mars on the 8th is the perfect recipe for "if you loved me, you would" syndrome, Aries—which, to be honest, isn't famous for working out well in the long haul. That said, if you need to call in a long-overdue favor and employing a bit of guilt is the only way to get it done—well, so be it. Remind them of what they honestly owe you.

Money and Success

The Sun and Saturn will get into a testy, irritating square aspect on the 25th, Aries, urging you to go to war with one particular person who seems to be standing in the way of your success. Before you alienate anyone permanently, however, be sure you have your facts straight. There's nothing worse than going off in a righteous manner and finding out later that you were entirely wrong.

Tricky Transits

Saturn will station on the 6th, set to move forward after months of forcing you to review how you're handling your career and your reputation, as well as many other professional matters. The good news is that if you've paid your dues, you won't need to wait much longer for your rewards to arrive. If not—well, I'm sure you know what might be coming. Either way, prepare yourself.

Rewarding Days

3, 7, 11, 12, 24

Challenging Days

5, 6, 8, 18, 23, 25

Aries | October

Relaxation and Recreation

The Full Moon of the 24th in earthy Taurus will provide you with a nice, solid emotional backdrop for gatherings with those you may have had rather fiery disputes with in the past. The best part is that Venus and Saturn will join in, an even calmer and more rational team that always votes for conciliation over continued warfare. This is a terrific month to mend fences, then kick back and catch up.

Lovers and Friends

The New Moon on the 8th will set up shop in your solar seventh house of relationships, urging you to make nice with anyone you've recently been warring with—okay, and even those you've been at odds with for some time now. The point is, if you really want closure, it may be necessary to initiate a reconciliation. No, that's not your strong suit, but think of how much better you'll feel when you two are speaking again.

Money and Success

That Venus-Saturn sextile aspect on the 24th will also come in handy if you're considering or negotiating a financial deal—even if it looked to be pretty much impossible to settle over the past few weeks. Sit down at the table again, and with these two on duty, cooler heads will prevail. Stop fighting it. Let go, shake hands, and move forward. It's for the best.

Tricky Transits

If you're out and about on Halloween, you should know that your costume may not be the only surprise on the agenda. An opposition between Venus and startling Uranus could bring along an encounter you weren't expecting, most likely with someone from the past you most definitely hadn't planned on ever speaking with again. Stay calm, smile pretty, and move along.

Rewarding Days

12, 13, 22, 24, 27

Challenging Days

2, 5, 11, 23, 28, 31

Aries | November

Relaxation and Recreation

On the 8th, fun-loving Jupiter will set off for Sagittarius—his home turf. This marks the beginning of an entire year of experiencing the urge to wander, explore, and have adventures. Talk about a good time! Sure, you'll have to take care of business and tend to responsibilities, but man, when you're off duty, you'll have a huge smile on your face. Just go easy on the partying.

Lovers and Friends

If there's any unfinished business you really want to put to bed between you and a dear one that wasn't solved last month, Aries, here's another shot at the title. Loving Venus will spend the entire month in Libra and your solar seventh house of one-to-one relationships, urging you to make nice. Oh, you know you're ready. Why put it off any longer?

Money and Success

If you're wrangling a deal or trying to make a joint financial venture work, you'd do well to look to the 9th to get it done, Aries. Venus will get together with Mars, bringing just the right amount of cooperation and assertion to the table, providing the perfect astrological formula for peaceful compromises. Just be sure to check your ego at the door.

Tricky Transits

Just when you thought all was said and done and peace had been restored in the kingdom, an unpredictable opposition between Venus and Uranus on the 30th could stir up the dust once again between you and a dear one—despite your best efforts. If that's the case and you've already done everything possible, relax. This too shall pass. If you need to make some relationship changes, however, don't wait any longer. It's prime time.

Rewarding Days

8, 9, 10, 11, 27

Challenging Days

16, 17, 19, 26, 30

Aries | December

Relaxation and Recreation

The Universe has seen fit to send along an enthusiastic, fiery, and fun-loving Leo Moon on the 24th and 25th, the perfect energy to ensure a wonderful holiday that won't soon be forgotten. Your mission is to use the Mercury-Neptune contact on the 24th to get the party started. Sit the whole gang down for a serious dose of sweet memories and pleasant nostalgia, and maybe bring along some photos or scrapbooks.

Lovers and Friends

On the 6th, Mercury will turn direct after three weeks of retrograde movement through intense, sexy Scorpio, urging you to stop pushing away the past and accept the fact that it's all contributed to who you are right now. Ready or not, it's time to forgive yourself—okay, and those closest to you that you're a bit peeved with, too. Oh, c'mon. 'Tis the season.

Money and Success

If you have last-minute shopping to do around the 21st, don't go nuts with your plastic or your checkbook. Mercury and Jupiter will be in cahoots, trying to convince you that nothing exceeds liked excess, but that's really not the case. A thoughtful gift—and your company, by the way—is really the best way to make someone's day. And week. And year. Use your intuition, not your credit line.

Tricky Transits

Bright and early on the 1st, Mercury will retrograde back into intense Scorpio and your solar eighth house of intimate matters. Yes, it's time to deal with unfinished business, and that's exactly what you'll be doing for the next couple weeks. Do yourself a favor and initiate closure with old lovers and recent fails. Clear the decks, kiddo. There's a lot more to come, but not until you get yourself free.

Rewarding Days

12, 13, 16, 24, 25

Challenging Days

1, 2, 3, 6, 7

Aries Action Table

These dates reflect the best—but not the only—times for success and ease in these activities, according to your Sun sign.

	JAN	FEB	MAR	APR	MAY	JUN	JUL	AUG	SEP	OCT	NOV	DEC
Move	2					22	5					
Start a class		15							7	22		20
Join a club		2			23			18				16
Ask for a raise			16	29	15			25				
Get professional advice	10	15		29			14		12		11	
Get a loan			15	7			22	19	11	27	9	
New romance	8, 9		19			6				28		21
Vacation		3			29	19					8	

Taurus

The Bull
April 21 to May 21

ᛏ

Element: Earth

Quality: Fixed

Polarity: Yin/feminine

Planetary Ruler: Venus

Meditation: I trust myself and others

Gemstone: Emerald

Power Stones: Diamond, blue lace agate, rose quartz

Key Phrase: I have

Glyph: Bull's head

Anatomy: Throat, neck

Color: Green

Animal: Cattle

Myths/Legends: Isis and Osiris, Ceridwen, Bull of Minos

House: Second

Opposite Sign: Scorpio

Flower: Violet

Keyword: Conservation

The Taurus Personality

Your Strengths, Gifts, and Challenges

Well, Taurus, let's get right to the heart of the matter: that famous stubborn streak. It influences everything in every facet of your life, from work to relationships. There's just no denying it. You are as determined as the day is long, capable of focusing completely on what's important to you. So what's wrong with that? Your steady, grounded nature makes you a sought-after catch—romantically, professionally, and emotionally—because others come swiftly to realize that when you make a promise, you keep it, no matter what. If that's being stubborn, it's a shame more of us aren't. Okay, so you do occasionally get "stuck" in a situation that isn't good for you because you don't want to throw away the time, effort, or emotions you've invested. In your mind, holding on to what you've got is far better than risking it all to try something new. In other words, you believe that the devil you know is better than the one you've yet to meet.

That doesn't mean you're absolutely anti-change of any kind, however. If you see futility in a current circumstance, especially if you are losing more than you are gaining, you will put your foot down and walk away—permanently. There is no such thing as a second chance for you. If it didn't work once, it won't work the second time. That solid, sensible approach to life in general makes you an excellent advisor and confidant and an even better long-term friend or partner.

Romance and Other Relationships

Speaking of relationships, let's talk about Venus, your ruling planet, who just so happens to be in charge of love, comfort, and money, all of which you, Taurus, absolutely must have to be truly happy. Venus's influence will simply not allow you to spend your time with those who do not pull their own weight in some way. You admire and respect commitment and a strong work ethic, and you tend to surround yourself with those who feel the same. You know what you're worth, and if others don't appreciate you, you're gone, especially with regard to acquaintances who have yet to prove themselves.

There is one exception to that rule, however, which only occurs when you meet someone who is just too physically delicious to ignore—someone you immediately want to call your own. Mercury may rule the senses in general, but Venus decides what makes each of them feel best—our appetites, that is. And since you folks are the undisputed touch-meisters—the most sensual, comfort-loving creatures on the planet—when you spot someone who arouses your urge to get up close and personal, sense and sensibility often fly out the window, much to the amazement of those who know you to be far more practical. The good news is that once you're attached to a partner, you stop looking. The tough part is allowing them to live their own lives. You like to take charge—and you're good at it, too—but that may be interpreted as possessiveness or excessive jealousy. Telling you to hold on with an open palm is impossible—but do try to let your partner make their own choices, for better or worse. After all, what you really want is someone as solid and sturdy as yourself, and that gift is earned most memorably through experience.

Career and Work

When it comes to work, Taurus, your affiliation with Venus often brings you to Venusian places and situations. Your knack for what looks like making money effortlessly makes you the perfect financial advisor, invest-ment analyst, or banker, but if you tend more toward the aesthetic side of your ruling planet's territory, you may opt for a career in beauty, art, or music. Regardless of which you choose, you will throw yourself into it, full speed ahead, and not stop until you are firmly situated at the very top of your field. Once that's done, you'll set about expanding your assets according to a cautious, calculated plan that doesn't allow for backtrack-ing or mistakes.

Many of you are also drawn to professions in the real estate field, which makes sense. You are a big believer in your home being your castle, and you know how important it is to feel grounded and stable in it—so what you're really doing is helping others to find that one patch of earth that suits them best. How rewarding!

Money and Possessions

Giving up what you love and have worked hard to have is just about impossible, which often extends not just to savings, but to possessions as well. When you're trying to force yourself to let an object or attachment go, remember that getting rid of what has become obsolete creates space for something new and better—something you can proudly show off to envious others.

You do love luxury, Taurus, and when it comes to choosing between quality and quantity, quality always wins out. You'd rather have one expensive, premium item than a roomful of cheap substitutes. You don't mind paying more, and you're not afraid to work hard to have the best that life has to offer.

Your Lighter Side

Pleasure and creature comforts, Taurus—that's what life is all about for you. So ideally, your perfect situation includes the absolute fulfillment of all your senses. Good music, beautiful surroundings, and a physically desirable companion are the essential elements to total happiness— along with a nice, fat bank account to help you feel secure and allow you to live every day with a solid safety net in place.

Taurus Celebrities

Your sign rules the throat in the physical body, Taurus, from whence all great voices are born. So it's not surprising that Enya, Cher, Adele, Bono, and Liberace are so well known for the magic their vocal chords produce that just one word is enough to conjure them up. Of course, the legendary Stevie Wonder and Willie Nelson are also Taurus, as was James Brown, the Godfather of Soul. There's a certain inimitable sensuality that you folks exude too, aptly evidenced by George Clooney, Uma Thurman, Dwayne "The Rock" Johnson, and Pierce Brosnan. Oh, and your reputation for being money magnets certainly makes it understandable that Mark Zuckerberg is among the members of your club.

The Year Ahead for Taurus

Fiery Mars will trek through Aquarius and your solar tenth house for five months during 2018, Taurus, an assertive, aggressive kind of energy that never fails to stir things up when he's in the vicinity. Now, this house has everything to do with your dealings with higher-ups, authority figures, and superiors, so you should probably expect a few arguments—or shall we say "heated differences of opinion"—to come up every now and then. In particular, it's May 16 through August 12 and September 10 through November 15 when your temper will be running on high, making it challenging to keep your opinions to yourself—even if you know it's in your best interest to do so. If you're at war with someone on the job because of personality or stylistic differences, make an effort to at least be civil. If the matter involves an important issue that's affecting your job performance, however, you absolutely won't be dissuaded from voicing your thoughts—as well you shouldn't. Either way, prepare for change. Planets in Aquarius tend to inspire sudden shifts and drastic turn-arounds, so don't be surprised if you suddenly change your mind—and, quite possibly, your career aspirations. Now, change doesn't usually come easily to you, so the ride to your new career could be a bumpy one. The good news, however, is that when it's you who initiates change, it's a whole different story, and a whole lot easier to handle. That said, when your antennae tell you it will soon be time to move along, don't sink those hooves into the ground and refuse to think about it. Look around, find a place or a situation that's more to your liking and better suited to your disposition, and trudge forward. It's the very best you can do.

Jupiter will change signs this year, but not until November 8, so you'll continue to enjoy his company in your solar seventh house of one-to-one relationships straight through that date. He'll be all done up in intense, sexy Scorpio, bringing along a veritable buffet of admirers—whether or not you're already attached. If you're settled and happy about it, resisting the urge to get out there and play may be challenging at times, but it likely won't be all that tough—because you're a rock, Taurus, and when you're with someone, you tend to stay put, sometimes even to a fault. If you're single, however, think of this as a delightful buffet. Your sign is famous for its love of sensual pleasures. Why not have just a taste of everything until you find exactly what you want?

Saturn

Saturn didn't get his reputation for being a stick-in-the-mud by accident, Taurus. The thing is, you're a fixed earth sign, so mud doesn't scare you. Matter of fact, ever since mid-December of 2017, when Saturn moved into an earth sign—Capricorn, by the way, which he just so happens to own—rather than feeling stuck or hindered, you've probably been feeling a lot more grounded and stable than you have in a while. Since Saturn rules career and professional matters and he'll be on duty in Capricorn for the next two and a half years, you should also expect to be quite involved in this area of life. Basically, you'll find that you're ready to stop playing around with "jobs" and instead devote yourself to getting ahead in the field that feels most natural for you. It might be real estate, or maybe dealing in fine art or music. Then again, fashion or beauty may become your focus. It really doesn't matter which profession you choose. The point is that with Saturn in this sign, you'll have a whole lot of astrological help to climb the ladder of success. Your mission is to take advantage of the advice and support of higher-ups who appreciate your talents and are willing to help you along the way. It won't be hard to spot these astrological guardian angels. They'll be the ones who'll listen to you describe your dreams, nod, smile, and tell you about their own journeys. Listen well. Experience is a terrific teacher.

Uranus

So let's get back to the whole concept of change—and, more importantly, the way you feel about it, Taurus. As we've already discussed, it's not your favorite thing, by any stretch of the imagination, but as of May 15, Uranus will enter your sign and change will become a way of life. That goes double for those of you born from May 21 through the 24th, since Uranus will be keeping close company with your Sun all this year and for a good part of next year, too. Now this, kids, is the stuff that major, sweeping change is made of—but don't be scared. You're growing as a person, and growth necessarily requires change. Sometimes change is comfortable and sometimes it's not, but it's inevitable. But I really can't stress enough how important it will be over the course of 2018 for you to grab the reins and initiate change in any area of life you see fit.

By nature, you're a practical, rational creature, but with Uranus shaking up your sign, some of your choices may not seem all that practical or rational to others. Forget about them, and pay no mind to their opinions. This is your life, and it's time to shake off anything—and anyone—who isn't helping you to become the person you really want to be. The good news is that there's really nothing quite as stimulating and invigorating as change, so your energy level will be running on high—and your imagination, too. Uranus is the planet that inspires genius. Pay attention to your gut, and don't be afraid to color outside the lines.

Neptune

Neptune will spend yet another year on duty in your solar eleventh house of group affiliations and friendships, Taurus—which, honestly, has been a bit of a double-edged sword for you. On the one hand, Neptune's talent for dissolving boundaries has endowed you with the ability to infiltrate the ranks in all kinds of social situations. Basically, you've been able to observe others from a distance from as far back as April of 2011—which adds up to a whole lot of grist for the mill. In short, at this point, when you don't want to be noticed, you won't be. Neptune has taught you how to make yourself invisible. Now, that can be a good thing—if you're around positive people, that is—but if you've wandered off into negative territory and exposed yourself to unkind, hurtful, or pessimistic energies—well, not so much.

Fortunately, Neptune in Pisces is forming an energetic, positive sextile to your Sun, so more often than not, your antennae have quickly talked you into backing away from unhelpful people and circumstances. The thing is, you're a psychic sponge right now—especially if you were born from May 1 through the 8th—so be careful not to hang around long enough to soak up anything negative. The good news is that if you've recently fallen in love, you two are probably fused at the hip and virtually inseparable—and able to read each other's minds, too. Your mission is to stay positive. Surround yourself with upbeat, spiritually uplifting people, and absorb all the good stuff you possibly can.

Pluto

Since 2008, Pluto has been working his way through earthy Capricorn and your solar ninth house, where opinions and higher thoughts are handled. In short, every time you sit still for a moment, whether it's to consider a current situation or muse a bit over the future, if you've been thinking about the big picture as it pertains to your life, it's Pluto who's been inspiring you. Now, this guy isn't for the faint of heart, so you'll be mulling over all kinds of subjects that really aren't fit for dinner conversation—your own mortality, for example, as well as that of others. Yes, that sounds a tad depressing, but on the other hand, Pluto also brings along the type of deep understanding that allows us to make peace with the past and clear a path toward the future, positioned as he is in an easy trine aspect to your Sun—and that goes double for those of you born between May 7 and 15.

Pluto is not the kind of guy who messes around, so anything that's meant to leave your life now will most certainly go, but if you assist the process, all will be well. Honest. Also, keep in mind that Pluto brings transformation and regeneration into our lives—on a very slow, deliberate level. Do yourself a favor and if you haven't already, put together a journal. When you look back and read it in a few years, you'll be amazed at the sweeping changes you made in your life that aren't obvious to you now. In short, you're molting—shedding your outer skin to grow someone new. Think of this time as your own personal evolution.

How Will This Year's Eclipses Affect You?

Think of eclipses as celestial exclamation points. They amp up the volume on ordinary life for us all when they occur, but the signs and houses they occupy show where the possibility exists for sudden, intense, and often quite surprising events. Eclipses occur in pairs, six months apart. Solar Eclipses are supercharged New Moons, bringing the Sun and Moon together and marking peak times for planting seeds in any department of life. Lunar Eclipses are high-energy Full Moons, times of dramatic culmination, fulfillment, and often new beginnings as well, provided the slate has been wiped clean.

There will be five eclipses during 2018, marking an extremely unpredictable year for one and all.

The first Lunar Eclipse of 2018 will occur in Leo on January 31, activating your solar fourth house of home and family matters in a very big, very dramatic way. A child or family member may reveal something you'd never, ever have expected in a million years—or you may uncover a family-oriented secret that few are privy to. Either way, the stage has been set for drama. Buckle up!

On February 15, a Solar Eclipse in startling Aquarius will arrive, set to plant a seed in your solar tenth house of higher-ups, elders, and authority figures. If you've been having trouble with someone who has control over a major part of your life, you may need to decide whether or not you want the relationship to continue—and you may need to make that decision in a hurry.

Another Solar Eclipse will occur on July 12 in home-loving Cancer and your solar third house of communications. A conversation with a dear one could turn quite emotional in a hurry, especially if something has been brewing between the two of you that neither of you has brought up yet. The Universe has decided it's time to stop ignoring the obvious. Talking things over is absolutely necessary.

On July 27, a second Lunar Eclipse will occur in Aquarius and your solar tenth house. This time around, you may be putting the finishing touches on a career-oriented project you began back in mid-February. If you're striking out on your own, rest assured that the Universe is willing to help—you may, however, need to retrace your steps at this time to work out the bugs. Don't be discouraged.

The final eclipse of the year will arrive on August 11, when the Sun and Moon will come together in Leo and your solar fourth house of home and family matters. Think back on what you were doing in mid-February and the changes that occurred then. This is your chance to bring closure to any emotional issues that didn't end well. Bury the hatchet and start over.

Taurus | January

Relaxation and Recreation

No less than five planets will make their mark on your solar ninth house of far-off places and distant loved ones this month, Taurus, all of them done up in Capricorn, a practical, sensual earth sign like your own. Does this mean you'll be off for a trip or receiving visitors from another shore? Sure could. If there's someone out there you've been missing for far too long, put an end to that nonsense now.

Lovers and Friends

If you've been waiting to express your feelings to someone—because you're currently "just friends" or because you work together—well, the astrological aspects of the 8th or 9th will probably convince you to speak your mind. Of course, you'll want to be gentle about it—but not so much that the object of your affection doesn't get the message. Be tactful, not coy.

Money and Success

When it comes to handling finances, you kids wrote the book, Taurus. You're so good at it that you're often referred to as "money magnets." That said, you'll still need to be careful with your credit cards after the 26th, when impulsive Mars in excessive Sagittarius will urge you to overextend, most likely for a toy you've been dying to bring home. Careful!

Tricky Transits

Authority figures and higher-ups may toss some rather surprising demands your way around the Lunar Eclipse of the 31st, Taurus, and even though you were born with the strongest work ethic of all twelve signs—well, even you may end up feeling a bit overwhelmed. Of course, that doesn't mean you won't rise to meet the challenge, so afterward, please do allow yourself a bit of strictly hedonistic downtime.

Rewarding Days

2, 6, 8, 9, 21, 25

Challenging Days

13, 14, 17, 27, 30, 31

Taurus | February

Relaxation and Recreation

If you're in the mood for an adventure, Taurus, plan it for the weekend of the 9th, when a fiery, fun-loving Sagittarius Moon will be on duty, urging you to break out of your routine and have some serious fun. The 9th also looks to be quite a romantic day, by the way, so if you're attached and it's time for some quality time alone together, this is a golden opportunity. If you're single, make yourself available. You never know who you might run into while you're out and about.

Lovers and Friends

If you're single, Taurus, prepare to be hit by a cosmic lightning bolt on the 3rd. This doesn't mean you'll be running into the love of your life, but it certainly does improve your chances, so get dressed and get out there. Some serious socializing is most definitely in order. If you're happily attached, this is the perfect weekend to plan a romantic getaway—and please do turn your phones off!

Money and Success

Venus will get into a sextile aspect with innovative Uranus on the 6th, Taurus, the stuff that sudden career-oriented opportunities are made of—especially since you've laid the groundwork already and seen to it that higher-ups can't possibly ignore your recent accomplishments. Well, good for you. You may be pleasantly surprised with a raise, bonus, or promotion on the 10th—or very soon afterward.

Tricky Transits

Venus will square off with expansive Jupiter on the 3rd, Taurus, creating an all-or-nothing team that specializes in going way, way overboard. You're going to be excessive. Your mission is to choose the right department for an all-out splurge. Your only ground rules are (a) to be sure you can afford it and (b) to do no harm to yourself or others. Otherwise, go for it!

Rewarding Days
6, 8, 9, 10, 21, 27

Challenging Days
1, 13, 15, 25

Taurus | March

Relaxation and Recreation

The Sun will spend most of the month in woozy, dreamy Pisces, the sign that's the personal property of Neptune—who also happens to be on duty in Pisces. Now, this is the ultimate water sign, so no matter what's ailing you—and even if everything is just fine—getting yourself outside by a lake or river or spending some time at the beach will be extremely therapeutic.

Lovers and Friends

Your ruling planet is Venus, and she'll be feeling pretty darn feisty this month, Taurus. On the 6th, she'll take off for fiery, assertive Aries—who, you'll remember, was the ancient Greek God of War. Does this mean you'll be arguing with your sweetheart? Maybe a little. But Aries planets are really just into passion, so... well, there are other options. Use your imagination.

Money and Success

Arguments over finances are quite possible on the 23rd, when Venus and Pluto will get into a square—which is basically an astrological shouting match. Now, Venus is your ruler, and she's in charge of finances, so if you're doing battle with someone over money matters, you'll probably win. Just be sure you won't lose anything more important in the process.

Tricky Transits

Jupiter will station on the 8th to turn retrograde, and when he does, he'll be wearing sexy Scorpio—oh, and standing still in your solar seventh house of one-to-one relationships. Now, Jupiter is famous for being excessive, so if you're not attached, you should expect a flurry of activity in the department of ardent new admirers. If you're seeing someone? Well, that flurry of activity will then most likely occur in a very tender department... if you catch my drift.

Rewarding Days

1, 2, 4, 8, 30, 31

Challenging Days

10, 11, 13, 22, 23, 25

Taurus | April

Relaxation and Recreation

It's time to take a break, Taurus—and around the 12th, 13th, and 14th, the Universe will be happy to provide you with some wonderful opportunities to really enjoy life. Mercury will turn direct on the 15th, so things will start to pick up soon afterward. Your mission is to enjoy this break in the action with a dear one who shares your love of the best things in life.

Lovers and Friends

This is it, Taurus—your favorite time of year. The lovely lady Venus—your ruling planet—will join hands with the Sun in your sign to make this a delightfully sensuous month. No matter how hard you're working or how many tasks you have to complete, I really have to insist that you make your earthy little heart happy. Make time to get outdoors to enjoy nature, or take in an event that's related to music or art. This is mandatory. Really.

Money and Success

If an argument over money comes up on the 4th or 5th, you'd do well to table the matter and put some distance between you two. The good news is that by the 7th, cooler heads will prevail and coming up with a solution that's agreeable to one and all will come far more easily. By the 10th, you may even be laughing about it all.

Tricky Transits

On the 2nd, fiery Mars will team up with serious, responsible Saturn in Capricorn, the sign that most loves the rules. Yes, this means you'll probably either have to lay down the law with respect to a relationship, or that someone else will present you with a bit of an ultimatum. If it's the latter, don't just storm off into the sunset. Take a bit of time to consider their point of view.

Rewarding Days

7, 12, 13, 14

Challenging Days

4, 5, 10, 15, 25

Taurus | May

Relaxation and Recreation

Mercury will zip through your sign in just over two weeks this month, Taurus, from the 13th through the 29th. Fortunately, he's moving direct, so any financial transactions you're handling should go along quite well, provided you avoid the 28th. If you're not sure about your next move, don't make any decisions or sign anything important until you talk to a trusted elder or professional around the 18th.

Lovers and Friends

On the 16th, fiery Mars and shocking Uranus will square off, activating what could end up being a very testy confrontation between you and a higher-up you're sure has been out to get you for some time now. This matter really does need to be handled, and soon, and even if an argument ensues, it's all for the best. Clear the air and move on. You'll feel so relieved!

Money and Success

Conversations about money matters may not go easily on the 1st, 7th, or 9th, Taurus—yes, even though money is one of your sign's specialties. This doesn't mean you won't be able to come to an agreement, only that you may have to table the discussion until much later in the month—say, around the 18th. You've never been famous for rushing. Don't start now.

Tricky Transits

The Full Moon on the 29th will occur in Sagittarius, illuminating your solar axis of finances, possessions, and personal values. This could mean that you're about to invest in a partnership, and if so, no matter what the reason, be it personal or professional, before you sign up, be sure you're sure. You're famous for hanging in there—sometimes well past the time when most would throw in the towel. Do you really want to be in this for the long haul?

Rewarding Days
18, 19, 22, 23, 25

Challenging Days
1, 7, 9, 15, 16, 28

Taurus | June

Relaxation and Recreation

The emotional Moon will spend the weekend of the 9th and 10th in your sign, Taurus, urging you to express your feelings. Now, spring is your season and food is your thing, and since the Moon is in charge of home and family matters, it will be easy to lure your dear ones over to your place for a cookout—especially if you mention the fact that you'll be doing the cooking.

Lovers and Friends

On the 1st and 2nd, loving Venus will get together with expansive Jupiter and dreamy Neptune, the stuff that very full and happy hearts are made of. Spend your time with loved ones who are tried and true, pass out lots of hugs, and be sure to express your appreciation. Don't worry about making any fancy speeches. Just let them know they're cherished—and expect to hear the same.

Money and Success

If you can't arrive at an agreement with a financial partner on the 1st—regardless of whether it's strictly business or pretty darn personal—table the matter until the New Moon of the 13th. At that point, a whole new solution will occur to one of you, and it will probably be exactly what you need to come to an amiable arrangement.

Tricky Transits

Mercury will square off with unpredictable, spontaneous Uranus on the 30th, urging you quite strongly and insistently to say exactly what's on your mind, regardless of the consequences—and a whole lot of yelling could be involved. Now, this type of behavior may not be your usual m.o., so it might not be possible for you to even force yourself to do it. In that case, you'll need to blow off some steam. Find an appropriate physical outlet.

Rewarding Days

1, 2, 12, 13, 20, 22

Challenging Days

5, 6, 8, 11, 19, 30

Taurus | July

Relaxation and Recreation

On Sunday the 8th, the Sun and Neptune will get into an easy, relaxing trine aspect, urging you to find a temporary escape hatch—just to ditch the harshness of reality for a little while. No matter which method you choose, please note the use of the word "temporary." It's healthy to draw back and regroup every now and then, but don't make this a habit.

Lovers and Friends

If you're not attached, Taurus, get out there and make yourself available around the weekend of the 21st and 22nd. You'll have several planetary allies on duty who'll see to it that you're in the right place at the right time to meet someone special. You may not fall in love at first sight, but then again, all conditions are right for it—and, as you well know, you can't win if you don't play.

Money and Success

The Lunar Eclipse on the 27th could be a bit problematic for you—career-wise, that is. It will occur in your solar tenth house, all done up in startling Aquarius, so one never knows what events might come along that will get you thinking that it's time to move on—maybe not without much notice, if any. Well, sudden change can certainly be liberating and invigorating, so as long as plan B is in place, knock yourself out!

Tricky Transits

The Solar Eclipse of the 12th will occur with intense Pluto on board, and since it's your solar third house of conversations and communications that will be activated, a serious conversation could cause a whole lot of change in your world—in rapid-fire fashion. We've established that you're not a fan of change, unless you've initiated it yourself. Fortunately, you've probably seen this coming for a while now. Don't worry. You've got this.

Rewarding Days
5, 8, 11, 22, 24, 28

Challenging Days
1, 2, 25, 26, 27

Taurus | August

Relaxation and Recreation

If you're after some quality time with friends and family and can't decide when this month to schedule the event, look no further. Circle the 24th and 25th on your calendar, and plan your gathering then. A pack of lovely, cooperative earth energies like your own will see to it that all parties involved will behave properly—even if there have been feuds in the past. No, you're not a mediator, but then again, being responsible for a truce would be kinda nice, yes?

Lovers and Friends

Your ruling planet, Venus, will set off for partner-oriented Libra on the 6th, a cooperative energy that has no problem with compromise. That said, if you've been doing battle with a dear one—regardless of the reason—know that there's hope on the horizon. If one of you would need to drastically change your mind for peace to occur, that may even be possible on the 7th.

Money and Success

Another benefit coming your way via Venus's entry into Libra is that you'll be able to balance out your finances far more easily. So if you need to cut corners in one area of life to expand your budget in others, it will be doable. Make it easy on yourself. Sit down with a trusted professional and go over the numbers—realistically, please.

Tricky Transits

Venus and Neptune will get into an inconjunct aspect on the 22nd—the stuff that confusing relationship messages are made of. If you're not sure why your sweetheart is acting a certain way, don't sit quietly and wonder. Ask. Matter of fact, be emphatic about it. It may take you two a while to get to the heart of the matter, but spending your time working on that together is better than sitting home alone stewing.

Rewarding Days
6, 7, 18, 19, 25, 26

Challenging Days
4, 8, 9, 10, 11, 22, 29

Taurus | September

Relaxation and Recreation

The New Moon on the 9th will combine forces with Venus in Scorpio to put you in the mood to play, Taurus—and as we all know, when it comes to putting on a party, you folks own the patent on the perfect recipe for that sort of thing. The good news is that you will also feel especially close to your current partner, so you two can make quite the fun project out of planning this event.

Lovers and Friends

Any badly needed negotiations—of any kind, but most especially involving you and your nearest and dearest—will go along quite well if you plan them around the 7th. New solutions for old problems will suddenly seem easy to agree to, and even the crankiest elder among you will be willing to at least consider the opinions of others. Seriously. Schedule it now.

Money and Success

A brief financial ripple that will initially seem to be earth-shattering will work out just fine on the 12th, Taurus—provided that you ask for and, more importantly, accept help from higher-ups or experienced professionals who can remain calm and advise you properly. Before you let loose or have a tirade, make a phone call to someone in the know.

Tricky Transits

Saturn will station on the 6th, and since he's the kind of guy who just loves to stall, frustrate, and delay even our best-laid plans, moving forward with your financial or business-oriented proposals may not be possible now. Matter of fact, if what you've been planning is a very big, very bold financial move for you, you'd do well to do some stalling yourself. You may not have all the information you need to make an informed decision.

Rewarding Days

3, 7, 9, 11, 12, 16

Challenging Days

6, 8, 23, 25, 30

Taurus | October

Relaxation and Recreation

The Full Moon on the 24th will get together with Venus and Saturn to make this quite the delightful day for you, Taurus. You'll be astrologically gifted with the ability to be hedonistic and yet controlled enough to enjoy just a bit of everything without going too far overboard. Don't laugh. A sense of moderation is a rare boon for you. Take advantage of it.

Lovers and Friends

Your ruling planet, Venus, will station to turn retrograde on the 5th, and she'll be in your solar seventh house at the time. Whether you're single or attached, expect a whole lot of voices from the past to return to your world—for better or worse—over the next six-ish weeks. Does this mean you'll be getting back together with the one who got away? Maybe. Just be sure you have new solutions to old problems before you sign up again.

Money and Success

On Saturday the 27th, you'll enjoy the benefits of a Sun-Saturn sextile aspect—the stuff that solid handshakes are made of. If you've been nego-tiating and renegotiating a deal and had just about given up hope that it would ever come to fruition, you can relax now. Have a nice lunch with all parties concerned and resolve problems from the past.

Tricky Transits

Power struggles that come up surrounding relationship issues around the 11th may seem far more serious than they really are, Taurus. If you and your sweetheart are having one of those "silent arguments" before then, don't challenge them or force the issue. Wait until everyone's temper has calmed down, bring the matter up in uber-gentle fashion, and let your partner speak their mind first. Trust me on this.

Rewarding Days

4, 12, 13, 15, 22, 24

Challenging Days

2, 10, 11, 30, 31

Taurus | November

Relaxation and Recreation

Talk about a good time! Outgoing, generous Jupiter will set off for playful, adventurous, and endlessly curious Sagittarius on the 8th, urging you to do some investigating—into what you really, really love to do and how you like to do it. Now, this certainly does pertain to the most tender areas of life, but your curiosity will extend into all other life departments as well. So what's the holdup? Start asking your questions.

Lovers and Friends

A wonderful, easygoing trine aspect between loving Venus and passionate Mars will come along on the 9th, urging you to make peace with a dear one you've been at odds with lately. The good news is that reconciliation will come about easily now—provided that one of you is brave enough to propose it. The best news is that you'll soon wonder why you were fighting at all.

Money and Success

If you're set to launch a project—especially if it involves shared finances and personal partnerships—do yourself a great big favor and avoid the 15th through the 17th at all costs, Taurus. Both Venus and Mercury will be stationing on the 16th to turn direction—so basically, starting anything new isn't a good idea. Hey, you're famous for being persistent. How about using some of that famous patience now?

Tricky Transits

Fiery Mars will square off with expansive Jupiter on the 19th, a giant boom of energy that just so happens to be in the neighborhood when all kinds of sudden events occur—for better or worse. In your case, it seems that a former friend may suddenly make it known that they're interested in a bit more from your relationship. Are you up for it? Fine. Just be sure it won't ruin your friendship if it doesn't work out.

Rewarding Days

2, 8, 9, 10, 11, 27

Challenging Days

3, 7, 16, 17, 19, 28

Taurus | December

Relaxation and Recreation

This month, the Sun, Mercury, and Jupiter will take turns passing through playful Sagittarius, a hooved sign like your own that enjoys its connection to the earth and all her sensory treasures. If you haven't yet given yourself a few days off to enjoy the holidays with friends and loved ones, it's time to plan it. Just wait until after the 6th to make it happen.

Lovers and Friends

The line between platonic and romantic relationships will muddy up a bit around the 7th, Taurus, as someone close to you makes a move to let you know they're interested in switching departments. Whether you're letting go of a romance or allowing a friend to become a lover doesn't matter. Just be sure you two can stay in each other's lives if things don't work out as planned.

Money and Success

On Friday the 21st, Venus and Neptune will get together in an easy trine aspect, the stuff that romanticized notions are made of. If you're trying to find the perfect gift for someone close to you, don't bother being extravagant. Sit back and think about what would make them smile. It's fond memories you're out to create, after all. The price on the sticker really doesn't matter.

Tricky Transits

Mercury will turn direct on the 6th, all done up in sexy Scorpio and your solar seventh house of one-to-one relationships. That said, you should probably expect to hear at least one voice from the past you were pretty sure you'd never be privy to ever again. How should you handle it? Well, first off, if they were unstable in the past, don't automatically assume they're here to stay. Bide your time and see what's what before involving your heart.

Rewarding Days

15, 16, 21, 24, 25, 28

Challenging Days

2, 5, 7, 31

Taurus Action Table

These dates reflect the best—but not the only—times for success and ease in these activities, according to your Sun sign.

	JAN	FEB	MAR	APR	MAY	JUN	JUL	AUG	SEP	OCT	NOV	DEC
Move			2		29				16			
Start a class	25									15		15
Join a club		9	1	17		22		25	9			
Ask for a raise		10		13			5					16
Get professional advice			4	11	18, 19		8		7, 12	24	11	
Get a loan		10			18	13		6, 7		27		28
New romance	8, 9	3					22				9, 10	
Vacation	2							19			8	

Gemini

The Twins
May 22 to June 21

Ⅱ

Element: Air

Quality: Mutable

Polarity: Yang/masculine

Planetary Ruler: Mercury

Meditation: I explore my
inner worlds

Gemstone: Tourmaline

Power Stones: Ametrine, citrine,
emerald, spectrolite, agate

Key Phrase: I think

Glyph: Pillars of duality,
the Twins

Anatomy: Shoulders, arms,
hands, lungs, nervous system

Colors: Bright colors, orange,
yellow, magenta

Animals: Monkeys, talking birds,
flying insects

Myths/Legends: Peter Pan,
Castor and Pollux

House: Third

Opposite Sign: Sagittarius

Flower: Lily of the valley

Keyword: Versatility

The Gemini Personality

Your Strengths, Gifts, and Challenges

You, Gemini, are among the most curious and easily bored critters on our lovely planet. Of course, that might be due to your affinity with Mercury, the movement-loving god with the wings on his head and his heels who just so happens to rule your sign. This fast-moving fellow has endowed you not just with an amazingly quick mind but enviable navigational skills as well. Yes, you certainly do think fast, move fast, and act fast, and yes, you're really, really good at multitasking, so in your case "thinking on your feet" isn't just a cliché—it's a habit. This explains why you kids are so good at texting, regardless of what else you're doing (but please do resist the urge to do it while driving). The thing is, most of us aren't quite as good at juggling as you happen to be, so try to be patient.

You're a big fan of activity and variety—because, after all, variety really is the spice of life—so in your book, there's nothing better than nonstop stimuli. Basically, when your brain is amused, even if you're so badly in need of a nap that your eyes are stinging, you'll force yourself to stay up to catch the show. Being "on" at all times can be physically and mentally exhausting, though, so every now and then, refuse all invitations and just stay home. Zone out in front of the television or put on your favorite music, turn off the lights, and turn in early. Your overworked brain will thank you by being even sharper than usual tomorrow. This boundless curiosity makes you versatile, flexible, and changeable—which only makes sense. You're acutely aware of what you'd miss out on if you forced yourself into a rigid schedule that never changed. Oh, and let's chat about puzzles, word games, and riddles, all of which are wonderful ways for you to exercise your brain. Indulge often, especially when you can't sleep. Giving your brain a project—and finishing it—is the best way to convince it to shut down for a bit.

Romance and Other Relationships

In your book, Gemini, regardless of whether someone wants to be a platonic playmate or a long-term spouse, the only deal breakers are these: First off, they absolutely must be interesting—hopefully, so interesting that they simultaneously entertain and amuse—which, to you, is nirvana. The thing is, you can tolerate just about anything but boredom, so putting aside all electronic devices and trusting another person to keep your restless spirit occupied is a very big deal—and quite the compliment, too. If you're attached, choosing hours when you two absolutely won't use phones, tablets, or computers may be critical to your relationship—but just think of the other wonderful ways you can spend your time together! If you're single, it's equally important that you look up from the keyboard every now and then. There may be an actual human being in the vicinity who'd like to get to know you better!

Of course, since you're such an intellectual creature, the way to your heart is through your brain, so the other air signs—Libra and Aquarius—are often good choices. Libra may become a tad too attached at times, but if you let it be known early on that you do love your freedom, you'll be able to work it out. Aquarius loves computers the way you do, so becoming intimate will take a bit of work on both your parts. If you want actual human connections, complete with sparks, look to the fire signs—Sagittarius and Aries, in particular—whose love of real-world, real-time adventure will easily lure you away from the electronics, maybe even for the long haul.

Career and Work

Since you kids are already the honorary heads of the communications department, Gemini, it's easy to picture you working in a profession that allows you to chat, type, or email—basically, anything that allows you to use a keyboard, a computer, or a phone. Sales, advertising, and marketing all come to mind, along with, of course, working online as a writer or setting and maintaining web pages. The thing is, you're easily bored, so if you're going to spend roughly one full third of the hours in a day toiling away, you'll only be able to tolerate it if you're interested in what you're doing. So no matter what field you choose, it must allow you to put your cerebral skills to use in a totally enjoyable way. Once that's done, you're sure to excel.

Money and Possessions

Your sign is pretty darn spontaneous, Gemini, so you'd think that your way of handling finances would be equally spontaneous—and not at all calculated. That's often the case, especially if you're flying solo with only yourself to care for. Still, even if you're happily attached, while you do have that impulsive side—especially when it comes to spending on someone you love (and most especially family members)—you're usually not quite so indulgent when it comes to yourself. Well, unless you're talking about electronic toys—in which case, you'll conjure up the cash in a New York minute. It's only fair, though. E-toys were created by members of your tribe who understand your needs, so of course you should be among the first to own them!

Your Lighter Side

What's fun for you, Gemini? Well, pretty much anything, provided it's new, colorful, or interesting. Festivals? Carnivals? Street fairs? Absolutely. In your mind, the people-watching part alone is well worth the price of admission. The same thing goes for malls, museums, classic car shows, or art galleries. The point is, anywhere a myriad of different types of people gather is your kind of place. All you need is a comfy perch—and maybe a latte—and you're good to go for hours. After the show, however, once you're home again, your restless brain still won't shut down. You'll immediately reach for one of your beloved gadgets, and chances are good it will either be a remote or a mouse—your favorites. Of course, even when you're offline, you enjoy playing around with other electronic toys and even cooking or cleaning gadgets—although, honestly, things that beep, blink, or talk back are most definitely your favorites.

Gemini Celebrities

You're a chatty creature, Gemini, so those born under your sign tend to have quite memorable voices. I can offer you no finer example than Morgan Freeman, whose voice is so famous that just about anybody can identify it. But then, think of Mel Blanc, who voiced not just the immortal Bugs Bunny and Daffy Duck but also the entire Looney Tunes crew. Oh, and then there's Clint Eastwood, who acts, directs, produces, and creates the soundtracks for his films. Talk about versatility! And then there's the classic vocal chords of Ian McKellan, Paul McCartney, Marilyn Monroe ("Happy birthday, Mr. President"), and Paula Abdul. Comedians Joan Rivers and Amy Schumer are uber-witty word wizards, another trait your sign is famous for. Of course, there's more to communication than just speaking, so let's consider the legendary writers born under your sign—like Anne Frank, Salman Rushdie, and Sir Arthur Conan Doyle, who created Sherlock Holmes. You also share your sign with expert, multifaceted communicators like Anderson Cooper, Laverne Cox, Prince, and Kanye West.

The Year Ahead for Gemini

As we already chatted about, you folks are natural-born multitaskers, so when it comes to juggling responsibilities, you're most definitely up for the challenge. This year, however, with excessive Jupiter in uber-focused Scorpio making his way through your solar sixth house of work and other daily duties, you might have your hands full. This house describes the typical rhythm of our day—that is, what we usually do and when we do it—which, of course, features our work schedule. So, since Jupiter expands and increases, you should expect your position on the job to take up a whole lot more of your time than usual. Not that you'll mind, not even for a minute. When planets wearing Scorpio come to visit, they inspire us to become fixated—and quite driven to have what we want. In your case, you'll be moved to perform above and beyond your pay grade, which means that the raise, bonus or promotion that's well past due could be along shortly—or better still, that a new, better position will be offered. Either way, congratulations. On a personal level, however, keep in mind that along with these additional benefits, some additional hours will also arrive, so prepare to deal with family members or dear friends who miss your company. Do yourself a favor. Every now and then, blow up your carefully made schedule, cut loose, and have some serious fun. Your light-hearted, fun-loving soul demands entertainment. Often. Don't deprive yourself, especially during this hardworking time.

Here's another thing: Assertive, aggressive Mars will spend no less than five months in your solar ninth house, Gemini, where opinions are formed—say, about religion, politics, and philosophies in general. That said, you should know that you'll be quite opinionated—and as per Mars, not at all shy about expressing those opinions—from May 16 through August 12, and again from September 10 through November 15. You're not shy about voicing your feelings, so those who know you well won't be at all surprised when you let loose, regardless of where you are or who happens to be in the vicinity. The good news is that you're in the mood to do some serious house-cleaning with regard to fair-weather friends and temporary acquaintances, so once you express yourself to one and all, you'll know who your real friends and allies are—and who they aren't.

Saturn

Good news, Gemini—and I mean really good news. After two and a half years of erecting roadblocks between you and your nearest and dearests via his presence in your solar seventh house of one-to-one relationships, Saturn has moved on. Just a week before 2018 began, he set off for Capricorn—his home turf—where this serious fellow will be operating quite happily until the spring of 2020. And believe me, if there's any planet you really want to keep happy, it's Saturn. The thing is, wherever he happens to be, the purpose of his visit is to teach you the art of caution, self-discipline, and patience, even if that means upsetting your best-laid plans and causing you a whole lot of frustration in the process.

Saturn also shows us what's useful and what's not, so if you've become estranged from someone recently, you can stop beating yourself up about it. If they're gone by Saturn's hand, they were meant to leave. Mourn them, if you haven't yet, but get it done soon, because it's time to move on. With Saturn currently holding court for the next two and half years in your solar eighth house—where sharing occurs—you have far bigger fish to fry. It's time for a crash course in true intimacy and everything required to maintain it. That goes for all personal relationships, from platonic confidants to sexual partners. Basically, this transit is all about trust—how to earn it, how to keep it, and how to know when it is and isn't deserved by others. You've become a bit of an expert on relationships, which will naturally make you even more cautious when it comes to inviting someone to join your inner circle. Just don't become so hesitant to trust that you back away from folks with qualities like integrity, decency, and reliability. That's what you're looking for.

Uranus

Think back to May of 2010, Gemini, because that's when Uranus first made his planetary debut at the door of your solar eleventh house of friendships and group affiliations and you began to reconsider how legitimate your peers were. Over the course of Uranus's time there, you've probably become quite attached to certain groups and other circles, and if the causes that brought you together are truly important in all your hearts, you won't be leaving each other's lives—not for a while, anyway. You've probably also gradually disappeared from gatherings that were no longer productive to you, and left friendships behind when you realized you were no longer on the same page. That's okay. It's part of the growth process.

The thing is, Uranus will leave this house behind on May 15, opting to spend the next seven years in your solar twelfth house—a very private place where few are invited and even fewer are allowed. This is the house of retreat, sanctuary, and silence, so after that date, if you suddenly have the urge to spend a whole lot more time alone, not to worry. That's exactly what you should be doing. Uranus is a bit of a mad scientist, and in this secluded place you'll find yourself wanting to putter around, either alone or in the company of someone you trust implicitly. It's time to start a journal, too. The insights that Uranus brings along during his trek through this house will be amazing, but they'll come and go in a second. Keep a pen and paper with you, and keep your journal next to your bed. Your dreams will also be inspirational, not to mention prophetic.

Neptune

At this point, Gemini, you're quite familiar with Neptune's energy. This woozy, dreamy goddess just loves to blur the lines between fantasy and reality, and she's been squaring your Sun sign from her spot in equally woozy, dreamy Pisces since April of 2011. Ever since then, you've probably been so confused about what's real and what's not that at times you've actually made up your own version of reality. On the positive side, if that happened because you decided to trust your gut—your intuition, that is—rather than simply obeying the rules because you've been told to—well, wonderful. After all, historically speaking, isn't it usually when you don't listen to your intuition that you get into trouble? If, however, you opted to ignore what was going on around you because you were doing everything you possibly could to avoid making a decision—well, that's where it might get dicey. Like it or not, a confrontation may be coming, and you won't be able to run away from it—and on some level, you really don't want to.

Do yourself a favor. Indulge yourself in all the Neptunian escape hatches you like from time to time—say, the movies, an adult beverage or two, and maybe even a day or two away from the madding crowds. Fine. Just don't remove yourself so far from the real world that you don't take care of business, or become so intimidated or disappointed by the real world that you withdraw. Yes, you're uber-sensitive right now, and yes, loud sounds and bright lights may actually physically hurt. Still, I don't need to tell someone who plays so well with the five senses that there are many, many lovely experiences on our wonderful planet you haven't had yet. Make it your mission during 2018 to get out there, find the gentler ones, and allow them to soothe you. If you were born between May 31 and June 7, all this goes double—and do try to treat yourself gently this year.

Pluto

Back in 2008, Pluto began his trek through Capricorn and your solar eighth house of intimate matters and shared resources, Gemini. Now, this is where we deal with issues related to intimacy and sharing, so on a surface level, while I'd like to tell you that shared financial matters like loans, inheritances, and mortgages will suddenly become easy to deal with—well, that's just not the case. That doesn't mean that you won't get the results you're after in these categories, but only that it most likely won't be easy—especially if you were born between June 9 and June 12. Regardless of when you made your debut, however, power struggles of some kind over money, resources, and possessions will likely be part of your landscape for the coming year. Your mission is to decide what's truly important and what's not—and to keep in mind that once you clear the decks and make way for new growth, Pluto will see to it that new growth occurs. Keep that in mind when you're trying to talk yourself into admitting that it's time to ditch a situation or relationship that just isn't working. It's cool. Sweep up, then sit back and see what happens.

How Will This Year's Eclipses Affect You?

Think of eclipses as celestial exclamation points. They amp up the volume on ordinary life for us all when they occur, but the signs and houses they occupy show where the possibility exists for sudden, intense, and often quite surprising events. Eclipses occur in pairs, six months apart. Solar Eclipses are supercharged New Moons, bringing the Sun and Moon together and marking peak times for planting seeds in any department of life. Lunar Eclipses are high-energy Full Moons, times of dramatic culmination, fulfillment, and often new beginnings as well, provided the slate has been wiped clean.

There will be five eclipses during 2018, marking an extremely unpredictable year for one and all.

The first Lunar Eclipse of the year will occur in romantic Leo on January 31, activating your solar third house of conversations and communications in a very big way. You single folks should prepare to be swept off your feet by a charming new admirer—unless you're already seeing someone, that is, in which case the relationship may be due to intensify in a wonderfully romantic and totally surprising way. On the other hand, if you're ready to make a dramatic statement and move on, don't hesitate.

Do it nicely, though, so you'll have no regrets and never feel the need to wonder, "What if?"

On February 15, a Solar Eclipse in Aquarius will plant a supercharged seed of new beginnings and your solar ninth house of long-distance friends and lovers. If the folks you're currently associating with aren't on the same page, the Universe will make it clear to you now that it's time to branch out. Investigate online sites where kindred spirits gather to exchange opinions and aspirations. It's time to see to it that stage one of your five-year plan is on the right path, and surrounding yourself with those who share your beliefs will most certainly help.

On July 12, a Solar Eclipse will arrive in home- and family-oriented Cancer and your solar second house of financial issues. This is a tricky one, Gemini—first of all, because eclipses are erratic by nature, but also because this one is quite literally hitting close to home. Your mission is to keep your cool—no, not your usual style, but you can handle it—and do what you can to ensure that your financial picture stays intact and your nest remains safe and secure.

The Lunar Eclipse in Aquarius on July 27 will set up shop in your solar ninth house, bringing about closure—or, at the very least, an amazing amount of progress—regarding a long-distance relationship you became involved in back in February. Sit back and think about all you've invested in this partnership since then, and if it's not working out, resolve to let go—once and for all—of anyone who's dragging you down. Wash your hands of it all and move forward.

The third and final Solar Eclipse of the year will occur on August 11, all done up in fiery Leo. If you found yourself single back in late January, or shed something that was holding you back from personal growth, circumstances that arise now will give you plenty of reasons to pat yourself on the back. Oh, and you'll be able to understand why the process was set in motion exactly when and how it happened, too. It might be time for a celebration—or, at the least, for a few moments of proud reflection before you set off on your new path.

Gemini | January

Relaxation and Recreation

The weekend of the 5th through the 7th looks to be great fun for you, provided that you take care of your responsibilities before you kick back and head for the hills. The emotional Moon in Libra will make Sunday even more delightful—especially if you can manage to spend it with one particular someone who's been sorely missing your intimate attention.

Lovers and Friends

Both Venus and the Sun will get into active squares with startling Uranus on the 13th and 14th, Gemini, so no matter what you had planned, better have plan B ready. There's a good chance that what you had scheduled will be changed—abruptly, too. Not to worry, though. You're famous for spontaneity, and after all, aren't some of your best memories the result of last-minute turn-arounds?

Money and Success

Money matters that have been rather confusing of late will suddenly become clear on the 1st, thanks to the bright light of the Full Moon in Cancer in your solar second house of finances. This boon may arrive with a bit of a cost, however, especially if you've been mulling over a decision about home improvements, a move, or the financial needs of a dependent.

Tricky Transits

The Lunar Eclipse on the 31st will occur in fiery, dramatic Leo and your solar third house of conversations and communications, Gemini, insisting that you open your eyes and accept that someone hasn't been entirely honest with you lately. No, it may not be pleasant—especially if you care a great deal for them—but no matter how tough the news might be, knowing what's really up will help you to move forward.

Rewarding Days

2, 3, 6, 8, 15, 19, 25

Challenging Days

9, 12, 13, 14, 26, 27

Gemini | February

Relaxation and Recreation

With the Sun, Mercury, and Venus set to dash through your solar ninth house this month, it's easy to imagine you being bitten, big time, by the travel bug. Places you've never been to will be especially appealing to your wanderlust, but if you can't take off for parts unknown just yet, do yourself a favor. Indulge your restless spirit by learning something new. It doesn't matter what it is, as long as it's something you've always been curious about.

Lovers and Friends

Around the 21st, loving Venus and dreamy Neptune will put you in the mood for love. Now, that mood may come about because you've just run across someone who's absolutely everything you've ever dreamed of. In that case, wonderful. Congratulations on your good fortune. Take your time getting to know them, though. Being alone for a little while is better than being with someone who won't make you happy in the long run.

Money and Success

If you're tempted to do a bit of shopping for a friend around the 3rd, Gemini, let it be known that you probably won't be a font of willpower—especially if you're trying to make up for something. Don't allow guilt to affect your judgment—and by all means, if you need to apologize, just do so and forget about extravagant gifts. Your sincere "I'm sorry" will mean much, much more in the long run.

Tricky Transits

On the 15th, a Solar Eclipse will arrive, Gemini—and yes, eclipses are extremely erratic creatures. This time around, however, a nice, stable Venus-Saturn sextile aspect will be in the neighborhood, ready to help you adjust to any major changes that come your way. Think of this pair as an astrological safety net. No matter how abrupt or sudden the events that arise, you'll have the support you need from dear ones.

Rewarding Days

5, 6, 27

Challenging Days

3, 13, 15, 17, 24

Gemini | March

Relaxation and Recreation

Four planets will make their way through your solar eleventh house this month, all done up in fiery, spontaneous Aries. Needless to say, after dealing with the added responsibilities Saturn in Capricorn has brought along over the past few months, you're due for some serious fun. Fortunately, you have a nice, long list of friends who'll want to join you. Get on the phone and make some exciting plans.

Lovers and Friends

If you get the feeling there's a bit of jealousy or resentment brewing between you and a loved one around the 23rd, don't question your instincts. It's not just your imagination. Mercury (your ruling planet) will be stationing to turn retrograde, dredging up all kinds of memories—and the accompanying emotions. You have three weeks to think this over, and either ditch the grudge or make a clean break.

Money and Success

Getting what you want around the 13th—both financially and with regard to possessions—may be a lot tougher than it initially seems, even if all systems seem to be go and you're just about ready to sign on the dotted line, make a major purchase, or finalize a deal. Prepare yourself for the possibility of temporary disappointment, but don't worry. This too shall pass.

Tricky Transits

The Full Moon in partner-oriented Libra on the 31st will illuminate your solar fifth house of lovers and playmates, Gemini, urging you to figure out what will make you and yours happiest—and then take steps to make it happen. We're not necessarily talking about a long-term solution to an ongoing problem—although that would be ideal, and if the possibility arises, you should jump on it. For now, though, just focus on having a peaceful weekend.

Rewarding Days

2, 3, 6, 16, 27, 31

Challenging Days

10, 11, 13, 23, 24, 29

Gemini | April

Relaxation and Recreation
If a friend decides to pull a prank on you for April Fools' Day, don't be too mad about it, Gemini. With Mars and Saturn holding court together in diligent, responsible Capricorn, it's been a while since you've had a good, spontaneous giggle. And since the lighter side of life is what makes your soul smile—well, let go, just for a bit, and laugh.

Lovers and Friends
Up until at least the 15th, your ruling planet, Mercury, will continue to bring old friends and long-lost loved ones back into your life, Gemini—for better or worse. If someone you've been missing doesn't make contact by the 12th, however, don't wait any longer. Take advantage of this transit to reach out first.

Money and Success
On the 22nd, intense Pluto will stop in his tracks in your solar eighth house of shared resources and joint finances, Gemini. If someone owes you and has been deliberately putting you off for no good reason, get in touch with them now and let them know you haven't forgotten about their debt. This planet doesn't mess around, so they'll hear you, understand, and get busy.

Tricky Transits
Loving Venus will take off for your sign on the 24th, and since she'll be bringing all her charm and magnetism to your solar first house of personality, you can count on attracting at least one rather adamant admirer. If you're single, clear your calendar. Think of the next three weeks as prime time to conduct interviews for the position of significant other.

Rewarding Days
6, 7, 12, 23, 24

Challenging Days
1, 2, 10, 18, 25

Gemini | May

Relaxation and Recreation

A friend's quite spontaneous invitation on the 13th could end up becoming a memory you'll never forget, Gemini. Yes, you're working hard, but that doesn't mean you can't remain true to your nature and have some serious fun when you've earned it. Oh, come on. When was the last time you had a chance to be unpredictable? Go for it!

Lovers and Friends

Communicating your needs to a loved one could be tough around the 9th, Gemini, so if you feel as if you're hitting a brick wall, rather than becoming totally frustrated and walking away angry, table the discussion for another day—and maybe even another week, for that matter. You two simply aren't speaking the same language at the moment. Take a bit of time apart. It's amazing how easily a bit of distance can bring us together.

Money and Success

Money matters that have been on hold stand a very good chance of turning out well around the 18th, Gemini, provided you've been able to keep quiet about a tip or suggestion a financially oriented friend or advisor recently whispered in your ear. You may even see a return on your investment—whether it be time or money—as soon as the 22nd.

Tricky Transits

Separating imagination from reality may be tough around the 7th, Gemini, especially if you've been seeing someone lately who you're sure hasn't quite been totally honest with you. You may be right—but just in case you're not, stay quiet and do some digging before you push them away. If the facts prove you right, don't bother ghosting them. Tell them off and walk away. No, strut away.

Rewarding Days

6, 8, 13, 14, 23

Challenging Days

1, 7, 9, 12, 16, 28

Gemini | June

Relaxation and Recreation

Bright and early on the 1st, the Universe will give you all the excuses anyone has ever needed to have yet another terrific weekend with friends, Gemini. You've been feeling quite spontaneous lately, and for the most part, those last-minute adventures have turned out well. That said, you might want to buckle up and prepare yourself, because the ride isn't over just yet.

Lovers and Friends

Prepare yourself, Gemini. Around the 25th, a certain someone who's been failing to capture your attention may take things to a whole new level. There may be a bit of drama involved, which can be charming, depending on how it's done. If you're interested and the display isn't over the top, wonderful. If you're not, better nip this in the bud—right now.

Money and Success

Getting your point across to coworkers won't be easy around the 6th or 8th, Gemini—but that doesn't mean you should give up. It would be best to put the negotiations on hold, just for a week or so, until all the proper astrological tools you'll need will be available to you. Yes, it will be frustrating, but trust me, you'll get over it. Be patient.

Tricky Transits

Mars will stop in his tracks in your solar ninth house on the 26th, Gemini, a place where opinions are formed, changed, and reformed. It seems you may soon be ready to reverse your sentiments about an issue that's been near and dear to your heart for a very long time. If it's because new information has come up, wonderful. Just be sure that you're not changing your mind because someone else has talked you into it.

Rewarding Days

1, 2, 3, 22, 25

Challenging Days

6, 8, 11, 14, 29, 30

Gemini | July

Relaxation and Recreation

The Sun, Mercury, and Venus will light up your solar third house during July, Gemini, a team that can't help but bring along all kinds of interesting, exciting news. On the positive side, you most certainly won't be bored. In particular, it's your siblings and neighbors who'll keep you on your toes—big time. Of course, the kind of drama they'll bring along may cause an interruption in your daily schedule, so pencil in some extra time on hectic days and prepare for distractions.

Lovers and Friends

Around the 22nd, someone you've had a secret crush on for some time now will finally acknowledge the fact that they knew about it the whole time. If you're single, this is the moment you've been waiting for. It's time to ask about lunch. Or dinner. Or coffee. If one or both of you is attached, before you speak up, better be sure you're ready to face some pretty darn serious consequences before you take this flirtation to an entirely different level.

Money and Success

Your luck may change suddenly on or around the 11th, Gemini, thanks to an easy trine aspect between Venus and startling Uranus—oh, and a Solar Eclipse, too. Now would be a terrific time to invest in a lottery ticket—but don't get crazy. It only takes one lottery ticket to win.

Tricky Transits

Someone from the past may suddenly make an appearance in your life around the 27th, Gemini. Does this mean you're obligated in any way, shape, or form to let them back in? Nope. Not at all. In fact, you should think really hard before you reopen any doors you shut for very good reasons. Don't indulge in selective remembering. Call to mind both the good and the bad before you sign up again.

Rewarding Days
10, 11, 21, 22

Challenging Days
1, 2, 6, 12, 25, 26, 27

Gemini | August

Relaxation and Recreation

A lovely configuration known as a Grand Trine will occur on the 25th, Gemini, bringing together three planets who'll all be in the mood to make overnight success entirely possible—provided you've been working hard for a very long time, of course. All kidding aside, if you've put in your time and paid your dues, you can expect to be richly rewarded now. Likewise if you've just come up with a way to solve a nagging work-related problem.

Lovers and Friends

Venus, the Goddess of Love herself, will take off for your solar fifth house of lovers and playmates on the 6th, Gemini. If you're single, think of the next three weeks as a buffet of sorts, and take your time choosing what you'd like to taste. If you're attached, take advantage of this time to court your sweetheart all over again. There are times when fires can be rekindled. This is one of those times. Go for it.

Money and Success

On the 9th, Venus and Saturn will square off, putting your need for security at odds with your urge to take a chance. If you're thinking of investing—even if you're sure you have all the facts down pat—just for the heck of it, and before you plunk down any of your hard-earned dollars, ask a professional for advice. That goes double if you're about to take a chance with money you really can't afford to lose.

Tricky Transits

Assertive Mars will station on the 27th in your solar eighth house of shared possessions and joint resources, Gemini—and with this warrior god on duty, heaven help anyone who's been trying to take advantage of you. Even if you haven't seen through them before, their agenda will become crystal-clear over the next couple of months, if not immediately. Your mission is to remain calm and alert the authorities.

Rewarding Days

5, 6, 7, 24, 25

Challenging Days

1, 4, 8, 9, 11, 12, 18

Gemini | September

Relaxation and Recreation

If you're thinking of entertaining family members at your place or visiting family or old, dear friends, look to the weekend of the 14th, Gemini. The emotional Moon will be in playful, outgoing Sag, with four helpful planets on board to ensure that your conversations and communications go smoothly—even if you're discussing matters that might ordinarily be a tad problematic.

Lovers and Friends

Venus will sidle off silently into sexy Scorpio on the 9th, urging you to take a current relationship to a whole new level. It might be that you're ready to become more intimately involved. It might be that you're willing to share a bit more about yourself in conversation. Regardless of how it happens, when the urge strikes you, be sure you trust this person implicitly.

Money and Success

Conversations about joint finances and shared possessions will go well around the 12th, Gemini, especially if you're negotiating a promotion that comes with a raise. Around the 23rd or 25th, though? Well, not so much. If you absolutely must make appointments with higher-ups toward the end of the month, aim for the 27th, when the Sun and fiery Mars will help you make your case energetically and emphatically—to say the least.

Tricky Transits

The Full Moon in Aries on the 24th will open your eyes to the very real possibility of taking charge of a group you've been enjoying for months now—and maybe even years. The good news is that while you may need to jump through a few hoops to please the higher-ups in charge of it all, if you're up for it, you could be a serious agent for change over the next two to three years.

Rewarding Days

14, 15, 16, 20, 21, 22

Challenging Days

6, 9, 18, 19, 23, 25

Gemini | October

Relaxation and Recreation

Roadblocks that come along around the 10th and 11th will be quite frustrating, and if someone you love is holding something over your head, you'll need to find a way to eliminate that problem. It might be that you'll have to come clean and confess something. It might also be that confronting someone with facts you've recently unearthed will become necessary. Regardless, don't shy away. Meet the situation head on.

Lovers and Friends

If you're feeling stalled or delayed with regard to a relationship situation, Gemini, don't blame yourself. After the 5th, when Venus turns retrograde, moving forward with your plans to become monogamous or to cohabitate won't go along easily. It's okay, though. Don't rush, and most definitely don't push your sweetheart. It's time to mull things over. Take some time—both of you—and be sure you're prepared for this.

Money and Success

The Full Moon on the 24th will occur in Taurus, the sign that's known for being a money magnet. If you're negotiating a contract—especially if this isn't the first time you've had this conversation with a higher-up—just be sure you've got all your ducks in a row before you sit down to defend your case. That expression "the devil is in the details" will prove to be true. Be sure you're prepared for anything.

Tricky Transits

A Sun-Uranus opposition on the 23rd could inspire coworkers to be unpredictable, erratic, or impulsive, Gemini, so if you've been working with someone in a partnership role, do yourself a favor and be sure that you can handle the whole project—just in case. If all goes well, you won't have to lift a finger. In fact, your cohort may pleasantly surprise you.

Rewarding Days

12, 13, 14, 22, 24, 27

Challenging Days

2, 5, 10, 11, 31

Gemini | November

Relaxation and Recreation

Talk about a good time! Jupiter will set off for Sagittarius on the 8th, set to keep you entertained, amused, and oh-so-happy throughout the coming year via his presence in your solar seventh house of one-to-one relationships. If you're seeing someone casually, that status could change in a wonderful way. If you're single and you don't want to be, this is a terrific time to resume the hunt.

Lovers and Friends

Optimistic Jupiter will set off for your solar seventh house on the 8th, Gemini, promising a year of positive and promising focus on your closest one-to-one relationships. The good news is that if you're seeing someone casually now and you'd like things to progress, you won't have to do much to make that happen. The best part? Once you ask for a more permanent, monogamous situation, you won't have to worry about being refused.

Money and Success

A shopping trip with a friend will be great fun around the weekend of the 9th. If you're off after a large item, take your BFF along, have a battle plan, and take your time. Resolve not to buy anything right away—or at least not until well after Venus turns direct on the 16th. Think of this as a scouting mission.

Tricky Transits

Venus will turn direct on the 16th, a few hours before Mercury—who you'll remember is in charge of communication—turns retrograde. These two planetary stations could make things quite complicated in the departments of love and money. Your mission is to be as patient as possible—which, admittedly, is a lot to ask from restless little you. The good news is that if you can wait a bit, things might just turn out exactly the way you want them to.

Rewarding Days
8, 9, 10, 11, 24, 25

Challenging Days
6, 7, 16, 17, 19, 30

Gemini | December

Relaxation and Recreation

The Full Moon of the 22nd will get your holiday weekend off to a terrific start, Gemini. It will occur in home- and family-oriented Cancer, so you should probably expect to do a bit of entertaining at your place—that is, if you're not kidnapped by loved ones who want to turn the tables and force you to enjoy yourself without putting any real work into holiday gatherings for a change. Let them spoil you. It's time!

Lovers and Friends

'Tis the season for fun, Gemini, for getting together with friends, family, and lighthearted acquaintances to celebrate—and with the Sun, Mercury, and Jupiter passing through fun-loving, outgoing Sagittarius, a good time is sure to be had by all. Of course, they'll all be moving through your solar seventh house, so it may be that one particular person is the reason for that perpetual grin you'll be wearing. Enjoy!

Money and Success

If you have last-minute shopping to do, schedule it for the 16th. That may seem a bit too close to the holidays for comfort, but a lovely sextile aspect between Venus and Saturn will make it easy for you to find exactly what you need at a price you can afford. Afterward, reward yourself with an evening out. Oh, and if you're still searching for a gift around the 21st, forget extravagance. Aim for something personal that will tell them you pay attention.

Tricky Transits

Mercury will retrograde back into Scorpio and your solar sixth house on the 1st, offering you another chance to fix a work-oriented project that's been problematic. If you're working with a partner, so much the better. Put your heads together and figure out what you need to do to wrap things up. You probably won't have to start over entirely, but don't get upset if you need to retrace your steps a bit further back than you'd like.

Rewarding Days

7, 8, 12, 16, 21, 24, 25, 28

Challenging Days

1, 2, 5, 6, 30, 31

Gemini Action Table

These dates reflect the best—but not the only—times for success and ease in these activities, according to your Sun sign.

	JAN	FEB	MAR	APR	MAY	JUN	JUL	AUG	SEP	OCT	NOV	DEC
Move								7		27		
Start a class		6	2	12		3		6	16			
Join a club							22				9	
Ask for a raise	2				14		11	24, 25	12			
Get professional advice			3, 4	6, 7						15		16
Get a loan	3		6							26		21
New romance		21		23, 24		25	21, 22				8	24, 25
Vacation	5–7	5			13	1, 2			14, 15		8, 9	

Cancer

The Crab
June 22 to July 22

Element: Water

Quality: Cardinal

Polarity: Yin/feminine

Planetary Ruler: The Moon

Meditation: I have faith in the promptings of my heart

Gemstone: Pearl

Power Stones: Moonstone, Chrysocolla

Key Phrase: I feel

Glyph: Crab's claws

Anatomy: Stomach, breasts

Colors: Silver, pearl white

Animals: Crustaceans, cows, chickens

Myths/Legends: Hercules and the Crab, Asherah, Hecate

House: Fourth

Opposite Sign: Capricorn

Flower: Larkspur

Keyword: Receptivity

The Cancer Personality

Your Strengths, Gifts, and Challenges

Your planet is the Moon, Cancer, the Queen of Emotions herself. She waxes, wanes, disappears entirely every two weeks, then becomes the star of the show when she's full. So are you moody? Of course you are! It's your job. But while you may be changeable, just like the Moon, you're also quite predictable in the eyes of those few carefully selected others who are lucky enough to know you well. The energy of the Moon isn't as obvious as that of her partner, the Sun, but just like the ocean tides she controls, she's quietly powerful and a force to be reckoned with. Sound familiar? It should. When you're on a mission, especially if it involves nurturing, defending, or protecting a child or other loved one, you can be extremely intimidating. Whether you realize it or not, you exude a quiet power that's quite formidable—which might be why family members and even your kids will only push you so far.

Now, speaking of family, let's talk about home. Your symbol is the crab, a creature so cautious it carries its home with it wherever it goes, and so vulnerable its shell also doubles as protection. Similarly, your home is your sanctuary—your nest—and anyone or anything who lives under your roof can't help but feel safe there. But you also make it clear right from the git-go that your home is definitely your castle, and you are definitely King or Queen.

Romance and Other Relationships

When you love someone, Cancer, there's absolutely no way they can possibly miss it. You tend their wounds, listen to their problems, feed them comfort food, and always, always have their back. Anyone who enjoys that kind of treatment from you won't come by it easily, however. You are cautious and private, and you take your time getting to know others. If and when you let your guard down, it's a tremendous compliment. In exchange for all that, you ask only that you are respected and that your rules are obeyed in your home.

Your family members are nearest and dearest to your heart. They come before anyone or anything else. That goes double for your children, the light of your life. You treat your pets as kids, too, and lavish them with the same TLC your human children enjoy.

Now, your highly emotional nature means your feelings can easily be hurt, although often unintentionally. That's when you sidle off and disappear for a while to lick your wounds and "moon" over the offense. As you get older, you tend not to take everything quite so personally, but as a young adult, you are often extremely sensitive. In fact, it may take years for you to literally come out of your shell and give friendships or romance a try.

The Moon's influence also makes you quite instinctive, and you usually operate on feelings rather than facts, trusting your gut above all else. So while you're searching for your soul mate, you move quickly from one possible candidate to the next. Those keen antennae of yours tell you almost immediately whether or not there's a reason to stick around. Sturdy Taurus and responsible Capricorn often fit the bill just fine when it comes to long-term relationships, and you'll feel an instant bond with perceptive Scorpio and intuitive Pisces.

Career and Work

As home-oriented as you are, Cancer, your ideal job situation will always be working from home. But if that's not possible, you'll need to find a work environment that feels like home. In that case, you end up thinking of your coworkers as part of your extended family. Occupations that deal with real estate or domestic situations are a nice fit for you, but you might also enjoy the food-service industry, especially if it's one of your own secret recipes that's served up.

Since your sign is so closely associated with kids and families, you might initially be drawn to work that involves children—a natural match. You appreciate their innocence and candor, and they bring out the protective side in you, which is one of the qualities you are proudest of. If you decide to teach, it will likely be the little ones you prefer to work with, since they accept love and guidance so willingly. You might also be drawn toward work that brings you into the homes of others, perhaps to decorate or, if you're metaphysically inclined, to practice feng shui.

Money and Possessions

Financially speaking, as with many other areas of life, security is very important, Cancer. Your home is precious to you, and you know the value of having a safety net in place to be sure you keep it. You have no problem putting money aside for a rainy day, and when you do pull out your wallet or credit card, it's usually because you've found The Real Deal—or because one of the kids has finally worn you down!

Your Lighter Side

Having your family and dearest friends over to your place is what you love best, Cancer, and if they're gathered cozily around the dinner table or in front of the fireplace, so much the better. Either way, you're a gracious and generous host. When you leave your nest in pursuit of some fun, it's often to share activities with your children.

Cancer Celebrities

The emotional Moon is your patron planet, Cancer, and she's very fond of silver, which is quite the reflective element. So think mirrors and then impressionists—and then consider that you were born under the same sign as both Robin Williams and Meryl Streep, the master and mistress of ducking out of their own bodies and taking on another persona. But you folks also have a way of making your way into our hearts in a very big way. Like Tom Cruise, Ricky Gervais, Jessica Simpson, Princess Diana, Tom Hanks, Liv Tyler, Will Ferrell, and Malala Yousafzai, for example.

The Year Ahead for Cancer

Your solar eighth house will play host to fiery, passionate Mars for no less than five months this year, Cancer, and since he's quite the assertive, aggressive energy, you should expect to be quite "active" with regard to this area of life. So what does the eighth house rule? Well, for starters, physical intimacy—so having Mars here could be quite a delightful situation. In fact, if you're attached and have been for a while, since Mars is in Aquarius, you two might decide to do some experimenting … if you catch my drift. Of course, Aquarius has also been known to appear a bit detached every now and then, so if you or your partner suddenly becomes too absorbed in a cerebral activity—say, because you're attached to your computer, phone, or other electronic device—one of you will need to put your foot down and demand that all electronics be shut off at a certain time. These e-trinkets are great fun, but if they're driving a wedge between you and the person who's actually right there in the room with you, it's time to cut way, way back on the time you spend using them. Now, you're an emotional sign, Cancer, so it's nearly as tough to convince you of this fact as it might be to talk others into it, but still, make a conscious effort to be present with the actual living human beings in the vicinity, and don't be afraid to ask—no, demand—that anyone who wants to spend time with you do the same. You may also run across someone interesting via an online venue, and if you have lots of interests in common, it will be tough to pull yourself away. There's nothing wrong with getting tight with someone online, but before you exchange any intimate information, be sure you spend some actual face time with them—even if it's only via Skype or Facetime.

I'm emphasizing relationship matters because Jupiter will spend the year in sexy Scorpio and your solar fifth house of lovers, so you'll be in the mood to fall in love—or become infatuated, at the very least. The thing is, in this sign and house, Jupiter doesn't tend to bring out the most realistic, practical side of human nature, so you'll need to pay careful attention to your feelings. If you're falling too far, too fast, apply the brakes. If it's real, a few deep breaths won't change a single thing.

Saturn

Just weeks before 2018 began, Saturn moved off into your solar seventh house of one-to-one relationships, Cancer, all done up in serious, respectable Capricorn. Now, this energy is nothing if not committed to commitment—no pun intended—so if you've been seeing someone causally but haven't yet made it exclusive, not to worry. You'll be in the mood to settle down, sign up, and put down some roots—big time—as the year goes on, and there's little doubt that you'll be refused. In fact, the really good news is that all parties concerned—family, kids, etc.—will be tickled that you two have finally decided to make things official.

If you're single, however, Saturn can act in one of two ways. First off, he may send someone along who's a great deal older or younger than you—in which case, dealing with the typically Saturnian issue of "who's in charge here?" will be your first hurdle. Most likely, the answer will be that you switch off, as do most couples. If that's the case, don't let anyone judge your relationship, no matter how odd or unusual it seems to them. If you're both happy and no one is being harmed, there's no reason for you to make excuses—or even feel like you should. On the other hand, if you're involved in a relationship that's not healthy and you feel repressed, stifled, or inhibited, don't allow it to continue, and don't make up excuses for why you "can't" move on. Face the facts. If this is a bad situation and you need to oust yourself from it, why wait a second longer?

Uranus

If you were born at the tail end of your sign, Cancer, your Sun will be experiencing a square aspect from Uranus—a very tense, very irritating energy that absolutely insists that we move, change, and transform. Of course, regardless of when you were born, your Sun sign has been feeling the pressure from Uranus for close to seven years now, so stress and tension probably aren't alien emotions. The thing is, when Uranus contacts your Sun, ignoring who and what you want to be becomes absolutely impossible—regardless of the rules and regulations you've been trying your best to abide by. If you've been feeling especially repressed or held back, whether by a person or a situation, you won't be willing to put up with it for much longer.

The good news is that Uranus will stay on duty here in Aries until May 15, so if you haven't yet declared your independence, you'll do it soon. Just don't let this chance to free yourself up pass you by. Get out from under the thumb of anyone who's been holding you down. Leave the job that's made you feel totally unappreciated. Don't just jump, though. You have half a year to come up with an alternate plan. The good news is that once you've liberated yourself, you won't believe the energy and enthusiasm for life you'll experience. Think of it as being reborn, and don't let shouldas, wouldas, or couldas get in the way.

Neptune

Neptune is still on duty in Pisces and your solar ninth house of education, higher beliefs, and opinions, where she's been since April of 2011. This spiritual, intuitive energy will be whispering to you all year long, urging you to pay attention to what's going on around you—and maybe even take a stance about issues that are near and dear to your heart. If you were born between July 1 and 10, her voice will be especially hard to ignore. Neptune will spend the year in an easy, inspirational trine aspect to your Sun, inspiring you to investigate spiritual and/or metaphysical matters, and your already keen antennae will be running on high. Needless to say, if you've been thinking about taking classes in those areas, this is the time to sign up. You're set to make contact with gurus, mentors, and advisors during 2018. Your only mission now is to be sure that you're ready, willing, and able to open up your mind and your heart—which, of course, has never been much of a challenge for compassionate little you. When you're not in class or immersed within a group of kindred spirits, be sure to find some time to spend either in or by the water. It's your element, after all, and when you're troubled, there's nothing that can soothe you faster or bring your emotions back into balance more easily.

Pluto

Pluto in Capricorn will spend yet another year in your solar seventh house of one-to-one relationships, an extremely intense guy in an extremely important place. Now, Pluto is in charge of life, death, and rebirth, so if you've had the feeling that people have been entering and exiting from your life in rather dramatic fashion for the past few years—well, you're absolutely right. Pluto is a big fan of clearing away what's no longer necessary to make room for bigger and better things. His methods leave a bit to be desired at times—in fact, most of the time—but that doesn't change the fact that he's basically on duty to push you toward getting rid of what's no longer working in your life.

The thing is, the harder you try to hang on, the more urgently—and ungently—Pluto will force you to let go. With this planet in the seventh house, it's best for you to understand that anyone who leaves your life now was absolutely meant to go. On the other hand, anyone who stays is here for a reason—to help you evolve into the person you need to be. If you've lost someone recently through death, try not to dwell on it. Yes, that's far easier said than done, but it won't do anyone any good for you to stay attached to the past—and you know your dear one wouldn't want that anyway. Pluto rules regeneration, so rest assured that your heart will heal. It may take a while, but it will happen. Grieve your losses for a respectable amount of time, then move on.

How Will This Year's Eclipses Affect You?

Think of eclipses as celestial exclamation points. They amp up the volume on ordinary life for us all when they occur, but the signs and houses they occupy show where the possibility exists for sudden, intense, and often quite surprising events. Eclipses occur in pairs, six months apart. Solar Eclipses are supercharged New Moons, bringing the Sun and Moon together and marking peak times for planting seeds in any department of life. Lunar Eclipses are high-energy Full Moons, times of dramatic culmination, fulfillment, and often new beginnings as well, provided the slate has been wiped clean.

There will be five eclipses during 2018, marking an extremely unpredictable year for one and all—but you, Cancer, will be directly affected by the Solar Eclipse on July 12. Read on...

On January 31, the Lunar Eclipse in Leo will activate your solar second house of personal finances and valued possessions, Cancer—and eclipses are anything but predictable, so you may be taken off guard by something tossed your way via someone you were sure you could trust. Ah, well. Life is full of surprises—some good, some not so good. At this time, your mission is to decide what's truly important.

On February 15, a Solar Eclipse in startling Aquarius will invade your solar eighth house of joint finances, the kind of energy that tends to tear down restrictions and completely discount the rules. If you've been feeling repressed or overwhelmed by duties you're performing that really don't belong to you, it's only a matter of time before you decide that enough is enough. Go ahead. Make a break for it, and make a show of it.

On July 12, a Solar Eclipse in your very own sign and your solar first house of personality and appearance will urge you to make whatever changes are necessary to ensure that your physical self and your personal presentation more aptly represent who you really are. Now, this may mean that you'll cut, dye, or style your hair in an unusual way, get a tattoo, or pierce something. Or it might just be a drastic wardrobe change. It doesn't matter. The point is for you to walk around feeling like your true self.

A Lunar Eclipse in Aquarius will arrive on July 27, once again activating your solar eighth house. If events from mid-February are rearing their little heads again, don't be a bit surprised. It's time to release the past. You'll have the closure you need, as well as an opportunity to make a fresh, clean start. Don't resist. Let go and look forward.

On August 11, a Solar Eclipse in Leo and your solar second house will help you put an end to a financial matter that's been pending in some way since late January. Enough is enough. If you're tired of the rigmarole, don't let it go on any longer. Let all parties concerned know that you're done. Period.

Cancer | January

Relaxation and Recreation

Your solar fifth house of lovers—casual flirtations and the like, that is—will be a very, very busy place this month, Cancer, as will your solar seventh house of more committed relationships. If you've been thinking about settling down, don't be surprised if your sweetheart mentions it even before you can. Yes, you're on the same page. Again. Nice, huh?

Lovers and Friends

The Sun and Venus in your solar seventh house of relationships will get together with dreamy, romantic Neptune on the 2nd and the 3rd, Cancer, making this the perfect time to find out exactly what happened to the one who got away. You know, the person you can't stop wondering about. Before you decide to reconnect, though, be sure you have new answers for the problems that split you up in the first place.

Money and Success

If you're thinking about investing in a business, whether it's yours or someone else's, the 8th and 9th are fine times to do it. A pack of earth and water energies will work together with practical Saturn to see to it that you're thinking clearly and moving ahead confidently. If you have any doubts about the fine print, however, the Universe will also see to it that someone who understands it will be along shortly.

Tricky Transits

The Lunar Eclipse on the 31st will occur in dramatic, fiery Leo—and since eclipses are already pretty darn fiery enough all on their own, you should probably prepare for a few fireworks, especially if you're in the middle of a financial battle. This doesn't mean that one of you will win or lose—not at the moment, anyway—but negotiating sure will be a bumpy ride for a few days.

Rewarding Days

8, 9, 10, 15, 16, 25

Challenging Days

7, 12, 13, 14, 24, 31

Cancer | February

Relaxation and Recreation

With outgoing Jupiter on duty in your solar fifth house of recreation, you've been a very big fan of going out to play lately, Cancer—as well you should be. But since you're a water sign, and Jupiter's wearing a water sign, why not soothe your soul by spending some quality time on the shore of a lake or river, or, best of all, walking barefoot on a beach? If all else fails, a good long soak in a hot tub certainly wouldn't hurt.

Lovers and Friends

Around the 24th, you may hear a voice from the past you were sure you'd never hear again. It might be that someone has tracked you down in hopes of getting another shot at the title—romantically speaking—but it could also be that you've finally found someone you've always been sad about losing. Either way, give it a shot. Have lunch—or coffee, at the very least.

Money and Success

Don't get too crazy with your plastic or your checkbook around the 3rd, Cancer—unless, of course, you've been saving up and tracking a certain item that's finally now on sale. In that case, be sure you're getting exactly what you want, and as far as any high-priced item goes, investing in the warranty wouldn't be a bad idea—you know, just in case.

Tricky Transits

A Solar Eclipse will occur in your solar eighth house of joint finances and shared resources on the 15th. Now, these lunations are notoriously erratic, tricky critters, so a certain someone you've been partners with may suddenly decide to ditch their responsibilities, leaving you with their share of the burden on very short notice. Prepare yourself, and be sure you're capable of managing the whole thing yourself before you agree.

Rewarding Days

6, 7, 14, 26, 27

Challenging Days

3, 10, 13, 17, 25, 28

Cancer | March

Relaxation and Recreation

If you've been thinking of taking a trip, whether it's to another state, another coast, or another country, the New Moon on the 17th will be a fine time to do it—especially if you're traveling with a partner. If you're attached, your choice of travel buddy is obvious. If not, consider your options carefully. Think about how long you two will be together. Is it pleasantly doable?

Lovers and Friends

During the first week of the month, a sky that's chock full of woozy, romantic Pisces energies will make it next to impossible for you to think rationally when your heart is involved. Does this mean you should refrain from making any decisions about relationships? Sure does. Coast. Tread water. Whatever you want to call it, stalling is entirely appropriate.

Money and Success

On the 6th, Venus—who's in charge of not just love but also money and possessions—will enter fiery, red-hot, and quite impatient Aries. She'll square off with Saturn on the 13th, which might stir things up between you and a higher-up. If you're not careful, a long-term feud may ensue. Keeping things on an even keel may not be easy, but it will be your best bet.

Tricky Transits

Mercury will turn retrograde on the 22nd, all done up in fiery Aries and your solar tenth house of higher-ups and authority figures. Yes, this certainly could mean you'll be at odds with elders and superiors, but only if you don't explain yourself to them well before Mercury makes this station. Sit down and talk things over. The 12th looks like your best bet.

Rewarding Days
1, 2, 8, 17, 30, 31

Challenging Days
10, 11, 13, 22, 23, 24

Cancer | April

Relaxation and Recreation
Mars and Saturn will collide on the 2nd in your solar seventh house of relationships, Cancer, urging you to either do some work on a current partnership or do what it takes to release a certain someone from the bonds you two have forged. No, it won't be easy, and please don't take it lightly, because these two planets play for keeps.

Lovers and Friends
A Sun-Pluto square on the 10th will make it tougher than usual for you to make amends with a dear one—any dear one, that is. If you're at odds with someone and trying to figure out a way to make it up to them, don't think gifts. Think heartfelt thoughts about how much you miss them.

Money and Success
On the 7th, Venus and Saturn will get into an easy trine aspect, the stuff that easy, profitable, and successful financial negotiations are made of. That's the good news. The best news is that Saturn represents authority figures, so if you need help and you're brave enough to ask for it, there will really be nothing you can't achieve. Now, clear your throat and pick up the phone.

Tricky Transits
On the 15th, the New Moon in Aries will arrive, just as Mercury in that same sign stops in his tracks to turn direct. These astrological occurrences sound like new beginnings, and they are—the thing is, the beginnings won't be coming along just yet. You're planting seeds now, not harvesting the results. Hang in there—career-wise, especially—for at least a few more weeks.

Rewarding Days
6, 7, 12, 13, 14, 23

Challenging Days
3, 4, 5, 10, 11, 25, 26

Cancer | May

Relaxation and Recreation

Once Venus sets off for your sign on the 19th, having fun will be pretty darn hard to avoid, Cancer. Between now and then, your mission is to be sure that you've done all your work and finished up all your projects so you'll be able to enjoy it all guilt-free. Staying up late on a school night is more fun when you know you deserve it.

Lovers and Friends

Around the 6th, someone who lives quite a distance from you and hasn't been in touch for some time now might just reach out to you, Cancer. If you left things on less than good terms, letting this person back into your world could be stressful—and maybe even impossible for you, emotionally speaking. Don't allow yourself to be pressured into anything you don't want to do.

Money and Success

Don't even try to negotiate a contract around the 9th, Cancer. You'll quickly find that whoever you're trying to do business with either doesn't understand you or doesn't want to understand you. That said, there's no reason you can't do business in the future. Your mission is to gather more information and schedule your meeting for the 17th or 18th.

Tricky Transits

If you get into an argument with a loved one around the 12th or 13th, forget about winning—and that goes for both of you. The Universe has arranged for a stalemate of sorts, and no matter how much you whine, yell, or carry on, your adversary will either match you or refuse to be moved. Sounds frustrating, right? Well, then, table the discussion until the 18th, when stable Saturn and Mercury will help to iron things out.

Rewarding Days

1, 10, 18, 19, 25

Challenging Days

1, 7, 8, 12, 16, 31

Cancer | June

Relaxation and Recreation

On the 1st and 2nd, you'll have plenty of chances to spend time at your place with your nearest and dearest—and since it's the weekend, there's a good chance they'll be able to accept your invitation. Enjoy whoever shows up, and understand if the rest of the crew is working—but rest assured that you most certainly won't be lonely.

Lovers and Friends

On the 15th, a very serious discussion between you and a dear one could end up turning into a long-lasting feud of sorts. Your mission is to be very careful what you say, and to try your very best not to take anything a loved one says in anger too personally. No, that's not easy for you, and yes, you'd be right to pout for at least six months, but just this once, try to nip it in the bud.

Money and Success

Assertive Mars has stormed off into Aquarius and your solar eighth house of shared resources, Cancer—and as per usual, he's in the mood to do battle. He'll be moving through this sign and house for several months, so if you've been going back and forth with a dear one over a money matter, be warned, because it may not end soon. Your mission will be to stay calm and stick to your guns.

Tricky Transits

On the 25th, loving Venus will get into an active square aspect with excessive Jupiter, who loves nothing more than going overboard in at least one department of life. In your case, it may be that you're out shopping for a gift for a dear one and you're suddenly struck by the urge to make a rather extravagant purchase. Don't do that if you can't reasonably afford it. You have nothing to prove.

Rewarding Days

1, 12, 13, 20, 22

Challenging Days

2, 5, 8, 16, 18, 23

Cancer | July

Relaxation and Recreation

The week of the 4th looks to be great fun for you, Cancer, especially if you can manage to take a few extra days off. Start on the 4th, and make it a long, extravagant weekend with loved ones—at your place, of course. After all, what could be better than celebrating the birth of our country with someone so home- and family-oriented?

Lovers and Friends

On the 5th, the Sun and Jupiter will get together to help you make peace with just about anyone, Cancer, even if you've been at odds with them emotionally for some time now. Your mission is to do your best to forget the past—especially if you're sure they weren't out to hurt you deliberately—and to move forward with a forgiving heart. Think of it as an emotional cleanse.

Money and Success

Friday the 13th isn't traditionally a lucky day, Cancer, but this month, it will be very, very lucky for you—especially when it comes to financial matters. Venus will get together with stable, practical Saturn, urging you to settle an old money matter that's come up once again, refusing to be ignored any longer. Whether it's a debt you owe or one that's owed to you, don't blow it off for a second more.

Tricky Transits

On the 25th, just as the Sun gets into a square aspect with startling Uranus, Mercury will stop in his tracks to turn retrograde. The thing is, most of this activity will affect you in the area of finances and possessions, so you should expect a few snafus with regard to settling up on money matters. Of course, your antennae have already alerted you to the situation, so you'll most likely be quite well prepared when it comes along.

Rewarding Days

5, 10, 11, 13, 22

Challenging Days

1, 2, 12, 24, 25, 26, 27

Cancer | August

Relaxation and Recreation

You've been working very hard lately, Cancer, and you've accomplished a lot, but it's time for you to sit still and enjoy a bit of time off—guiltless time off, that is. With Pluto and Saturn in your solar seventh house of relationships, convincing yourself that you've done all you can do won't come easily to you, but to move forward, you need to review the good things you've done and forgive yourself for what you feel you haven't done.

Lovers and Friends

The emotional Moon—who, you'll remember, just so happens to be your ruling planet—will spend the 8th and 9th in your very own sign, Cancer, and your solar first house of personality and appearance. Does this mean you may end up being a tad more emotional than usual? Yep. Sure does. It's up to you to decide when and how to let those feelings show.

Money and Success

A Grand Earth Trine will form in the heavens above on the 25th, the stuff that easygoing, pleasant times are made of. In your case, this aspect pattern also means that it will be easy to bring closure to a financial issue that's been a problem for a while now. Do what you can to facilitate the process, but don't feel obligated to cave to anyone's demands if you're not ready.

Tricky Transits

Fiery Mars—who's never been known for being especially patient—will stop in his tracks on the 27th, Cancer, set to turn direct after weeks of forcing you to think over a relationship issue you thought was past the point of no return. If you're trying to work things out with someone you love, have hope. Nothing is set in stone, especially if you're both willing to compromise.

Rewarding Days

7, 19, 24, 25

Challenging Days

4, 6, 9, 10, 26, 29

Cancer | September

Relaxation and Recreation

Once Venus moves off into your solar fifth house of fun times and recreation on the 9th, Cancer, it won't be hard to talk you into enjoying a little quality time alone with those who are nearest and dearest to your heart. It may be that you've been separated from them for a while, but one hug will be all it will take to bring you together again. Get ready, now. Open up your arms.

Lovers and Friends

Expenses that pertain to your home and family could come about around the 3rd, Cancer, but not to worry. Either you'll find a way to juggle things to your advantage, or someone close to you will offer to help out at the very last minute, when you least expect it and most need it. Think of this as positive karma, and don't feel guilty about accepting the favor.

Money and Success

On the 10th, Mars will storm off into Aquarius and your solar eighth house of shared finances, Cancer—and remember, he's a very feisty kind of guy. That said, if you've been involved in a financial war of sorts—or even just a minor dispute—you should know that things will soon come to a head, for better or worse. It's your mission to decide how to handle the situation while being fair to yourself and all parties involved.

Tricky Transits

On the 25th, the Sun and Saturn will get into a testy square aspect, the stuff that arguments and power struggles with authority figures and higher-ups are made of. Does this mean you'll be quitting your job or maybe even be fired? Maybe. The good news is that if this occurs, you'll be quite happy with the outcome. After all, isn't it time for you to become your own boss?

Rewarding Days
7, 11, 12, 15, 24

Challenging Days
5, 6, 22, 23, 30

Cancer | October

Relaxation and Recreation

On the 9th, Mercury will make his way into your solar fifth house of recreational activities and playmates, Cancer—and remember, this is the guy who's famous for being "the Trickster." Needless to say, games of all kinds will be on your agenda. Just be sure not to play with anyone's feelings, especially if you know for a fact that they're very, very fond of you and very, very hopeful that you feel the same way.

Lovers and Friends

Loving Venus will station to turn retrograde on the 5th, Cancer—in your solar fifth house of lovers, no less. She'll be all done up in sexy Scorpio for the rest of this month, so someone you were quite fond of and amazingly attracted to in the not-so-recent past may suddenly reenter your world. If you're still interested, don't wait for them to call you first. Find them yourself, and see what they're up to. No harm done by having a chat to catch up, right?

Money and Success

If you've decided to share your resources with someone—perhaps by cohabitating or combining your incomes—the best time to put those plans into play would be the 24th, Cancer. On that day, a sturdy, even-handed Venus-Saturn sextile aspect will join forces with the Full Moon in Taurus—the sign that's famous for being successful and prosperous—to extend their blessing to all financial matters.

Tricky Transits

Choose your words carefully around the 15th, Cancer, when chatty Mercury will collide with relationship-oriented Venus in sexy, intense Scorpio. Yes, you'll want to discuss the finer points of your relationship with a certain someone, and yes, the subject of intimacy may come up. Just be sure you trust them implicitly before you reveal too much. Some things are truly meant to be kept to yourself.

Rewarding Days
12, 13, 22, 24, 27

Challenging Days
2, 10, 11, 15, 31

Cancer | November

Relaxation and Recreation

On the 8th, Jupiter will take off for fun-loving Sagittarius—which is home turf for this guy, by the way—which means he'll be especially comfortable and even more able to talk you into being totally excessive in at least one life department. He'll be here for an entire year, however, so if you've been waiting for a good reason to let your hair down and have some fun, go for it—but please do pace yourself.

Lovers and Friends

An easy trine aspect between loving Venus and passionate Mars will make for quite the weekend on the 9th. If you're single and looking, stop putting it off. The right one won't just show up on your doorstep. Get up, get out there, and mingle. If you're attached, that's a different story. In that case, rustle up a selection from your enviable repertoire of comfort foods and have a Netflix-and-chill kind of evening—or two.

Money and Success

With Mars—the God of War, you'll remember—set to spend the first two weeks of November in your solar eighth house of joint finances and shared resources, Cancer, it's not hard to imagine you becoming embroiled in a testy and maybe even volatile situation. It might be due to a loan, an inheritance, or simply a promise to share the financial burden that hasn't been kept. Regardless, it's time to reassess this relationship. Take your time.

Tricky Transits

On the 16th, both Venus and Mercury will station, set to change direction. The thing is, Venus will begin to move forward, but Mercury will begin to move in reverse. Confusing? Oh yeah. This is most definitely not the best time to make any decisions whatsoever with regard to love or money. If it seems like everything has become far too complicated, rest assured that it's not you, and sit tight for at least four days.

Rewarding Days
8, 9, 10, 11, 27

Challenging Days
7, 15, 16, 17, 18, 19, 30

Cancer | December

Relaxation and Recreation

The Universe has seen fit to send along no less than five wonderful days this month, Cancer, masterfully scheduled from the 21st through the 25th. There will even be a Full Moon in Cancer on the 22nd—so your ruling planet will be on duty in your very own sign. Expect your emotions to be heightened in a very big way, but not to worry. Looks like all your feelings will be upbeat and positive.

Lovers and Friends

Loving Venus will spend the month in your solar fifth house of lovers, Cancer, urging you to consider the possibility of giving a certain someone another shot at the title. That's been a common theme in your life lately—dear ones from the past returning, that is—and since it's the holiday season, you'll be especially willing to open up your heart to them again. Don't make any promises, though. Not just yet.

Money and Success

The 16th is the perfect time for you to put together a budget you can stick to over the coming year, Cancer. If one of your resolutions has been to tend more carefully to your financial situation, don't let this opportunity pass you by. The astrological culprits involved are Venus—who's in charge of money—and Saturn—who's really, really good at planning. Seriously, it doesn't get any better than this when it comes to money matters.

Tricky Transits

Mercury will retrograde back into your solar fifth house of lovers and playmates on the 1st, Cancer, where he'll stay until the 12th. This will give you yet another opportunity to make nice with someone near and dear to you—and since it's the holiday season, that quest will go along quite easily. Your mission is to make the first move. Go ahead. You won't regret it.

Rewarding Days

15, 16, 21–25, 28

Challenging Days

1, 2, 5, 6, 30, 31

Cancer Action Table

These dates reflect the best—but not the only—times for success and ease in these activities, according to your Sun sign.

	JAN	FEB	MAR	APR	MAY	JUN	JUL	AUG	SEP	OCT	NOV	DEC
Move			2						7?			
Start a class		14			18				11	26	8	16
Join a club		6			19	12						
Ask for a raise			1	7?			10	24			25	
Get professional advice	9			6		20	13			22		
Get a loan	8			12, 15			5	25	12	24		15
New romance	2, 3	24									9, 10	
Vacation			17		19	1		19				21

L͜eo

The Lion
July 23 to August 22

Element: Fire

Quality: Fixed

Polarity: Yang/masculine

Planetary Ruler: The Sun

Meditation: I trust in the strength of my soul

Gemstone: Ruby

Power Stones: Topaz, sardonyx

Key Phrase: I will

Glyph: Lion's tail

Anatomy: Heart, upper back

Colors: Gold, scarlet

Animals: Lions, large cats

Myths/Legends: Apollo, Isis, Helios

House: Fifth

Opposite Sign: Aquarius

Flowers: Marigold, sunflower

Keyword: Magnetic

The Leo Personality

Your Strengths, Gifts, and Challenges

To say you're entertaining just doesn't cut it, Leo. First of all, your sign is fixed fire, making you the human equivalent of a bonfire. Ever try ignoring a bonfire? Exactly. You love attention, applause, and praise, and you're willing to work hard to win it—so tossing a few well-deserved kudos in your direction is a small price to pay for admittance. Your ruling planet is the Sun, so when you're pleased and you're pointing all the warmth and energy of your wonderful patron star directly toward us—well, there really aren't words to express how special that makes us feel.

And speaking of stars, let's talk about the spotlight, a place you're quite comfortable inhabiting. Yes, you were born to perform, and you've always known it. It comes easily to you. In fact, you probably started stealing the show at a very young age. At birthday parties, class plays, or recitals, you made your presence—and talent—known. Stage fright? Ha! You're frightened a lot more at the thought of blending into the background and never being noticed. The thing is, you've got to be careful with that whole attracting attention thing, because it happens, all by itself, all the time—for better or worse. Of course, in show biz, they say that bad publicity is better than none at all, but as for awkward or embarrassing displays? Those will hurt your pride—and there's nothing sadder than a Leo who feels humiliated. It simply breaks your big ol' heart. So do your best to keep a lid on public tantrums—even if they're well deserved. Find a private place to roar, then be sure to direct your anger and frustration where it's deserved.

Finally, like it nor not, let's be honest: you tend to be a tad vain every now and then, especially about your hair (I mean, "mane"), and criticism isn't something you handle very well. Pay attention to just a bit of it every now and then, though—as long as it's well intentioned. Constructive criticism leads to growth, and growth to excellence. Don't be afraid to change your act every now and then. It certainly works well for Madonna.

Romance and Other Relationships

Romance just so happens to be one of your specialties, Leo—in fact, you're a little too good at that particular sport. Once someone has experienced what it's like to be loved by you...well, it ruins them—for anyone else, for a very long time. Obviously, to say you're a hard act to follow is a bit of an understatement. Okay, so you can be a tad high-maintenance at times. Who cares? You pull out all the stops to make sure those you love know all about it. You dole out presents and compliments lavishly and nonstop, and have an enviable knack for knowing exactly what will make one of your beloveds blissfully happy. It might be a little something you came across at the mall quite by accident, but just as likely it's a big something you went out of your way to find. Tickets to a show your sweetie is dying to see, maybe, or a surprise trip—completely planned—to the place they've always wanted to visit. In short, if you're in love and you can make it happen, you will make it happen. Yes, you're extremely thoughtful toward those you love. That said, be kind to those who love you, even if the feelings aren't mutual. Don't make someone fall for you just because you can, and if you're done with a relationship, no fair ghosting them. Bravery in the face of confrontation is a quality you're famous for. Let them down gently, and do it in person.

So which signs are best for you? Well, generally speaking, the other fire signs and the air signs are at the top of the list. Fiery, passionate Aries and adventurous Sagittarius make for fun friends and terrific companions—and your relationship will never be boring. Airy, fast-moving Gemini and partner-loving Libra can keep you not just interested but amused. Scorpio is fixed and very intense—and so are you. Careful there.

Career and Work

Obviously, your fondness for center stage often translates into a career in performing, Leo—but remember, there are a whole lot of options out there that fall in that category, such as acting, music, and the arts. They're all satisfying, creative ways to express what's inside you, and as an added bonus, they're just about guaranteed to bring you a heap of love, appreciation, and admiration. Before you become a household name, however, you may need to take on a few more menial tasks, but if you tackle them with your usual fire and enthusiasm, you won't be plodding through for long. Allow yourself to shine—and please find yourself some kind of stage. A classroom. The working side of a bar. A local theater group. Regardless of what you choose, be sure there's room to grow, because talent and ambition like yours doesn't go unnoticed for long.

Money and Possessions

Being a Leo (and therefore a lion, and therefore uncontestable astrological royalty) means knowing in your heart—and right down to the bottom of your paws—that you deserve nothing but the best. You're not selfish, though. You've been known to splurge on yourself, but you're only too happy to share your blessings with the ones you love—and the more you love them, the more extravagant you'll be. That's lovely, and if you can afford it, please do continue to spoil your nearest and dearest in any way you can. Careful, though. Spending money to impress others—no matter who they are—is totally unnecessary. Put the plastic away and spend some time with them instead. Now that's a gift!

Your Lighter Side

You love kids, Leo, and you love having fun—two facts that add up to a whole lot of laughter, games, and explorations. Whether you're taking your little ones on a trek to a local museum or daring your friends to sign up with you for a photo safari, it's adventure you're after—and it's what you love best. Of course, one can have adventures in an armchair, by curling up alone with a good book, and your creative side is happy to spend quality time puttering away in your workshop. Once all is said and done, however, you're a social, fun-loving creature. Make your heart happy. Get out and about with like-minded friends who want to experience something new and see all there is to be seen.

Leo Celebrities

Many of those born under your sign only need one name to be recognized, like Lucy, JLo, Madonna, Jagger, Whitney, and Iman. Then there's Robert De Niro and Dustin Hoffman, and two of our most recent and most entertaining presidents—Barack Obama and Bill Clinton—are also Leos, as are sports legends Tom Brady and Magic Johnson. Both Ben and Casey Affleck are lions, keeping good company with the likes of legendary Dame Helen Mirren and the astounding Wesley Snipes, James Cameron, and Viola Davis. See? You were born for the spotlight. Step on up!

The Year Ahead for Leo

If you're attached and hoping to keep it that way, Leo, you need to sit up and pay attention to this astrological headline: "Fiery Mars Stays on Duty in Unpredictable Aquarius for Five Full Months in 2018." Now, that in itself is enough to shake the foundations of even the most solid, loving, and drama-free of relationships, simply because, in this sign, the crankiness and urge to rebel that Mars will be pumping out (from May 16 through August 12 and again from September 10 through November 15) will be unsettling to one and all—to say the very least. In your case, however, it's your solar seventh house of one-to-one relationships that will play host to the extraordinarily long transit of this assertive, aggressive, and often angry god—so yes, your connections with your nearest and dearest loved ones will most certainly be tried and tested.

You or your sweetie—or both—may decide to push the envelope, to see exactly where the boundaries lie in your relationship. Sure, it sounds exciting, and yes, you'll have your fair share of adrenaline rushes, but if you're not up for the drama this time around, do yourself a favor and talk to each other. Aquarius planets herald change, and that may be inevitable, but if you can create new rules, you two will be able to get through this and be stronger for it. If you're single and looking—well, regardless of what you've ever considered to be your "type," you can forget about that now. At least one unruly, unusual, and unorthodox new admirer will come your way. Should you get to know them better or just observe for now? Up to you— of course. Do enjoy the hunt, though. Oh, and with expansive Jupiter in Scorpio and your solar fourth house of home, emotions, and domestic matters, you'll be reacting from an extremely intense place—which may conjure extremely intense scenarios. Be prepared.

Saturn

You've been dealing with the energy of this eminently serious planet in your solar fifth house of playmates and recreation for two and a half years, Leo—which has probably felt like two and a half years too long, especially for a sign that loves to play as much as you do. Needless to say, you've probably had to curtail your social activities a bit—okay, a lot—but you can relax now. Saturn has moved on into his very own sign, Capricorn, putting this stern, hardworking fellow in a house where you can make good use of his energies: your solar sixth house of work. Of course, Saturn just loves heaping chores on us to see what we're made of, so before you can get back to partying, traveling, and boldly seeking out one adventure after another, you'll have to completely finish your daily to-do list. The good news is that once you've checked off that last item, you'll be able to kick back and enjoy a bit of real, actual downtime—and it's certainly not like you haven't earned it, so feel free to make up for lost time. On the other hand, love affairs are also handled in this house, so if you've been seeing someone for a while now and all is well, you two may decide to go exclusive, move in together, or even discuss the M word. Don't be scared to put a ring on it (Saturnian pun intended). If they're your favorite playmate and they've put up with your schedule this long, you've obviously got something good going on.

Uranus

This unpredictable guy began holding court in impulsive Aries in early 2012, Leo, bringing his fondness for the sudden, startling, and abrupt into your solar ninth house. Now, this is where education and travel are handled—or basically, any events, encounters, or relationships that broaden our horizons, form our opinions, and widen our understanding of the big picture. Anyway, I'm willing to bet that ever since, you've had some experiences that were eye-opening, if not all-out life-altering. You've probably changed your mind about all kinds of things you never thought you'd even consider wavering on, and you're probably a very different person now than when this transit began.

If you were born at the tail end of your sign, these exciting, electric life lessons aren't over just yet, either. Uranus will stay put in this house until May 15, so keep your pencils sharpened and your wits about you. Then get ready to start a whole new series of sudden, unconventional changes, this time in the department of career, professional ambitions, and dealings with authority figures. The thing is, what you've learned since 2012 has affected your opinions—big time—which in turn will affect your attitude about your current line of work. In short, if it doesn't resonate with the new you, you'll be looking for something that will. Keep in mind, however, that this too is a seven-year transit, during which time you'll probably try on a variety of careers or change positions often within your current field. The point is to keep at it until you find the perfect fit. Above all else, stay flexible and remain true to your ideals.

Neptune

Back in April of 2011, Neptune tiptoed off into your solar eighth house, a dimly lit place where your deepest feelings take refuge and your most intense emotional and physical encounters occur. Over the course of this transit—specially designed to gradually awaken you to what you're willing and able to share with an intimate partner—falling in and out of love a few times is pretty much a given, and maybe even mandatory. Neptune is a dreamy, woozy energy, a huge fan of romance and fantasy—so it only stands to reason that you'd be doing a bit of fantasizing yourself. Nothing wrong with that—as long as you don't allow yourself to believe that the fantasy has come true before it actually has, which is always a temptation when we're under Neptune's spell.

If you haven't yet met "the one," then don't worry, because this transit will give you plenty of opportunities to rectify that situation. Prepare to do a whole lot of interviewing, and resolve to keep your personal boundaries up until you've met someone you're sure is not just sexy as hell, but also completely worthy of your trust. Yes, they do exist. The trick is to take your time, consider all your options, and pay attention to qualities that really appeal to you. Think of this as a buffet. Have just a wee taste of this and a wee taste of that until you know what you like. If you were born between August 2 and 9, you'll be even more susceptible to Neptune's energy. Your mission is to round up a friend who's never been afraid to tell you the truth, regardless of the situation, and give them full permission to inform you, in no uncertain terms, if you begin to drift away from reality.

Pluto

Pluto is the kind of guy who doesn't mess around, Leo. He's in charge of death, destruction, and decay—so yeah, he's not usually invited to Mom's Sunday dinner. The thing is, he's also the ruler of regeneration, rejuvenation, and the recycling of energy in general—but no one really sticks around to hear that last part. Still, whether you like Pluto or not, birth, death, and rebirth are all highlighted in his job description—just as they are in ours. Obviously, then, wherever it is in your solar chart that this intensely powerful planet is making his presence known at the moment is where you're a force to be reckoned with. Right now, it's your solar sixth house of work—where, you'll remember, your no-nonsense ruling planet, Saturn, is also hanging out. In a nutshell, these two are pushing you to take control of your life by taking control of what you do during the part of your day that you spend working. Are you sure you believe in your work? If so, awesome. Carry on. If not, and you need to end a bad job situation to get yourself free from the nonsense, that's okay, too. Yes, you need to earn your daily bread, but if you're not happy with how that's happening, trash the situation as soon as reasonably possible and move on. It's true—the Universe doesn't care for voids, and Pluto just loves to start over from the ashes. This is your chance for a gigantic do-over.

How Will This Year's Eclipses Affect You?

Think of eclipses as celestial exclamation points. They amp up the volume on ordinary life for us all when they occur, but the signs and houses they occupy show where the possibility exists for sudden, intense, and often quite surprising events. Eclipses occur in pairs, six months apart. Solar Eclipses are supercharged New Moons, bringing the Sun and Moon together and marking peak times for planting seeds in any department of life. Lunar Eclipses are high-energy Full Moons, times of dramatic culmination, fulfillment, and often new beginnings as well, provided the slate has been wiped clean.

There will be five eclipses during 2018, marking an extremely unpredictable year for one and all—but you, Leo, will be directly affected by at least two of them.

For starters, on January 31, the first Lunar Eclipse of the year will occur in your sign, urging you to take a good, long look at yourself and make some much-needed changes—in rapid-fire fashion. Now, you've been slowly and silently mulling over these changes for a while, so whatever you suddenly decide to begin—or end, or both—you'll feel just fine about it. Those close to you who aren't inside your head, however? Well, they may be a tad startled. If you decide to do something drastic to your appearance—whether it's piercing something, cutting your mane, or redoing your entire wardrobe—expect to raise some eyebrows, and be kind. Warn anyone who hasn't seen you in a while. All this goes double—no, triple—for those of you born around August 4, by the way.

On February 15, a Solar Eclipse will arrive in unpredictable Aquarius and your solar seventh house of relationships, Leo. This could most definitely cause an unexpected rift in an existing partnership—but don't worry. It will also clear the way for a whole new relationship that's far more freedom-oriented—which, to be honest, is exactly what you've been craving anyway, isn't it? Don't hang on to the past. Look to the near future. Let go of negative connections and move forward. All kinds of new friends and admirers are out there. Ditch anyone who doesn't appreciate you, and don't look back. This goes double for those of you born around August 16.

The second Solar Eclipse of 2018 on July 12 will super-charge the sign of home- and family-oriented Cancer, activating your solar twelfth house of secrets and behind-the-scenes activities. If you've been hiding something and praying it won't come to light, better prepare yourself, because eclipses aren't famous for keeping secrets. If you've been good so far, but someone is relentlessly tempting you to stray away from your home turf, think it over carefully before you cave. Be sure the consequences are truly worth the risk you'll be taking. Exactly how much are you willing to gamble?

The Lunar Eclipse on July 27 will set up shop in Aquarius and your solar seventh house—which is exactly where the Solar Eclipse occurred back on February 15. Think about what you put into motion back then. If it involved getting closure after a long ordeal, it might be time for you to wash your hands of it once and for all—yes, even if it still smarts a little. This pertains most especially to July 25th-ish babies.

On August 11, the third Solar Eclipse of the year will arrive, once again activating your very own sign. Think back to the events that the eclipse of January 31 helped you set in motion. Have you truly washed your hands of what you discarded back then? That better be the case, because the Universe is about to send you something new and improved in that very department, and if you haven't already, you'll need to make room for it in your life. Have a yard sale if you need to, or bid someone a fond (or not-so-fond) farewell. Then stand aside and watch your future unfold. If you were born around August 11, fasten your seat belt, because all this and more is on your agenda.

Leo | January

Relaxation and Recreation

If you need to get away from it all—which would be perfectly under-standable right about now—the weekend of the 19th is the perfect time to plan your escape. You'll be able to count on playful Mercury, dreamy Neptune, and the Sun's passage into easily bored Aquarius to steer you toward fun, new adventures and total relaxation, all mixed into one. What's not to love?

Lovers and Friends

Searching for the perfect time to plan a romantic getaway? Well, if you can't manage it around the 19th, then take a couple of personal days around the 8th and 9th and allow yourself to enjoy life, and talk your sweetheart into doing the same. Truth be told, you may be getting yourself involved in some extremely intense emotional situations—but you'll probably enjoy every moment.

Money and Success

On the 15th, Jupiter will form an exciting, stimulating sextile aspect to Pluto, activating your solar sixth house of work in a very big way. It's time to sit down with a higher-up who has control of your paycheck to let them know exactly what you contribute and how essential you are to your place of business. Don't worry about being taken the wrong way. If you're calm, cool, and collected—and all your paperwork is in order—there's really no way they won't hear your message.

Tricky Transits

The Lunar Eclipse on the 31st will occur in your solar first house of person-ality and appearance, Leo. If you're been silently thinking about recreating yourself via a major physical change—be it via piercings, tattoos, hair dye, wardrobe changes, or whatever—well, wait no longer. This is most definitely the time. Just be prepared for a whole lot of raised eyebrows and a whole lot of questions.

Rewarding Days

2, 3, 15, 19, 25

Challenging Days

7, 12, 13, 14, 24, 27, 31

Leo | February

Relaxation and Recreation

With so much astrological energy passing through your solar seventh house of relationships, Leo, there's no way that your attention won't be drawn to partnership issues—especially when you're out for a good time. If you're attached, make it a point to do something new and unusual together. If not, get out there and get to know all kinds of new and unusual people. One of them might be the soulmate you've been searching for.

Lovers and Friends

The lovely lady Venus will remain in your solar seventh house of relationships until the 10th, and after weeks of turning up the thermostat in this extremely partner-oriented place, she'll move on into dreamy, woozy Pisces and your solar eighth house of intimate relationships. Obviously, if you've been toying around with whether or not to take a relationship to the next level, you'll toy no longer.

Money and Success

Venus is in charge of not just love but also money, Leo, so when she moves off into dreamy Pisces on the 10th, keeping track of bills and the paperwork that follows won't be easy. Still, as careful as you usually are with your personal financial dealings, you'll be up for the challenge. The thing is, if you discover that someone you care about is being less than honest with you, you'll have to dismiss them—and letting go of dear ones is always tough for you.

Tricky Transits

On the 15th, a Solar Eclipse will activate your solar seventh house of relationships—yes, again—urging you to get yourself free if you haven't already, or take steps to entangle yourself with an "other," if you haven't already—or maybe both. One thing's for sure. Your current partnerships will be under a magnifying glass, and any that don't make the cut won't last long—and why would you allow that, anyway?

Rewarding Days

5, 6, 7, 20, 21, 22, 27

Challenging Days

1, 2, 3, 10, 13, 25

Leo | March

Relaxation and Recreation

You'll be on the hunt for adventure this month, Leo. Your solar ninth house will be activated by no less than four planets in fiery Aries, urging you to hit the road and do some serious exploring. If you can't go right now, planning a vacation may keep you happy for the moment. In the meantime, expand your horizons by taking classes in a subject that's always fascinated you.

Lovers and Friends

On the 6th, Venus will storm off into impulsive Aries, a combination that's capable of convincing even the most cautious among us to take a chance on a new lover. If you're happily attached, weigh the consequences before you decide to act on these urges. If you're not, don't be surprised if you fall in love fast. This is the stuff that love at first sight is made of.

Money and Success

Jupiter will stop in his tracks on the 8th to turn retrograde, and since he's the purveyor of success and triumphs, even your best-laid plans may be put on hold. If that's the case, try not to get frustrated. Think of this delay as a chance to do more investigation—not to mention troubleshooting—to ensure that all will go well when the time is right.

Tricky Transits

The Sun in Aries will square off with Mars on the 24th, Leo, creating the potential for all kinds of disputes—some of which could turn volatile quite quickly. Do yourself a favor. If you feel the atmosphere charging up around you and you're afraid you might say something you'll regret, put some distance between you and whoever seems determined to yank your chain.

Rewarding Days

1, 2, 4, 14, 31

Challenging Days

8, 10, 22, 23, 24, 29

Leo | April

Relaxation and Recreation

With Mars and Saturn in hardworking Capricorn, you may not have a chance to kick back and relax this month, Leo—but when you finally do…well, let's just say you'll do it right. Look to the weekend of the 7th for the possibility of switching job duties with someone you know you can trust to take care of things just as well as you would.

Lovers and Friends

If you've been thinking about making a commitment, look to the Venus-Saturn trine aspect on the 7th to put those wheels in motion. These two planets are the stuff that lovely, stable, long-term devotion is made of. The more positive you are about your feelings, the less you should worry about settling down. What could possibly be better than a permanent playmate who adores you?

Money and Success

Venus will spend most of the month in solid, practical Taurus and your solar tenth house of career matters, Leo—which is terrific news for those of you who've been waiting for the powers that be to finally recognize your accomplishments. Don't hesitate to schedule meetings with higher-ups and other authority figures. Impressing them will be a walk in the park.

Tricky Transits

Chatty Mercury will square off with serious Saturn on the 25th, just a day before the volcanic conjunction of passionate Mars and intense Pluto. Now, Mars is famous for being the God of War, so when he's active, anger is always a possibility. But when Pluto steps in, that anger can easily turn to rage. Think before you speak.

Rewarding Days

6, 7, 8, 12, 14, 24

Challenging Days

1, 2, 4, 5, 25, 26

Leo | May

Relaxation and Recreation

On the 19th, loving Venus will set off for home- and family-oriented Cancer, urging you to pull back a bit on your social life, Leo. No one's saying you have to entirely ditch your friends, and if you invite them to family reunions and other domestic events, they won't think you're neglecting them. Just be sure to spend some quality time with your pride.

Lovers and Friends

Until the 19th, Venus will stay on in lighthearted, chatty Gemini, a fun-loving energy that's sure to turn up the volume on your social life—and your curiosity—in a very big way. Expect to run across some amazing people—and to have some pretty darn fascinating conversations, too. Don't hesitate to exchange ideas with others, even if you're most definitely on the same page.

Money and Success

Venus will oppose Saturn on the 25th, Leo, setting you up for what may be a pay hike you totally deserve—or the necessity to tighten your belt, big time. If you need to cut back and put yourself on a budget, don't pout about it. This too shall pass—and anyway, it's about time that others started treating you to lunch for a change, yes?

Tricky Transits

Startling Uranus will trudge off into earthy Taurus on the 15th, Leo, just hours after a New Moon arrives in that very same sign. This will activate your solar tenth house of career matters, so sudden changes could be on your agenda. If you've been secretly plotting to leave your job but trying to hold on for just a bit longer, that may not be possible much longer. Just have plan B ready before you storm out.

Rewarding Days
11, 18, 19, 22, 23

Challenging Days
7, 8, 15, 16, 26, 27

Leo | June

Relaxation and Recreation

For the first couple weeks of June, you may still be in stay-at-home mode, Leo. Don't fight it. Tend to your nest and its inhabitants and show them the kind of super-love only you can dish out. Then just watch, and bask in the happiness and comfort you've provided to those nearest and dearest to your heart. You'll feel good enough to purr.

Lovers and Friends

Venus and Jupiter will get together in an action-oriented square aspect on the 25th, and since the lovely Goddess of Love will be on duty in your very own sign at the time, this looks like quite a romantic day. Jupiter amps up the energy of any planet he encounters, so expect your heart to be quite full and to receive a whole lot of praise and admiration from your fans.

Money and Success

Taking care of business may not be as easy as it should be around the 19th, Leo, but that's no reason to become discouraged. Venus and Saturn may toss an obstacle or two in your way, but let's face it—you've handled far more challenging obstacles before. Stick to your guns and keep your eye on the prize.

Tricky Transits

With chatty Mercury opposing serious-minded Saturn on the 15th, you may need to have an equally serious sit-down with a family member who's just not pulling their weight. If they're making an effort, fine. Let them know it's appreciated. If they're not, there's no reason for you to put up with it. Lay down the law—and say it like you mean it.

Rewarding Days

1, 2, 13, 20, 21

Challenging Days

6, 8, 14, 15, 19, 23

Leo | July

Relaxation and Recreation

The Solar Eclipse on the 12th will occur in home- and family-loving Cancer and your solar twelfth house of behind-the-scenes activities, Leo—so if you've been keeping a secret or helping someone else to keep one, prepare for your cover to be blown. Not to worry, though. Someone may simply be preparing to make a happy announcement—say a marriage, or the birth of a child.

Lovers and Friends

That passionate roll you're on will continue this month, Leo, thanks to three planets in your very own romantic sign. And since one of them is magnetic Venus, who'll stay on duty in your sign until the 9th, you should expect to attract a great deal of attention. If you're single, mingle. It's prime time for the right one to come along. If not, mind your manners and behave yourself.

Money and Success

Venus will head off into precise, calculating Virgo on the 9th—which just so happens to be your solar second house of money matters. That said, you may need to pull some paperwork together quickly to finalize a financial deal. Do yourself a favor and get your ducks in a row early on. Think of the stress you'll avoid if you're prepared.

Tricky Transits

The Lunar Eclipse on the 27th may be a bit unsettling for you, Leo. It will occur in your solar seventh house of one-to-one relationships, all done up in startling Aquarius, so someone near and dear to you may present you with some extremely surprising news. Now, this doesn't mean the news will be bad—only that you should prepare yourself for a great big surprise.

Rewarding Days
5, 11, 13, 22, 23, 28

Challenging Days
1, 2, 9, 12, 16, 25, 27

Leo | August

Relaxation and Recreation

The Sun and Mercury will make their way through your fun-loving sign this month, Leo, which bodes well for your recreational adventures. But with the Solar Eclipse of the 11th in your sign, it might be best to rein in any overly risky activities. Better to err on the side of caution and wake up intact than to become famous on Instagram for your injuries, right?

Lovers and Friends

Once Venus tiptoes off into ultra-charming Libra and your solar third house of conversations and communications, you'll be even more lethal than usual, Leo—and that's what's going to happen on the 6th. It will be far too easy for you to entice and seduce—yes, even more than usual—so please don't turn this energy onto anyone who's not what you'd seriously consider a long-term prospect.

Money and Success

On the 6th, the lovely lady Venus will set off for your solar third house, a place that's ordinarily devoted to simple day-to-day dealings with neighbors and others we see on a regular basis. If you're looking for a career path, it's time to wake up and have a look around. Your future success could be right under your nose! Why not exchange more than niceties next time you meet up with someone who is successful in your line of work?

Tricky Transits

The Solar Eclipse on the 11th will occur in your very own sign, Leo, urging you to make some rapid-fire changes to your personality or appearance. If you've been mulling over a drastically different hairstyle or you've come to appreciate a whole new wardrobe style, this will be the time you trash everything you were—physically speaking, of course—to outwardly become who you want to be.

Rewarding Days

7, 13, 14, 15, 18, 25

Challenging Days

1, 4, 6, 8, 10, 11, 26, 27

Leo | September

Relaxation and Recreation

Playful Mercury has just one more week to spend in your fun-loving sign, Leo, so if you're planning an adventure, heading out by the 5th would be best. If you're homebound but still feeling restless, be assured that any plans you make now will fall under the heading of "exciting quests yet to be experienced" in the eyes of the Universe. Pull out all the stops, and make it happen.

Lovers and Friends

Venus will set off for sexy Scorpio and your solar fourth house of home and domestic situations on the 9th, Leo, so if you haven't already decided to cohabitate with your sweetie, this may well be the time you choose to fix all that. If you're happily attached, you might need to make room in your home—and your life—for a new arrival of some kind.

Money and Success

The New Moon on the 9th will plant a seed of new beginnings in your solar second house of personal money matters, helping you to either put together or perfect a financial plan that's perfectly suited to your personal needs. If you don't already have those wheels in motion, talk to a knowledgeable friend you trust implicitly, or a professional advisor with a sterling reputation.

Tricky Transits

Mars is the planet of passion, Leo, so once he enters your solar seventh house of relationships on the 10th, expect the thermostat on all your encounters to be cranked up on high—for better or worse. If you're happily attached, better block out a good amount of quality time alone with your sweetheart. If not, get dressed. It's time to resume the hunt.

Rewarding Days
3, 7, 11, 12, 15, 24

Challenging Days
8, 17, 18, 22, 23, 25

Leo | October

Relaxation and Recreation

Seven of the ten traditional planets will hold court in earth and water signs this month, Leo, creating—for the most part—a friendly, cooperative atmosphere. If you're suddenly moved to extend a long-overdue apology—or, better still, to finally accept one—don't hesitate, especially if the offense was unintentional. Life's too short for this nonsense.

Lovers and Friends

Loving Venus will station on the 5th, preparing for a six-week retrograde journey. It's not uncommon for long-lost dear ones to turn up during these times, or to be struck by the urge to contact someone from the past who answers that description. If it's an old love, before you rekindle it, be sure you have a practical, realistic plan to avoid reliving the less pleasant parts of your time together.

Money and Success

Venus is in charge of not just love but also money, so as of the 5th, you may need to dig up some seriously old financial records to get closer to finalizing a deal that looks pretty darn good. If you can't seem to find them, seek out a professional with experience in that area—ideally around the Full Moon in prosperous Taurus on the 24th.

Tricky Transits

Watch what you say around the 2nd, Leo. Mercury will form a contentious square aspect with intense Pluto, and if you've been properly provoked, you could be moved to say some rather hurtful things—so hurtful, in fact, that you won't be able to take them back or apologize. If you feel an argument quickly turning passionate, think before you shout.

Rewarding Days

12, 13, 14, 22, 24, 27, 29

Challenging Days

2, 10, 11, 31

Leo | November

Relaxation and Recreation

Jupiter, that fun-loving, benevolent King of the Gods, will return to his home turf—aka Sagittarius—on the 8th, marking the beginning of a very good year for you, Leo, especially in the department of playmates, recreation, and dealings with children. If you're single and looking for a partner, expect a veritable parade of applicants for the position—many of whom will arrive with a terrific accent.

Lovers and Friends

And speaking of Jupiter, this outgoing guy will turn up the volume on your social life in general in a very big way. If you've been toiling away for the past year or so, you'll finally have a chance to unwind—which will probably include opportunities to travel, take classes, and expand your horizons in equally delightful ways. Better rest up, kids!

Money and Success

Venus will turn direct on the 16th, and all those pesky financial roadblocks and hindrances to your success will begin to gradually subside. Now, Mercury will also be stationing to turn retrograde, so remember the word "gradually," and don't expect too much too soon, but do rest assured that celestial help is on the way, and you'll be able to move forward with your plans soon. Be patient—for just a little longer.

Tricky Transits

The 16th, again, will be a very tricky day—for all of us—but in your case, Leo, it may be not just money but relationships that are hard to pin down. Someone you adore might not be geographically close, or they might not even be available because they're still edging away from a current relationship. Again, patience is the only tack to take—and don't make any long-term plans you can't change.

Rewarding Days
5, 6, 8, 9, 11, 22, 27

Challenging Days
15, 16, 17, 19, 30

Leo | December

Relaxation and Recreation

With three planets making their way through funny, optimistic Sagittarius and your solar fifth house of playmates and recreation—well, I don't need to tell you that it's going to be a holiday season to remember, Leo. Clear your schedule as much as possible, because opportunities to play with dear ones will abound. Oh, and if you have the chance to travel, go for it!

Lovers and Friends

With the Moon in Gemini from the 20th through the 22nd, it's clear that you won't have to wait for the actual holidays this month to begin having fun. Wrap up work as early as possible and enjoy the spirit of the season. You're a generous, loving, and playful soul, and it's the perfect time of year to show off those qualities and enjoy the good feelings coming your way.

Money and Success

On the 7th, Mars and Neptune will get together in your solar eighth house, where loans are handled. If you're out shopping and thinking of committing to a long-term payment plan for a dear one—well, that's fine and very generous, provided you can realistically keep up with the payments. Otherwise, please do keep in mind that the warmth of your love is the very best gift of all.

Tricky Transits

When it comes to New Year's Eve, what we're all after is the energy to make a whole new start in one way or another, and with Mars set to enter Aries, that's exactly what we'll get. The thing is, this guy in this sign tends to be a bit confrontational, so if you're out and about, be sure not to get too involved in situations that could turn volatile. Keep your antennae turned up to high.

Rewarding Days
12, 13, 16, 21, 24, 25, 28

Challenging Days
5, 6, 7, 31

Leo Action Table

These dates reflect the best–but not the only–times for success and ease in these activities, according to your Sun sign.

	JAN	FEB	MAR	APR	MAY	JUN	JUL	AUG	SEP	OCT	NOV	DEC
Move			2			2		25				20
Start a class		21			18	13	23		15			
Join a club		6			19		5			14	26	
Ask for a raise	15			8							22	
Get professional advice	2, 3		4	7	11			18	11	24		
Get a loan		27	1	6				7	12		27	21
New romance			1	6				7				
Vacation	19					1	22			27		16

Virgo

The Virgin
August 23 to September 22

Element: Earth

Glyph: Greek symbol
for containment

Quality: Mutable

Anatomy: Abdomen,
gallbladder, intestines

Polarity: Yin/feminine

Colors: Taupe, gray, navy blue

Planetary Ruler: Mercury

Animals: Domesticated animals

Meditation: I can allow
time for myself

Myths/Legends: Demeter,
Astraea, Hygeia

Gemstone: Sapphire

House: Sixth

Power Stones: Peridot,
amazonite, rhodochrosite

Opposite Sign: Pisces

Flower: Pansy

Key Phrase: I analyze

Keyword: Discriminating

The Virgo Personality

Your Strengths, Gifts, and Challenges

You've chosen quite the tricky celestial mission this lifetime around, Virgo: to pursue and achieve perfection. (Feel free to use that as ammunition the next time you overhear someone whining about how picky you are.) The thing is, perfection is an amazingly elusive and most likely mythical creature—kind of like a unicorn. Please keep that in mind the next time you're lying awake at night, beating yourself up because you can't remember if you put butter on the shopping list for tomorrow. Yes, you do hold yourself to the highest of standards—impossible ones at times—so telling you not to punish yourself for even the most minor infraction is an exercise in futility. But seriously, kids, it's time to let up on yourselves. You absolutely will not be able to create perfection in all areas of your life, and the sooner you accept that fact, the better. But take heart, because there's no doubt you'll come very close to perfection in at least one life department, most likely your work.

That said, you may be so precise, adept, and meticulous while performing your job that you're the stuff of legends among your coworkers—and if so, enjoy it, because you've earned it. Unbeknownst to the fans who worship, envy, and try to copy your organizational skills, however, you may secretly come home to a cluttered mess. Relax. I'm not criticizing. You channel so much of your energy into being precise and particular on the job that it's really not fair to expect you to be "on" 24/7, and you're an all or nothing kind of sign, so ... My advice? Every now and then, call a maid service. Go out for a long lunch with a much-loved, long-winded friend. Chew slowly, listen well, and come home to an orderly, sweet-smelling home. Then kick back in front of your newly Windexed television and call it a day. Having your nest organized and sanitized regularly will make for positive chi, which in turn will make you even more productive—and, by the way, if you're working as hard as you usually do, you deserve it. Oh, and one last thing. When you encounter a person or a situation that's not quite right and you immediately feel that only you can fix the problem, stand back and think it over for at least one full minute. Heaven knows you do love to fix things, but you can't fix everything.

Romance and Other Relationships

Consciously or unconsciously, Virgo, you're always on the hunt for fixer-uppers. That applies to objects and situations, in particular, but this same attitude also seeps into your relationships. It's only natural, of course. In the Virgo mind, the only thing better than finding the perfect partner is finding the almost-perfect partner—someone who's jee-ust about there, loaded with potential, and willing to allow themselves to be sculpted into Ms./Mr. Right. So when you're single and looking, once you feel the click with someone new, you put on your rose-colored glasses right away. You sit back, observe, and begin to assess the possibilities—regardless of any immediately obvious character flaws others might say are far too big to ignore.

The thing is, not everyone can be "fixed," and lots of people don't think they need to be. Train yourself to accept others as they are. Flaws and imperfections are often the most endearing and most memorable qualities of all. When it comes to choosing a sign that works for you romantically, your most comfortable celestial matches are often the other earth signs—solid, practical Taurus and ambitious Capricorn. These folks make fine friends, too, but you folks tend to seek out the fire signs—Sagittarius and Leo, in particular—as playmates and lovers. If you're an especially intellectual Virgo, then thoughtful, witty Gemini could make for a fine friend—and depending on connections between your Venus and theirs, love isn't out of the question. Above all, regardless of what sign your sweetheart happens to have been born under, allow them to be imperfect, and cut yourself the same slack, please.

Career and Work

As I already mentioned, Virgo, you're quite meticulous about your work, which includes the tools, equipment, and supplies you need to do it. You strive for perfection, pay attention to the little things that create it, and feel tremendous pride when you've accomplished it. It doesn't matter what career path you've opted to pursue, either. It might be that you take your knack for spotting details into work that involves trouble-shooting, inspection, and correction. It might be that you love working with your hands—in which case, turning a favorite craft into a full-time income is where you should direct your focus. Regardless of your chosen field, you'll be well recognized—but quietly so. You see yourself as a tool—a specific tool that's tailored to a specific job. It's what makes you an expert, Virgo. Now, let's not forget about that whole "fixing stuff" thing, because while the urge to restore and repair is primary to your nature, it often leads to quite noble ends—that is, the healing arts. Whether you're a nurse or a physician, massage therapist, Reiki practitioner, or acu-puncturist, you'll be happiest if you truly believe in what you're doing especially if you can physically see the results of your efforts.

Money and Possessions

In general, you kids tend to be a tad on the frugal side and watch over your cash and plastic quite carefully. And since you're so famously detail-oriented, you usually have your eye just as carefully trained on your financial paperwork. You're not famous for splurging or being excessive, but when it comes to family members and your domestic situation, all bets are off. If you're going to break the piggy bank, it will most likely be to buy a home or help a friend or relative in need. You prefer to live on what you have, and since you're so aware of the little things that can go wrong in life, you're a big fan of insurance policies and warranties. Just be sure you're not so carefully prepared for what might happen that you're not enjoying what's going on in your life at this very moment.

Your Lighter Side

What's fun for you? Well, fixing things, for starters, followed closely by working on your crafts and puzzles. If it needs to be assembled, put in order, or repaired, you're in, and it won't feel at all like work. Still, nothing can replace a fast-moving conversation with a kindred spirit or a lively debate with a worthy opponent. Then, too, you're quite fond of the plant kingdom, and many of you are famous for your green thumb. You have a way with plants, but as you've probably explained to others a zillion times, it's because you pay attention to their preferences and tend to their needs. You're just as good with animals, by the way, who also respond to your tender touch and appreciate your understanding.

Virgo Celebrities

Let's go back to the concepts of precision and perfection, Virgo, and consider those while we have a look at the celebs who share your Sun sign. First off, imagine the physical precision it took for Michael Jackson to create the Moonwalk, or for comics Lily Tomlin, Adam Sandler, and Melissa McCarthy to so perfectly time their comedy, or for legendary dancers like Gene Kelly and performers like Beyoncé. Think of Stephen

King, who's made a living from meticulously sculpting words and details into sentences and paragraphs we just can't wait to read. And then there's Queen Elizabeth I—who presided over England alone, and did a pretty fair job of it—who was known as "the Virgin (Virgo) Queen." Oh, and then there's Rachael Ray, who makes a living from following and sharing precise and meticulous instructions—aka "recipes"—to create something that always tastes perfect.

The Year Ahead for Virgo

Mars will spend an extraordinarily long time in startling, rebellious Aquarius and your solar sixth house of work this year, Virgo. He's quite the fiery fellow, so if you've been quietly at war with a higher-up, quietly angry, itching to quit your job but practical enough to hang on to it—so far—well, prepare for all that to come to an end. Sure, this gig pays the bills, which is nice—but as radical as you'll be feeling, better have plan B set and ready to go, just in case. I mean, it's a given that it won't take much for you to grab your keys, relay a few parting sentiments, and say hasta la vista to anyone who pushes you too far, which most certainly includes the person who signs your paycheck. Mars is the planet of anger, assertion, and aggression, the ultimate me-first warrior. Needless to say, titles and positions don't impress him. Not at all. With his sword drawn in this house, he'll inspire you to do battle with whoever or whatever has been irritating you—no later than the exact second you decide you've had enough. You'll feel this urge to cut your losses and stalk away most especially from May 16 through August 12, and again from September 10 through November 15, so take note of those dates, especially if you're already thinking of making a move. Of course, the sixth house also pertains to matters of health, and Aquarius planets are changeable creatures, so if you've been mulling over a major physical overhaul—a diet or exercise program, for example—go for it. Mars will provide you with the fire and energy to get the job done—fast, too.

When it comes to your relationships with neighbors, as well as with other folks you see on a regular if not daily basis, prepare for some fireworks—but don't panic. Yes, there may be a bit of drama on the agenda, but, like fireworks, drama can also be quite romantic. If you're looking for love and passion, then don't ignore what's directly in front of your eyes—but do be careful. A friend could suddenly catch your interest for far more than platonic reasons—always a tough place to be—but if there's always been a spark between the two of you, it might be time to investigate. And speaking of drama and passion, let's not forget that Jupiter—who never fails to expand and amplify the traits of the sign he's wearing—will spend the year in intensely emotional Scorpio and your solar third house of conversations and communications. He'll turn up the volume on all your encounters—for better or worse. The old rule applies here: if you don't have anything nice to say, keeping quiet might be best.

Saturn

Serious Saturn will cross his arms and stay on official duty in your solar fifth house of fun times and recreation for the next two and a half years, Virgo—and yeah, I have to admit, that doesn't sound like a really good time. The good news, however, is that being put in charge of activities and clubs you were previously only a member of—even if you didn't start out wanting to be a higher-up in the situation—well, it's a compliment, and it means your efficiency and constancy are appreciated. Consider all of that before you decide whether or not to take up the reins, but spend an equal amount of time thinking about what you're truly capable of. If you want to handle the task, and you're sure you have the time and energy to do it well, don't be afraid to say yes. Otherwise, don't be afraid to say no—and don't feel obligated to provide additional information once you've refused. A simple no is enough. Besides, those of you born within the first ten days of your sign will have bigger and far more pleasant fish to fry.

Uranus

An extremely impulsive, impractical, and unpredictable energy has been on duty in your solar eighth house for several years now, Virgo—none other than shocking Uranus himself. The good news is that while you may have thought of yourself as squeamish or skittish in the face of urgent or emergent situations, life has probably taught you otherwise recently—that you're strong, sturdy, and more than capable of acting quickly and effectively under great duress. This testing period will last for a bit longer—say, up until mid-May—but there's no reason to hide out until then. First off, you know you can handle it. Second, if you don't step up, you'll always wish you had—especially since this quirky, rebellious energy will set off for your solar ninth house of opinions in May, at which point you'll want to go to sleep knowing that you've taken a stand for what you believe. Expect "the big picture" to become a very big part of your ordinarily detail-oriented life.

Neptune

This woozy, ultra-sensitive planet has been on duty in your solar seventh house of one-to-one relationships for years now, Virgo, urging you to let down your guard and allow others into your life. Nice—and hopefully, you've met and come to know a lot of wonderful people in the process. On the other hand, you may have let some rather unscrupulous types into your world as well—in which case, it's time to dismiss them and move on. Yes, you're the world's foremost expert on seeing the best in others, but you're often not so swell at seeing the worst—which can come back to bite you. It's up to you now to protect yourself by using your famous, ultra-sensitive antennae. If someone doesn't strike you as quite right or you suddenly have the nagging feeling that this encounter won't end well—and I don't care whether you've known this person for a month or a decade—please do trust your gut. Ghost them if you're not up for a direct confrontation. The good news is that Neptune is a trial-and-error kind of energy that provides you with lots of near-misses, so that you'll get to know exactly what you need—and what you don't. Your soulmate is out there, but finding them won't happen overnight. You'll recognize them when you see them. Until then, be patient and discriminating, especially if you were born at the tail end of your sign.

Pluto

This all-or-nothing guy has been holding court in your solar fifth house of lovers and fun times since 2008, turning every casual encounter, adult playdate, and family outing into a potentially intense emotional situation. And with Pluto in work-oriented, no-kidding-around Capricorn, even at supposedly recreational events you may not have had a whole lot of time to relax—or for anything even remotely resembling fun. Is that about to change? No. Sorry. In fact, with serious Saturn joining Pluto here for the next two and a half years, your duties and responsibilities may double—but the news isn't all bad. This house also rules hobbies and recreational pursuits, so if you've been thinking of making your hobby into a business, even if it's only a part-time thing at first, this is a great time to put those wheels in motion. Just don't quit your day job until you see a return on your creative investment. And don't worry—with these two on your team, it won't take long. Just be sure you're willing to put in the effort to make it all happen.

How Will This Year's Eclipses Affect You?

Think of eclipses as celestial exclamation points. They amp up the volume on ordinary life for us all when they occur, but the signs and houses they occupy show where the possibility exists for sudden, intense, and often quite surprising events. Eclipses occur in pairs, six months apart. Solar Eclipses are supercharged New Moons, bringing the Sun and Moon together and marking peak times for planting seeds in any department of life. Lunar Eclipses are high-energy Full Moons, times of dramatic culmination, fulfillment, and often new beginnings as well, provided the slate has been wiped clean.

There will be five eclipses during 2018, marking an extremely unpredictable year for one and all.

On January 31, a Lunar Eclipse will occur in Leo and your solar twelfth house of secrets, and with this bright light all done up in such a publicity-loving sign, it's a given that something you've been hiding—or helping a loved one to hide—may come to the surface, in rapid-fire fashion. If you're carrying on behind closed doors and most definitely don't want your activities to become known, better cease, desist, and cover your tracks while you can.

On February 15, a Solar Eclipse will storm the doors of abrupt Aquarius and your solar sixth house of work, health, and daily schedules. Something about the rhythm of your day is about to change in a very big way, and you may not have a whole lot of notice to adapt to it. It might be that you're initiating change by quitting your job or that you're sending out uber-strong signals that you'd really rather not be around your current employers—which will get you fired. It doesn't matter. In some way, shape, or form, you're ready to walk away and start over, and whether or not you're doing it consciously, it will happen. Don't hold yourself back for a second.

Your solar eleventh house of friendships and groups will receive the impact of a Solar Eclipse in protective Cancer on July 12, urging you to take up the reins with regard to a group you've perhaps only recently joined. If you're game, don't worry about being qualified. Think of yourself as the last piece in the puzzle, and do what you can to make it all perfect.

A Lunar Eclipse will occur in Aquarius on July 27, planting a most dramatic seed of new beginnings in your solar sixth house of work and urging you to finish what you started back in mid-February. If you began advertising what you do for a hobby back then, your efforts could come to fruition now. And even if you haven't been working hard on advertising, a haphazard meeting back then with someone who really enjoys what you do will turn out to be the best thing that's happened to you in a very long while.

Finally, on August 11, a Solar Eclipse will urge you to clear the boards and start all over in your solar twelfth house, the department of secrets. This is tender territory, so I won't tell you what to do—but do allow yourself to reveal anything you've been hiding that's weighing heavily on your mind and spirit to a trusted friend or adviser. Remember, confession is good for the soul.

Virgo | January

Relaxation and Recreation

With no less than four planets in Capricorn, a sign whose work ethic rivals your own, you may not find much time for parties this month, Virgo—but you'll feel good about yourself as you see another and yet another project come to fruition. You may need to postpone a vacation or leave late for the weekend because of work duties, but when you finally do get to kick back, you'll be able to enjoy your time guilt-free.

Lovers and Friends

With Mars in sexy Scorpio and loving Venus in steady-handed, practical Capricorn, you, Virgo, will probably be in the mood to settle down with your sexy someone. As an earth sign, you're good at staying put and making a relationship work, whenever possible, so if you sense that your prospective partner is on the same page—well, what's the holdup? Go for it—and congratulations.

Money and Success

On January 15, Jupiter and Pluto will get together in an exciting sextile aspect, bringing together strategy and unbelievably good luck. If you're thinking of investing, opening an IRA or similar account, or simply making a real estate deal—well, this is most definitely the day to do it. Just be sure you want this situation to last for a good, long time. This pair plays for keeps.

Tricky Transits

The Lunar Eclipse of January 31 will activate your solar twelfth house of secrets, Virgo, and since it will be all done up in attention-loving Leo, it's a good bet that something you've been hiding—or helping someone else hide—won't stay hidden for much longer. Keep that in mind, and remember, this is the last day of the month. You have thirty days to either adjust your behavior or get ready for the consequences.

Rewarding Days

2, 3, 8, 12, 15, 16, 19, 25

Challenging Days

13, 14, 17, 24, 27, 31

Virgo | February

Relaxation and Recreation

Around February 25 or 27, an event you've been looking forward to will turn out to be better than you could ever have possibly imagined, Virgo, so don't even think about rescheduling, no matter what the Universe tosses your way. Make it a point to get there. Matter of fact, put getting there before anything that doesn't urgently require your attention. You'll be so very glad you did.

Lovers and Friends

Venus will set off for woozy, romantic Pisces on the 10th, a wonderfully dreamy energy that inspires love at first sight. So when she touches base with Neptune on the 21st—in your solar seventh house of relationships, no less—be prepared to cross paths with someone you're immediately taken with. Oh, and expect the feeling to be mutual, too. Tread lightly if you're already attached!

Money and Success

Venus will square off with excessive Jupiter on the 3rd, a team that firmly believes that nothing exceeds like excess. That said, you Virgos who are on a strict budget should be absolutely sure to bring a steady-handed friend along on any shopping excursions—the kind of friend who won't be afraid to stop you before you go overboard because of a momentary impulse. Better still, have them hold your plastic.

Tricky Transits

The Solar Eclipse of the 15th will activate your solar sixth house, turning your attention toward work and health-related matters. If you've been thinking of quitting your job—provided you have something else lined up—it might be time to do just that. If you've been thinking about starting up a whole new physical regime, go for it. This is a terrific time for it.

Rewarding Days
3, 4, 10, 20, 21, 25, 27

Challenging Days
17, 24, 28

Virgo | March

Relaxation and Recreation

With four planets on duty this month in Aries—a sign that's never, ever been famous for being shy, holding back, or waiting—you'll be moved to take off after fun and adventure whenever the thought crosses your mind. The thing is, with Mars, Saturn, and Pluto in hard-working Capricorn, you'll first have to cover all your bases on the job. Not to worry. At least one someone owes you a favor. Call it in.

Lovers and Friends

Venus will take off for hot-heated, passionate Aries and your solar eighth house on the 6th, urging you to put an end to all those shy glances and get down to business. If you have something to say, one of you needs to say it. Stop with the shy, retiring thing. Yes, it's appealing at first, but right around now, making your intentions known will go a whole lot further toward getting a relationship on the road.

Money and Success

Any money matters or financial dealings that aren't turning out as well as you'd hoped after Mercury turns retrograde on the 22nd may need to be put on hold for a few weeks, Virgo. You'll need to muster up all the patience that only you earth signs famously possess, and it won't be easy, but do yourself a favor. Take a deep breath, talk with all parties involved, and wait.

Tricky Transits

Around the 11th, you stand a very good chance of clearing the air with someone you've been pretty much at war with for a very long time, Virgo. The only requirement is that you'll have to admit that you were part of the problem too—even if it galls you to do that. Of course, if you know in your heart that you really don't share in the fault, stand your ground—but don't refuse any sincere apologies.

Rewarding Days

1, 2, 4, 8, 30

Challenging Days

10, 11, 12, 13, 23, 29

Virgo | April

Relaxation and Recreation

Serious Saturn, feisty Mars, and extremely intense Pluto are currently on duty in your solar fifth house of fun times and playmates, Virgo—which doesn't sound like fun at all. The good news is that these planets may not let you relax without clearance from the authorities, but once your application has been cleared, they'll make it possible—especially around the 7th, 8th, and 23rd.

Lovers and Friends

On the 7th, loving Venus and dutiful Saturn will come together in an easy trine aspect, making this the perfect weekend to snuggle up with your sweetheart—and maybe even discuss the concept of settling down and settling in. Yes, that could mean cohabitation, and yes, it could also mean the M word, but if you're not prepared for all that, just having a chat about being exclusive is a step in the right direction.

Money and Success

As of the 24th, when Venus dashes off into Gemini and your solar tenth house of higher-ups and professional contacts, you may find that you're spending a bit more to entertain others, Virgo. The good news is that you'll be earning bonus points toward that bonus or promotion, and if you're after a new position entirely—well, it's amazing what a nice lunch and a pleasant getting-to-know-you chat session can accomplish.

Tricky Transits

The Full Moon in mysterious Scorpio on the 29th will occur in your solar third house of communications and conversations, Virgo, poised to make you privy to at least one secret—and possibly to blow your cover with regard to another. Remember, if you really want to keep something under wraps, the fewer people who know about it, the better. Resist the urge to talk about it.

Rewarding Days

6, 7, 8, 12, 23, 24, 29

Challenging Days

1, 2, 4, 5, 15, 25, 26, 27

Virgo | May

Relaxation and Recreation

You're an earth sign, Virgo, with extremely close ties to our lovely planet, but you're also quite cerebral. That said, the trine aspect between the Sun and Mars on the 23rd is set to ignite your curiosity in a very big way. In fact, if you've been looking for a career—or even just a temp job that will keep your wonderful brain amused—go out after it around this time.

Lovers and Friends

Talking things over with a dear friend won't go as planned around the weekend of the 12th, but don't give up hope. Wait a few days for Venus to make her escape from relentless Pluto and you'll have a far better chance to make nice. In fact, by the 18th, you'll likely find that a whole lot has changed—for the better.

Money and Success

If you're appealing to a higher-up for financial help, make your case before the 19th and you'll have a terrific chance of success, Virgo. Venus, who handles the planetary purse strings, will be on duty in your solar tenth house of authority figures until then—and I've yet to meet anyone who could resist her charms. Smile pretty, present your case factually, and be patient.

Tricky Transits

Talk about tricky! Fiery Mars and unpredictable Uranus will square off on the 16th, Virgo, bringing along the very last thing on earth you'd ever have expected. Now, there's not necessarily any need for alarm. Surprises can be either bad or good, as you know. Just be prepared for situations and circumstances to change in the blink of an eye.

Rewarding Days

6, 8, 11, 18, 19, 23

Challenging Days

1, 5, 9, 12, 16, 17

Virgo | June

Relaxation and Recreation

The Sun and Mercury in lighthearted Gemini will see to it that you enjoy yourself this month, Virgo—provided you can slip away from your duties for a bit, which may not be easy. Still, with lovely Venus making her way through fiery, playful Leo, it's a given that at least one charming someone will lure you away for at least an evening of guilt-free fun and adventure.

Lovers and Friends

Around the 2nd, a dear friend or family member may insist on introducing you to someone they firmly believe is "just perfect for you"—and no matter what happened the last time you accepted such an introduction, it would be in your best interest to at least make a date for coffee. At the very least, you may meet a new friend. Best-case scenario? They may have been right.

Money and Success

Four planets will get together on the 19th to make it an extremely "interesting" time to make a financial deal. The thing is, while all the facts may be in order and all parties involved may be in a cooperative frame of mind, you still may have to wait for the paperwork to come together. Yes, it's frustrating, but if you have faith in this venture, please do wait it out.

Tricky Transits

Neptune will station to turn retrograde in your solar seventh house of one-to-one relationships on the 18th, Virgo, a woozy, dreamy energy that can bring along the perfect partner. The thing is, moving retrograde, she may also nudge you into crossing paths with someone from your past. Be careful. Don't go down the same path if you're not sure you can make it work out this time around.

Rewarding Days
1, 2, 3, 20, 26

Challenging Days
5, 6, 8, 14, 19, 30

Virgo | July

Relaxation and Recreation

Three planets will make their fiery way through dramatic, playful Leo this month, Virgo, each of them set on pushing you toward having some serious fun. Now, anytime you're involved in a project, it's next to impossible for you to let go and allow yourself some time for recreation, but this time around—well, you know you deserve this, and it's summer, after all. Take the 4th off. Really. It will do you good.

Lovers and Friends

Around the 9th, when chatty Mercury squares off with expansive Jupiter, someone may confide a secret—which, ordinarily speaking, you're pretty good at keeping. This time around, however, keeping quiet will be tougher, possibly because someone you love is involved in a rather tangled web. Before you let them know what's up, be sure the news will help, not hurt.

Money and Success

On the 1st, Venus will get into a tricky inconjunct aspect with intense, relentless Pluto, conjuring up some circumstances that could be less than pleasant for you, Virgo—especially if you were trying to finish up a financial deal without alerting anyone who really doesn't need to hear about it. Ah, well. It's now your mission to ignore anyone who seems to have their own agenda with regard to your money matters.

Tricky Transits

On the 12th and 27th, a pair of eclipses will occur, Virgo—and these lunations are the stuff that sudden changes are made of. If you've been wondering about a loved one's true motives—or maybe even questioning their feelings for you—information could surface to prove to you, once and for all, that you were either very right to wonder or very wrong to doubt.

Rewarding Days

5, 11, 13, 22, 23, 24

Challenging Days

1, 2, 16, 25, 26, 27

Virgo | August

Relaxation and Recreation

Mars will back up into your solar fifth house of fun times, playmates, and recreation on the 12th, Virgo, giving you a second chance to either contact a former lover or respond to their request to get together again and give your relationship a second shot. Whether or not you decide to go for it is, of course, up to you, but be prepared to deal with past issues before you two can move forward together.

Lovers and Friends

Venus, the Goddess of Love, will remain in your sign until the 6th, Virgo, so don't expect that veritable parade of admirers to go anywhere just yet. In fact, one in particular may become rather adamant about getting to know you better. Ready or not, the Universe may have you set up for at least one more totally unexpected blind date.

Money and Success

Even if all systems seem to be go on the 18th with regard to a financial deal, loan, or mortgage, be sure you have all your paperwork in order. Mercury is set to stop in his tracks to turn direct on that day, and while this is good news, it often takes a few days for the best of this transit to occur. Expects delays, and force yourself to be patient.

Tricky Transits

On the 9th, cooperative, compromising Venus will square off with Saturn, who's never been famous for inspiring those sorts of things. Your mission will be to maintain a pleasant and agreeable demeanor—even if it means biting your tongue for a little while to keep the peace. You'll have your chance to speak up soon enough. For now, smile pretty and bide your time.

Rewarding Days

7, 8, 17, 24, 25

Challenging Days

1, 2, 9, 11, 12, 27

Virgo | September

Relaxation and Recreation

The weekend of the 15th looks to be just delightful for you to catch the R&R you're craving, Virgo. Oh, and if you're happily attached, that might not mean going out to paint the town red—in fact, it will probably be just the opposite. Yes, it's high time for some quality time alone. If you're single, however, call a friend, get dressed, and beat feet to a place where kindred spirits gather.

Lovers and Friends

On the 8th, loving Venus and assertive Mars will get into a square aspect—basically, the astrological equivalent of a shouting match. If you and someone you love are at odds, do your very best to resist the urge to say anything even remotely resembling "If you loved me, you would." Bribery and guilt have no place in this battle. Part ways for a while and let cooler heads prevail.

Money and Success

Negotiations you've been conducting behind closed doors related to a financial deal might come to a happy ending around the 3rd, Virgo, especially if you're both willing to give in—just a smidge—to make peace. No one's saying you have to cave entirely, but a show of willingness to compromise will go a very long way toward getting the situation peacefully resolved, once and for all.

Tricky Transits

On the 25th, the Sun and Saturn will form an edgy square—the stuff that arguments with higher-ups, elders, and authority figures are made of. The thing is, these two also play for keeps, so if you're not ready to make a break, watch what you say and do. There's nothing weak about opting to take some time alone to think before you speak.

Rewarding Days

3, 4, 7, 11, 12, 15, 16

Challenging Days

5, 6, 8, 22, 24, 25

Virgo | October

Relaxation and Recreation

The Full Moon of the 24th will set up shop in your solar ninth house of long-distance friends and lovers and far-off places, Virgo, urging you to either hop on a plane, train, or bus or bring someone you've been missing back into your own world. It will be easy to forgive and forget now—which is good, of course—but don't fall back into any patterns from the past that made you unhappy.

Lovers and Friends

Once again, just like on September 8th, Venus and Mars will get into a square on the 10th, and once again, you'll need to resist the urge to play the guilt card when dealing with a loved one you still feel owes you an apology—or a favor. Have a chat, get it settled, and call it even. There's no point to stretching this feud out any longer, and you know it.

Money and Success

Venus will stop in her tracks to turn retrograde on the 5th, Virgo, set to spend a month encouraging you to take a second look at relationships you ended but were never quite sure you'd reached a closure point about. If you have unfinished business with someone, don't be surprised if they contact you—or if you feel a very strong urge to reach out to them.

Tricky Transits

On Halloween Day, Venus will get into an opposition aspect with surprising Uranus. This is the perfect recipe for suddenly becoming someone else, and perfect for costume parties and masked balls—but you may also discover a side of yourself you like and want to hold on to. Pay attention to the "disguise" you choose. Is it the real you trying to emerge?

Rewarding Days

12, 13, 14, 15, 24, 27

Challenging Days

2, 3, 5, 10, 11, 31

Virgo | November

Relaxation and Recreation

Mighty, optimistic Jupiter will take off for your solar fourth house of home, family, and domestic matters on the 8th, Virgo, set and ready to make this a year to remember. If you've been thinking about putting in a pool, adding on a room, or expanding your family somehow—well, you won't have to wait much longer for the Universe to provide you with some wonderful opportunities to expand.

Lovers and Friends

No matter what type of disputes you've been going through with a loved one lately, Virgo, the two of you will find a way to come together and make nice around the 9th, thanks to an easy trine aspect between Venus and Mars—the stuff that reconciliations and successful negotiations are made of. Put down your weapons and have a cup of tea together. It's time to mend fences.

Money and Success

Watch out for financial deals that anyone insists must absolutely happen around the 16th. First off, there's no reason for you to feel rushed, and if your antennae tell you that something's wrong, they're probably right. Second, both Venus and Mercury will be stopped in their tracks on that day, urging you to stop, wait, and review. Listen carefully to your gut.

Tricky Transits

On the 30th, loving Venus will face off with startling Uranus, a meeting of astrological minds that can pretty much go either way—that is, between love at first sight or splitting up quite suddenly. Your mission is to go with the flow. If you're single, prepare yourself. If you're with someone but you've had it, forget hanging in there to see if anything changes. It's time to say goodbye. Now. Your future lovers are waiting.

Rewarding Days
5, 6, 8, 9, 11, 25

Challenging Days
16, 17, 19, 24, 30

Virgo | December

Relaxation and Recreation

The emotional Moon in warmhearted, family-loving Leo will hold court on the 24th and 25th, Virgo, and this is the stuff that big hugs, wonderful memories, and fabulous pictures are made of. Be sure to keep your phone handy to chronicle the good feelings. No texting, though. 'Tis the season for interacting with loved ones who are actually in your physical presence.

Lovers and Friends

The weekend of the 28th is an ideal time to do some interviews, Virgo—as regards the person or persons with whom you'll spend the first few moments of 2019. Don't make any plans at the beginning of the evening. New Year's Eve is a big night, and the right company is essential. Have some fun, look around, and save your invitations for later in the week.

Money and Success

If you have any last-minute shopping to do, look to the 16th for the best deals at the prices you're comfortable with. Loving Venus will get together with practical Saturn, the astrological formula that inspires careful spending and bargain-hunting. Keep in mind that no matter what you give, it's thoughtfulness—not extravagance—that will be remembered.

Tricky Transits

Communication- and navigation-oriented Mercury will station on the 6th, set to turn retrograde for the next three weeks. Now, this can be problematic, as far as traveling goes, but during the holiday season, it can also mean that you're due to hear at least one voice and see at least one person you've been sorely missing. Be sure your AAA membership is up to date, and take the good with the inconvenient.

Rewarding Days

12, 13, 15, 16, 21, 25, 28

Challenging Days

1, 2, 5, 6, 7, 23, 31

Virgo Action Table

These dates reflect the best—but not the only—times for success and ease in these activities, according to your Sun sign.

	JAN	FEB	MAR	APR	MAY	JUN	JUL	AUG	SEP	OCT	NOV	DEC
Move							22	·	15		8	
Start a class			2		23			7		15		
Join a club	3	10		12		22					5	
Ask for a raise				24	6				3			16
Get professional advice			4	7			8			27		
Get a loan	15				11		5	17	11			17
New romance		20, 21	1			2		25			9	
Vacation	2	3				25				24		20

Libra

The Scales
September 23 to October 22

♎

Element: Air

Quality: Cardinal

Polarity: Yang/masculine

Planetary Ruler: Venus

Meditation: I balance
conflicting desires

Gemstone: Opal

Power Stones: Tourmaline,
kunzite, blue lace agate

Key Phrase: I balance

Glyph: Scales of justice,
setting sun

Anatomy: Kidneys, lower back,
appendix

Colors: Blue, pink

Animals: Brightly plumed birds

Myths/Legends: Venus,
Cinderella, Hera

House: Seventh

Opposite Sign: Aries

Flower: Rose

Keyword: Harmony

The Libra Personality

Your Strengths, Gifts, and Challenges

You kids are amazing, Libra. To start with, your social skills are legendary—but then, they'd have to be. Your ruling planet is Venus, the Goddess of Love herself, who's gifted you with a truly awesome superpower: the ability to make nice. Now, as superpowers go, this talent might not sound like much, but underestimating it would be a mistake. How many of us—or should I say, how few of us—can chat comfortably with just about anyone, regardless of where you are, what you do or don't have in common, or how odd, stressful, or downright uncomfortable the situation might be? Exactly. You somehow manage to make it look easy, too. But then, your astrological symbol is the scales, and your astrological mission is to bring those scales into balance—and keep them that way. Basically, you've signed up for a lifetime of juggling—of smiling, nodding, and politely changing the subject at social gatherings as soon as your antennae alert you to trouble in paradise. You can't truly relax until you sense that everyone in the vicinity has been at least temporarily placated—long enough for you to come up with a more permanent solution.

In a nutshell, you're a natural-born peacemaker, Libra, and we're all grateful. The thing is, you didn't choose an easy job. In order to learn your trade—how to keep things on an even keel, that is—you'll necessarily find yourself in unbalanced and/or uneven situations and relationships. That said, you can now officially stop beating yourself up when your relationships don't go along smoothly, or if keeping your personal life stable often requires an exhaustive amount of effort. All this goes double if you're under thirty, by the way. But regardless of your age, like all of us, you're a work in progress. Count yourself fortunate to own your superpower. Use it only for good.

Romance and Other Relationships

Okay, then. Let's roll up our shirtsleeves and talk about your astrological major: relationships. First off, kudos! You were very brave to make this choice. One-to-one relationships are easily the most difficult, confusing, and challenging part of life on our lovely planet. Ask anyone. So how do you do it? How do you manage to soothe troubled waters, keep your sanity, and remain neutral—or at least impartial—even if you're emotionally attached? Well, there's Venus, for starters—your charming, sociable, even-handed patron planet—seeing to it that you walk into every social situation with a great big smile and never leave home without your trusty invisible olive branch tucked in your pocket. You have a knack for making others feel special, so you're not usually short on admirers, but please—you're positively enchanting when you want to be, so don't let anyone get used to it if you're not really interested. Keep in mind that you're an extremely hard act to follow, and be merciful. Oh, and be sure to never blow off your closest friends—not even if you've met someone you're thinking just might turn out to be The Eternal Beloved. What if you're wrong? Speaking of friends, the other air signs—Gemini and Aquarius—always make good, chatty companions, and they can be fun, flexible partners, too. If it's passion you're after, look to fiery Leo and Aries, or philosophical Sagittarius, who'll get your brain moving and keep your interest piqued. If you're drawn toward a Scorpio, fasten your seat belt and know that keeping the two of you on the same page may not be easy—but you most certainly won't be bored.

Money and Possessions

Equilibrium. That's what you're after in all departments of life, Libra, finances included. Fortunately, since Venus, your ruler, is in charge of not just love but also money, you tend to manage affairs just fine in this department—unless, of course, you're in love with someone who doesn't. In that case, please do listen up the very first time your best friend calls your attention to the fact that you always pick up the tab. They're not out to sabotage your budding relationship—just to help. Your mission is to find balance, remember? Likewise, if the situation is reversed and it's your sweetie who always grabs the check first, it wouldn't hurt for you to pony up every now and then. At any rate, as with all else, you'd do well to work with a partner if finances become overwhelming. Team up with someone you trust implicitly.

Your Lighter Side

You're a delightful, appealing creature, Libra, so you rarely spend time alone—unless you want to, of course, which doesn't happen often. You enjoy absolutely everything ten times more when you share it with someone else, and that includes sleeping. (Yes, just sleeping.) You set out to make every moment you spend with a dear friend or lover into a wonderful memory, so when it comes to time off, you're more than happy to adjust your schedule to accommodate theirs. Of course, you're a big fan of photos, souvenirs, and scrapbooks—the best way to immortalize those special moments. Spending your time off in naturally beautiful places, surrounded by music and art, with pleasant, amiable companions—well, what could be finer?

Career and Work

When it comes to the work you'll enjoy and the type of career in which you're just about guaranteed to excel, think of it this way, Libra: in a nutshell, you guys are natural-born cruise directors. Is everybody happy? No? Well then, you'll encourage them to tell you all about it and then do what it takes to make things better. That's your m.o. in real life, so one can only imagine how devoted you'll be to that cause when you're on the clock. Obviously, any variation on this hospitable occupation will work just fine (including actually being a cruise director or tour guide, by the way), provided it allows you to work one-on-one with others to help them settle their problems. On the other hand, that knack for bringing the scales of justice back into balance may lead you toward rather contentious legal occupations. Still, careers that involve mediation, negotiation, or diplomatic actions suit you best. Think human resources, counseling—and, yes, hostage negotiation.

Libra Celebrities

Judge Judy and attorney Nancy Grace are anything but peaceful types, but they certainly make it their business to keep the scales of justice balanced. But speaking of relationships, take a look at how many of your tribe are famous because they're part of a team: Paul Simon, Richard Carpenter, John Lennon, Sharon Osbourne, Matt Damon, Kelly Ripa, Catherine Zeta-Jones, and Michael Douglas. And let's not forget about Johnny Carson and Barbara Walters, both of whom built careers from having one-to-one chats—in front of a camera.

The Year Ahead for Libra

If you're a single Libra—an odd state of affairs indeed—you'll have plenty of opportunities to find a partner who's every bit as intelligent, sexy, and curious as you are. It seems that red-hot, passionate Mars has opted to spend no less than five months in your solar fifth house of romance and love affairs during 2018—from May 16 to August 12 and again from September 10 to November 15. Oh, and he'll be wearing surprising, unpredictable Aquarius for all of it. Needless to say, you should prepare yourself to bump into more than one potential partner under extremely unusual circumstances or in the last place on earth you'd ever expect to find someone fascinating. Now, the fifth house has everything to do with recreation and Aquarius just loves group energy, so signing up for classes or tagging along with a friend to gatherings of like-minded others is a terrific idea, whether or not you're looking for a mate. Mars makes everything exciting and he moves fast, too, so it's a given that charming little you will be accepted just about immediately. You happily attached Librans should follow this same advice—but if your partner can make it, take them along. If you know you could be spending this leisure time with them, you won't be able to truly enjoy yourself flying solo. Oh, and getting back to that "happily attached" situation? With expansive Jupiter set to remain on duty in sexy Scorpio until November 8, you two may be MIA quite a bit, opting for quiet evenings at home alone together rather than socializing with friends. Be kind. Surface every now and then, if only to reassure your friends that you're alive and well.

Saturn

Serious Saturn will spend the year on home turf, Libra—in Capricorn, that is. Now, when a planet occupies a sign it rules, it's operating in an extremely powerful way, so figuring out how to use that energy is extremely important. In your case, since this solemn, responsible, respectable fellow will be holding court in your solar fourth house of home and family matters, there may be some changes en route. You could decide to pare down your domestic expenses, or your family's size may change. One way or the other, you'll be in the mood to downsize, so a smaller or less expensive home could be in order. Saturn just loves feeling safe, so if making everyone in your nest feel more secure is something you've been thinking about, a new security system may be in order. Once that's done, you may agree to assume a whole lot more responsibility on the home front, perhaps because of the needs of a child or even a parent who's having problems taking care of themselves. However this energy manifests in your life, keeping a positive attitude is a must—and keeping careful records is mandatory. If you were born around October 1 or 2, Saturn will square your Sun from March through May, which could bring along quite a bit of pressure from higher-ups, elders, and authority figures. Stand your ground, and if you know you're right, don't you dare buckle.

Uranus

Unpredictable Uranus has spent the last seven years storming through fiery Aries and your solar seventh house of one-to-one relationships, Libra, where he'll remain until May 15 of this year. In the meantime, as he finishes up business in this partner-oriented house, you should expect one last round of highly unusual people to come your way—and that goes double if you were born at the tail end of your sign. At this point, after seven years of extremely odd but highly amusing (and oh-so-interesting) people dashing in and out of your life, you might think it's no longer possible to surprise you. Well, don't get attached to that theory. Planets on their way out of a sign or house tend to make splashy exits, so yet another freedom-oriented individual will undoubtedly be along shortly, set and ready to raise your eyebrows by insisting that you consider what life would be like with no shoulds, woulds, or have tos. If you've been thinking about getting out of a relationship that's not doing either of you any good, this may be when you decide to stop thinking and take action. Likewise, if a fairly new relationship has been quite positive and going along well, you two could decide to make it official.

But let's get back to May, when after laying the groundwork for a truly intense relationship that can stand the test of time—or showing you the way to complete personal freedom—Uranus will trudge off into practical Taurus and your solar eighth house of intimate relationships and shared resources. If you've recently become single and there are assets to divide, you'll want to do it quickly, but be careful not to move so fast that you cheat yourself out of what you deserve. Speak with a trusted counselor before you sign anything important.

Neptune

Neptune has been making her way through your solar sixth house of work for seven-ish years now, Libra, asking that you find a job that agrees with your belief system. In short, if you're not really into what you're doing for your paycheck, continuing to do it will become tougher and tougher as time goes by. Instead of forcing yourself to get used to it, choose a path that resonates with your soul and makes you feel good about yourself. Devote as much time and energy as you possibly can to make it happen, but don't quit your day job right away—definitely not until you can earn a living. In the meantime, get the show on the road.

Check out groups near you where kindred spirits gather to exchange ideas and experiences. Don't get too attached to your daily schedule this year. In the sixth house, Neptune subtly erodes your daily routine so you'll have time to think about what's really important—and what's not. She may also bring folks into your life who aren't as steady and reliable as they initially seemed to be, so prepare for a bit of disappointment, but don't give up. Neptune transits bring false alarms en route to realizing a dream, but eventually what you've been waiting for breathlessly will show up. Patience.

Pluto

If you were born between October 11 and 17, your Sun will receive a testy square from intense Pluto for at least part of the coming year, Libra, insisting that you make some major life changes. Now, squares in general don't ever allow us to get comfortable, but squares from transformative Pluto are absolutely relentless. Readjusting your position until you find one that's comfortable becomes a way of life, so much so that you probably won't even notice it. Still, the wheels are in motion to drastically change the way you see yourself and the first impressions you make on others. Don't think you can resist the urge to make huge changes in your life. This is mandatory. The thing is, you'll need to take a good hard look at yourself before you can start the process of transformation—to decide who you want to be when this transit is over—and this type of brutal honestly is tough to conjure up alone. So oftentimes, critical or urgent situations will arise, demanding that you take charge immediately, with little or no time to prepare, so that the person you are at your very core is the one in charge. Basically, Pluto wants you to dig down deep and rediscover yourself, and there's really nothing like a crisis to force us to wake up and open our eyes. Think of this as a time of self-discovery—big time. Remember, though, that Pluto is highly manipulative, so if you have the feeling that someone is trying to control you or influence your thinking, you're probably right, and you shouldn't let that happen. Likewise, resist the urge to control someone else simply because you can. That would be a shallow victory, at best.

How Will This Year's Eclipses Affect You?

Think of eclipses as celestial exclamation points. They amp up the volume on ordinary life for us all when they occur, but the signs and houses they occupy show where the possibility exists for sudden, intense, and often quite surprising events. Eclipses occur in pairs, six months apart. Solar Eclipses are supercharged New Moons, bringing the Sun and Moon together and marking peak times for planting seeds in any department of life. Lunar Eclipses are high-energy Full Moons, times of dramatic culmination, fulfillment, and often new beginnings as well, provided the slate has been wiped clean.

This year, there will be five eclipses. The first, a Lunar Eclipse, will occur on January 31 in romantic, dramatic, and oh-so-passionate Leo and your solar eleventh house of peer groups and goals for the future. If you've been flirting with someone you usually only see in the company of others, it might be time to lure them away from the madding crowds to share a more private conversation. Enough with the flirting. Sure, it's fun, but don't you want to know where you're at with them? If you're already quite happily settled, romantically speaking, consider taking on a work- or business-oriented partner who has as much passion as you do for a pet project.

On February 15, a Solar Eclipse will come along, activating Aquarius and your solar fifth house of love affairs. Yes, it sure does sound like you might decide to begin carrying on with someone, but keep in mind that this house is anything but secret—so please be careful, because what you have hidden won't stay that way for long. In fact, July's Lunar Eclipse will shine a spotlight in this department, so anything that's been under wraps could easily be revealed. Keeping that in mind, decide what you're willing to risk—and more importantly, what you're not. Consider also that you may simply be bored with your lifestyle, not your partner. At the very least, a heart-to-heart chat may be in order—and a weekly adventure alone together wouldn't hurt, either.

On July 12, a Solar Eclipse will set up shop in home- and family-loving Cancer and your solar tenth house of career and professional matters. Obviously, this could be tricky. Your family will want more of your time—but your work will, too. This is where that whole juggling thing you do so well will come in handy. It may not be easy, but you'll keep those plates spinning. You may even find a way to work from home—the ultimate balancing act. If that's always been a goal, pursuing it now is a good idea.

The second Lunar Eclipse will occur in Aquarius on July 27—and again, this is the one that may be problematic, especially if you've been hiding something. Fasten your seat belt, because a trine between Venus and Pluto that same day means that the the truth could be accidentally revealed by a well-meaning friend who thinks they're defending your honor. Do yourself a favor and get ahead of this. If there's something you need to confess, do it sooner rather than later. On the positive side, if you've been working on a creative project since last winter, a chance encounter could put you in contact with someone who can help you to finally find a proper audience for it.

The final eclipse of the year will arrive on August 11, a Solar Eclipse set once again to activate Leo and your solar eleventh house of groups. It may be "make it or break it" time for any relationships you started back in January, or time to end one partnership and start another. You may also be asked to take on added responsibilities with regard to a group you're quite closely involved with. If that's the case, be sure not to promise more than you can reasonably deliver. You're already juggling work and home. Can you realistically make time for more? If so, go for it. If not, be practical.

♎ Libra | January ♎

Relaxation and Recreation

On the 6th, Mercury and Uranus will team up to put surprises on your daily agenda. It might be the chance to go on an unexpected adventure with an exciting companion, or you might bump into someone you haven't seen in a very long time. Regardless, you'll be in the mood to try something new and have some serious fun. Don't hesitate for a single second—even if it means taking a personal day.

Lovers and Friends

Loving Venus and romantic Neptune will team up on the 3rd, Libra, a pair that often inspires infatuations that don't last. This time around, however, Venus—your ruling planet, by the way—will be wearing practical, realistic Capricorn, so that won't be the case. In fact, if you're still searching for the right one, this would be a great day to resume the hunt in earnest.

Money and Success

Investments get the green light on the 8th, thanks to four planets in the mood to wheel and deal. Unexpected expenses that arise on the 12th or 13th will need to be handled right away, Libra. You may need to call in a few favors or even ask for a loan to get them taken care of, but don't put this off.

Tricky Transits

Mars, a rather testy guy who likes to make his presence known, will storm the borders of your solar third house of communications and conversations on the 26th, Libra. If you're feeling testy yourself, take a break and put some distance between you and whoever you see as being especially irritating. It's better than saying something you'll regret.

Rewarding Days

2, 3, 6, 8, 15, 25

Challenging Days

12, 13, 14, 24, 27

Libra | February

Relaxation and Recreation
Three planets in startling Aquarius will take turns passing through your solar fifth house of playtime and playmates this month, Libra, urging you to try something new or mingle with a group you feel in sync with just about immediately. Don't be put off, even if they're not your usual type of friend. Variety is truly the spice of life.

Lovers and Friends
Venus will tiptoe off into tender-hearted Pisces on the 10th, Libra, just as the Sun in your solar fifth house of lovers gets together with Jupiter in sexy Scorpio. If you're attached, you two should seriously consider some quality time alone. There's more romance due to come your way on the 21st, when Venus and Neptune will bring along a whole lot of sighs, for all the right reasons.

Money and Success
The Moon will set off for Taurus on the 20th, a sign that's an absolute money magnet. If you've been waiting for a raise or bonus, you may receive some terrific news. It might be that you're in the running for a better-paid position. Regardless, try to wrangle a few minutes alone with the person who signs your checks—and turn on the charm!

Tricky Transits
Venus will square off with red-hot, assertive Mars on the 25th, an astrological setup that brings along sudden passion. On the one hand, you might end up in an argument with a loved one—in which case, watch what you say. On the other hand, however, passion can be just delightful if you're behind closed doors with the right person. Hey, I know what I'd aim for.

Rewarding Days
6, 16, 21, 25, 27

Challenging Days
1, 10, 11, 12, 13, 28

Libra | March

Relaxation and Recreation

The Sun, Mercury, and Venus will join dreamy, woozy Neptune in your solar sixth house of work for the first week of the month, Libra—which really isn't all that inspirational when it comes to putting your nose to the grindstone. Don't fight it. If you have time off coming, take as much of it as possible and relax. You've earned this respite, and you know it.

Lovers and Friends

The Full Moon in your sign on the 31st will activate your solar relationships axis, Libra, urging you to open your eyes and see a certain partnership as it really is, rather than how you wish it was or what you're hoping it might become. It's time to be practical. Is this good for you? If you're doubtful, back away for a while and assess the situation.

Money and Success

Feuds over money matters could come about between the 5th and the 7th, Libra, but if you keep a cool head and you're dealing with someone reasonable, you'll be able to work things out nicely—and quickly, too. Your mission is to resist the urge to gloat once you've gotten your way. Remember, gloating isn't attractive—and it's bad for your karma, too.

Tricky Transits

Mercury will station on the 22nd, Libra, in your solar seventh house of one-to-one relationships. Now, this guy in this condition is often in the neighborhood when delays and roadblocks occur, tossing a wrench into even the best of our best-laid plans. Try to be patient. This will pass. Enjoy the day, regardless of where you end up. The Universe has stalled you for a reason.

Rewarding Days

1, 2, 15, 16, 27

Challenging Days

11, 12, 13, 24, 25

Libra | April

Relaxation and Recreation

Venus will spend much of this month in luxury-loving Taurus, the sign that's fondest of creature comforts and shameless hedonism. If you find yourself longing for a glass of wine, a hot tub, and a delicious companion, forget the overtime. Punch out and relax—with someone you trust who's pretty much always ready to enjoy the best the senses have to offer. You know who I mean.

Lovers and Friends

With Venus on duty in Taurus, it's time for you to indulge yourself, Libra—but please don't get crazy and overspend. The best things in life may not all be free, but many of them can be enjoyed without breaking the bank. Of course, if you can afford it? Well then, it's first class all the way, for you and yours. Either way, enjoy!

Money and Success

If you're thinking of selling something, whether it's your home, your vehicle, or a whole bunch of things you no longer use, look to the Full Moon on the 29th for the perfect day to make it happen. Investigate your options with regard to refinancing, have a yard sale, or trade in your vehicle for something better.

Tricky Transits

The astrological agenda on the 1st and 2nd will most definitely be tricky to handle, Libra. Even someone as skilled at making and keeping peace as you are will find it challenging to stay out of trouble, so if arguments arise and your powers of mediation and negotiation don't seem to be working, relax. Believe it or not, you're not responsible for anyone's happiness but your own. Remember that.

Rewarding Days

14, 15, 22, 23, 29

Challenging Days

1, 2, 4, 5, 25, 26

Libra | May

Relaxation and Recreation

The weekend of the 18th looks to be peaceful, Libra, so if you've been trying to schedule some quality time with your family, your kids, or friends you haven't seen in far too long, this is prime time to make it happen. A barbecue or other gathering at your place is a terrific idea. Just be sure someone stays late to help with the cleanup!

Lovers and Friends

Loving Venus will spend her time in fast-moving, funny Gemini until the 19th, urging you to spend your time with lighthearted companions who'll lift your spirits and feed your curious mind. After that, however, she'll move off into Cancer, and family matters and domestic issues will bring you lots of warm, loving moments with those you hold dear.

Money and Success

The New Moon of the 15th will occur in Taurus and your solar eighth house of shared resources and joint finances—which bodes quite well for you with regard to investments. This lunation will present you with ample opportunities to make some cash, and with thoughtful Mercury and startling Uranus set to invade this same sign and house within days, it's important that you look over all financial offers carefully.

Tricky Transits

Mercury in fiery, impulsive Aries will get together with startling Uranus on the 13th, not long before they both set off for sturdy Taurus. If you've got something surprising or unexpected to announce and you've been waiting for the right time to do it, wait no longer. The Universe is calling you to the blackboard. Express yourself, but make it fast.

Rewarding Days

6, 11, 18, 19, 25

Challenging Days

4, 5, 7, 12, 16, 28

Libra | June

Relaxation and Recreation

The Sun and Mercury will move through your solar ninth house of far-off places and distant friends, Libra, urging you to hit the road in search of adventure—even if it's only to revisit your old stomping grounds. The thing is, they'll both be wearing fast-moving, easily bored Gemini, so your escapades will likely be quick ones—for example, a long weekend—but don't think that you'll be any less affected by where you are and what you see. It's time to expand your horizons.

Lovers and Friends

The weekend of the 2nd will be terrific, Libra. The emotional Moon in airy Aquarius will team up with the Sun and Mercury in equally airy Gemini to create nothing but the best of circumstances for you to launch a brand-new project—regardless of what it's about or when it's due to become available to the masses. All creative endeavors of the intellectual kind will work out well if you start them up now. Why wait?

Money and Success

A startling conjunction between the emotional Moon and startling Uranus will occur on the 9th, and since they'll both be in your solar eighth house of shared finances and joint resources, any financial dealings you're working on right around now could be problematic. That doesn't mean these deals won't work out well—only that there will be ups and downs along the way. Keep an eye out for fraud.

Tricky Transits

Venus and Saturn will get into an uncomfortable inconjunct aspect on the 19th, just about guaranteeing that whatever you're trying to put to rest—be it relationship-oriented or of a more financial nature—will be hard to do. This doesn't mean you won't be able to carry it off, but you'll have to adjust to circumstances beyond your control.

Rewarding Days

1, 2, 20, 22, 26

Challenging Days

5, 6, 8, 11, 14, 21, 29, 30

Libra | July

Relaxation and Recreation

Three planets will pass through playful Leo this month, Libra, a team that will absolutely insist that you get out there and have some fun with friends. You may be introduced to a creative circle of peers—in which case, you really shouldn't hesitate to show off your own skills. Let them know you'll be an asset to the group.

Lovers and Friends

Venus will tiptoe off into your solar twelfth house of secrets on the 9th—and you know what that means, Libra. You may be tempted to take up with someone who's not quite available, or it may be that you're already spoken for, but things aren't going smoothly at the moment. Either way, be very careful. The truth could come out rather suddenly around the 25th.

Money and Success

An unexpected windfall could come your way around the 11th or the 22nd, Libra. It might be that you're due to win something, or the raise you've been waiting for may finally come through. Don't get crazy and spend it all in one place, and think twice before you take on another monthly payment. Why not set a little something aside instead?

Tricky Transits

A Solar Eclipse on the 12th will occur in home- and family-oriented Cancer and your solar tenth house of professional matters, Libra. Eclipses tend to act suddenly, so a family emergency could temporarily distract you from being at your best on the job. Be sure to let higher-ups know exactly what's going on, so as not to damage your hard-earned reputation.

Rewarding Days

4, 8, 11, 17, 22

Challenging Days

1, 2, 12, 16, 19, 25, 26

Libra | August

Relaxation and Recreation

Oh, you're just going to love this, Libra. Venus, your ruler, will take off for your sign on the 6th, turning up the volume on your already lethal charm. She'll stay on duty here until September 9th, bringing along admirers of all shapes, sizes, and backgrounds. Be fair. Don't flirt if you're not truly interested or give someone false hope about your relationship turning romantic.

Lovers and Friends

After three long weeks retrograde, chatty Mercury will turn direct on the 19th, providing you with the information you've been waiting for. If a formerly platonic relationship has turned rather tender lately, you two should sit down and figure out exactly what's going on here—and what you'd both like to see happen. Be honest—and be sure you can be friends once again if things don't work out.

Money and Success

A family member with a financial problem could come to you around the 9th asking for help. Do what you can, but don't hurt yourself in the process. What's most important is to help them get on the right track and stay there. Oh, and don't let anyone manipulate your soft heart with a sob story that's not true around the Full Moon of the 26th.

Tricky Transits

Chatty Mercury will square off with Jupiter in secretive Scorpio on the 28th, Libra, when a tasty bit of gossip could reach your ears. Resist the urge to pass it along. Around the 29th, you may find that not one word of it was true. Keep quiet. On the other hand, if you're sure someone you care for will be badly hurt if they're not informed, sit them down and have a serious chat.

Rewarding Days

6, 7, 13, 14, 15, 24, 25

Challenging Days

4, 9, 10, 22, 26, 29

♎ Libra | September ♎

Relaxation and Recreation

A lovely sextile between loving Venus and Mercury in fun-loving, adventurous Leo on the 3rd will turn your attention toward a certain person who makes you feel special like no one ever has. If they invite you to a gathering of their friends and family members, go for it. It's time to try something new—and that might include changing your peer circle.

Lovers and Friends

An argument on the 23rd will have lasting repercussions, Libra, so no matter how unfairly you feel you're being treated, don't say anything you'll regret. Matter of fact, if you're really angry with someone, don't talk to them at all. Put some distance between you until cooler heads prevail—no matter how long it takes. It's better to miss them for a while than to alienate them for good.

Money and Success

On the 9th, Venus will set off for your solar second house of personal finances, Libra, turning your attention toward bank accounts, loans, and credit card obligations. It might be time to refinance, consolidate, or at least shop for a better interest rate. Seek the help of a trusted professional with rather unconventional talents around the 12th, but don't sign anything important. Take a day or two to think about it.

Tricky Transits

The Sun and Saturn will square off on the 25th, Libra, bringing along a test of sorts. Is your relationship with a higher-up, elder, or authority figure really solid? You'll find out soon. In the meantime, be sure to follow through on the promises you've made—no fair cutting corners, making elaborate excuses, or putting off your responsibilities. These two planets don't play.

Rewarding Days

3, 7, 12, 15, 16, 27

Challenging Days

5, 8, 17, 18, 24, 25

Libra | October

Relaxation and Recreation

Red-hot Mars in unpredictable Aquarius has taken up residence in your solar fifth house of playmates and fun times, Libra—and this guy is nothing if not the ultimate adrenaline junkie. Needless to say, you'll be looking for new adventures and exciting experiences—but no one says you'll have to climb Everest. In fact, challenges of the intellectual kind will be far more fun for you now.

Lovers and Friends

A Venus-Mars square on the 10th could be a touch problematic. That goes double if you or your sweetheart have been feeling unappreciated. At best, you can use this energy to talk things out and clear the air. Resist the urge to manipulate someone with "if you loved me, you would," and don't you dare let anyone pull that line on you. Work out your problems honestly.

Money and Success

You may need to rethink a financial commitment after the 5th, Libra, when Venus will turn retrograde in your solar second house of money matters. If you need to make a major purchase—and please don't if it's not absolutely necessary—save your receipt and make sure to keep track of all other related paperwork. Above all, don't ignore the fine print.

Tricky Transits

On the 12th, the Sun and intense and often relentless Pluto will square off, Libra, the stuff that serious and long-lasting disagreements are often made of. If someone close to you seems to be holding out on you or hiding something, don't be afraid to question them. You tend to avoid confrontations, but sometimes that's just not possible. Get the truth, and if need be, cut your losses.

Rewarding Days
4, 12, 13, 22, 24, 27

Challenging Days
2, 5, 7, 10, 11, 31

Libra | November

Relaxation and Recreation

Talk about a good time! Jupiter—the heavens' answer to Santa Claus—will dash off into merry, funny Sagittarius on the 8th, marking the beginning of a year-long trip through your solar third house. Now, this is where conversations, communications, and travel matters are handled—so obviously, your social life is about to become a whole lot more active. Expect a variety of new acquaintances, some of whom may be travel buddies.

Lovers and Friends

Venus will spend the month in your sign, Libra, once again bringing all kinds of new admirers your way. Up until the 16th, however, she'll be moving retrograde, so you should also expect quite a few voices from the past—and possibly even a reunion with the one who got away. If you're up for a second try, fine—just be sure you have new answers to the old problems that split you apart.

Money and Success

The Sun in your solar second house of finances will get into an easy sextile aspect with intense Pluto on the 11th, giving you the perfect opportunity to take another shot at solving a rather nagging financial issue. If you're not quite sure what to do, consult a friend who's a financial whiz, or better still, hire a professional. Don't make any money-oriented changes between the 14th and the 19th.

Tricky Transits

Both Venus and Mercury will stop in their tracks to change direction on the 16th, Libra. Now, when these stations occur, it often seems impossible to get anything done—at least, not the first time around. Don't be angry if others are late or absent. Delays and roadblocks will be everywhere. Likewise, don't be mad at yourself if you're waylaid by unexpected circumstances.

Rewarding Days

2, 4, 8, 9, 22, 23, 27, 28

Challenging Days

15, 16, 17, 18, 19, 30

Libra | December

Relaxation and Recreation

The Sun and Mercury will join Jupiter in outgoing Sagittarius and your third solar house this month, Libra, urging you to mingle, socialize, and get to know your neighbors. A party or reunion around the 21st will be warm and wonderful, and a Leo Moon will see to it that your heart is full and happy from the 24th to the 26th. Keep your loved ones close to you.

Lovers and Friends

A surprise call, message, or even visit could be on the agenda on the 12th or 13th, Libra, so keep your schedule open as much as possible. A certain person you've been dearly missing could be back in town for a few days, and you'll want to spend every minute you can with them. A romantic fantasy stands a good chance of becoming a delightful reality around the 21st.

Money and Success

If you've got last-minute shopping to do on the 7th, promise me you'll take a friend along, Libra—the kind who is brave enough to relieve you of your credit cards if you're about to be far more extravagant than your budget will reasonably allow. It really is the thought that counts. Be thoughtful and creative rather than excessive, and remember, your company is the best gift of all.

Tricky Transits

If tensions are riding high between you and a loved one from the 2nd through the 5th, solving the matter could be tough—especially if you're not exactly sure why you're angry. Take some time alone to figure it out—or better still, sit them down for a heart-to-heart chat on the 9th, when the emotional Moon and Saturn inspire you two to find a practical, reasonable solution.

Rewarding Days
8, 9, 16, 21, 24, 25, 28

Challenging Days
2, 3, 4, 5, 19

Libra Action Table

These dates reflect the best—but not the only—times for success and ease in these activities, according to your Sun sign.

	JAN	FEB	MAR	APR	MAY	JUN	JUL	AUG	SEP	OCT	NOV	DEC
Move				29				25				
Start a class			2		13	1, 2	4		15	22		
Join a club		6	1		18				3	26		20
Ask for a raise		21									11	16
Get professional advice			19	29		18			12	24		
Get a loan	8			14	15		22					
New romance	3	25						7			7	
Vacation	6					13	8	18			9	21

Scorpio

The Scorpion
October 23 to November 21

♏

Element: Water

Quality: Fixed

Polarity: Yin/feminine

Planetary Ruler: Pluto (Mars)

Meditation: I let go of the need to control

Gemstone: Topaz

Power Stones: Obsidian, garnet

Key Phrase: I create

Glyph: Scorpion's tail

Anatomy: Reproductive system

Colors: Burgundy, black

Animals: Reptiles, scorpions, birds of prey

Myths/Legends: The Phoenix, Hades and Persephone, Shiva

House: Eighth

Opposite Sign: Taurus

Flower: Chrysanthemum

Keyword: Intensity

The Scorpio Personality

Your Strengths, Gifts, and Challenges

Your ruling planet is Pluto, Scorpio, the mythical Lord of the Underworld—which certainly does explain your fondness for digging, on all levels. His jurisdiction over your sign also makes you magnetic, personally powerful, impossible to ignore, and, yes, quite secretive at times.

Those gifts make you a born researcher, analyst, and detective, with an amazing ability to notice and interpret clues that most of us miss. It might be an ordinary gesture, a subtle glance, a nod, or a flinch. Doesn't matter. Any tiny element of body language that catches your eye is enough to get your water-sign antenna twitching, and the more interested you are in your subject, the more determined you are to get to the bottom of things. It might take days, months, or decades, but you won't quit and you won't waver. You wrote the book on perseverance, willpower, and tenacity.

Those qualities are terrific assets when it comes to achieving your goals, but when you're bored, they can turn inward. That's when you find yourself lying in bed awake, fixating on something trivial. So, are you obsessive? You bet. That's why it's so important for you to find positive, appropriate channels for your particular brand of relentless, enduring energy. The more you use those natural abilities productively during your waking hours, the less likely you'll be consumed with someone or something that's really not worth your time.

Romance and Other Relationships

You're the human equivalent of a lie detector, Scorpio, and you take your equipment along on every encounter. So for someone to get to know you—the real you, that only a select few see—they have to pass your test. If something about a new friend or admirer doesn't seem quite right, you're out of there. That goes double for someone who asks too many personal questions too soon. Trusting others is a slow process for you, but if and when you do feel safe enough to open up, you'll tell all, right down to your deepest, darkest secrets.

Every sign rules a part of the human body, and you probably aren't surprised to hear that yours rules the genitals. So along with your innate craving for emotional intensity and deep connections, it only makes sense that you folks are highly sexual creatures—and that you tend to have significant others who grin a lot. When you fall for someone, it's usually because (a) they're incredibly sexy, and (b) you can't seem to solve the mystery of how they tick. The more fascinated you are in both departments, the more you'll keep coming back for more. The good news is that the vibes you put out when you're interested are magnetic, potent, and just about irresistible, so there usually isn't any shortage of intimacy in your life. One of your very best matches is Taurus, the most sensual sign in the zodiac—for obvious reasons. Not only does Taurus love to touch, but they're also just as stubborn as you are, and best of all, once they're committed, Taurus stays put. Virgos can be fun, since their eye for detail rivals your own, but Leos and Geminis aren't a match made in heaven for you.

Career and Work

Thanks again to the influence of Pluto, you're naturally gifted with the ability to understand invisible processes, Scorpio, and to see the inner workings of any situation. As such, you're the perfect employee—once you've devoted yourself, that is—and after just a few weeks on the job, you're perfectly capable of running the place alone. What you don't know, you'll figure out, or you'll interview coworkers who you're sure have the info you need. For that reason, you're often promoted early in your career and tend to use your quiet power to keep your workplace under control—wherever it is or whatever you happen to be doing.

Money and Possessions

Money-wise, things can go one of two ways, Scorpio. First off, you can become so obsessed with something—and please, please don't ever allow that to be drugs or alcohol—that you really don't care what it costs or what you have to put off to pay for it. On the other hand, thanks to the influence of excessive Sagittarius on your solar second house of finances, you might tend to overspend on fun stuff. Regardless, you'll need to have someone else manage your finances. Although that may be your occupation, handling your own money may not be your specialty.

Your Lighter Side

It's tough for you to relax, Scorpio, and even harder to stop doing what you do best and most naturally—investigating. So when you're unwinding, you often spend time alone, watching mysteries, solving puzzles, and poking around the Internet. Once you've been enticed out of the house, you let your keen wit, almost slapstick sense of humor, and blunt honesty have free rein with a select group of friends.

You're a natural-born strategist, Scorpio, so you love the intricacies of politics. You probably even find following this dangerous sport fun. When you actually allow yourself to relax—which isn't often—you indulge in mysteries. It might be a mystery weekend on a train, or it might be a well-done horror movie or the latest Stephen King novel. You plot so well and pick up on subtle clues so easily that no one could possibly be better suited to poker.

Scorpio Celebrities

You're not shy, Scorpio. Never have been, never will be. So it's not surprising to find you in the company of well-known activists like Leonardo Di Caprio, Whoopi Goldberg, and RuPaul, all of whom have never been shy about professing their thoughts about the big picture. Oh, and sexy? Well, how about Julia Roberts, Ethan Hawke, former Playboy model Jenny McCarthy, and Matthew McConaughey? Tracee Ellis Ross and Thandie Newton are also among the stars who share your Sun sign.

The Year Ahead for Scorpio

Fiery Mars, who never met an argument he didn't love, will set off for startling Aquarius on May 16, ready to set up shop in your solar fourth house of home and family matters. Now, this could mean that you'll be dealing with a bit of dissent from within the ranks over roughly half the coming year. In particular, look to May 16 through August 12 and September 10 through November 15 for the possibility of sudden disputes to arise on the home front. The thing is, when Mars comes along, it's time to make changes, and quickly—and sometimes that means someone needs to blow up and stalk off into the sunset. In this case, it probably won't be you who's doing the stalking, because it's probably you who's in charge of keeping things together on the domestic scene. Even so, if you've got to let go of someone you care for who's decided to remove themselves from your nest and strike out on their own, it won't be an easy transition. Your mission is to allow these changes to happen, whether or not you're fond of them.

Saturn will spend his first full year in Capricorn—his home turf—and in your solar third house of conversations and communications.

Does this mean you'll be a whole lot more serious and that you'll be choosing your words far more carefully from now on? Yep. Sure does. In fact, you may begin to think about taking classes to help you express yourself more fully and accurately in your chosen field. Are you up for a certificate course, or is night school in your future? If so, this is the time to do it. You'll be amazed at how much you've underestimated yourself. You already know a whole lot more than you thought you did!

Saturn

Just weeks before the year began, this serious planet set off for Capricorn, the sign it most prefers. This puts this no-nonsense energy on duty in your solar third house of conversations and communications for the next three years, Scorpio, so lest you think you'll be participating in any lighthearted chats, think again. The news isn't all dire, however. Your thoughts will be more serious, too, so what you'll be looking for is an intellectual equal—at least one—who can keep up with you, challenge you, and keep you on your toes when it comes to checking and rechecking your facts before entering into any discussion about them.

You may start this transit off by thinking that your lack of knowledge in certain areas of life is impossible to overcome, but not to worry. The Universe will arrange for a mentor—again, at least one—to come along when you least expect them, and they'll be bearing information you need to move forward. In the process, you'll probably also discover that you're not nearly as unskilled in this area of life as you thought you were. It's all about being validated now—about being taken seriously by others, and about learning what you need to know to advance on the career path you've chosen. And speaking of your career path, it's time to put together that five-year plan. Matter of fact, make it a ten-year plan. With Saturn in Capricorn, planning for the future is the very best thing you can do—and the thing he'll be most willing to offer his help for you to attain.

Uranus

Up until May 15, Uranus will continue on his path through fiery Aries and your solar sixth house of work and work-oriented relationships, Scorpio, giving you a chance to put the finishing touches on a project you've been pouring everything you've got into for a very long time. You may need to find a new business partner to help you complete the project, but not to worry—as per usual, your work ethic will stay intact, and you'll be more than able to take care of business. Once May arrives, however, a whole lot will change. Uranus will trudge off into Taurus and your solar seventh house, insisting that you reexamine the concept of relationships and decide which kind works best for you. Don't be surprised if you find that you're interested in a whole lot more freedom and independence after that date—which, sadly, may mean that you'll need to distance yourself from several people you thought would be in your life forever. Don't panic, though. Anyone who knows you well and understands you even better won't be going anywhere.

On the plus side, you'll begin meeting all kinds of new, unusual, and oh-so-interesting people, most likely through friends of friends or through seemingly coincidental encounters. Stay open to new experiences and new friends—and if you're single, don't rule anyone out because of their appearance or the first impression you have of them. Dig a little deeper. They may have been put in your world to bring you a message about how to enjoy life more fully—basically, by being absolutely true to yourself, no matter what anyone else has to say about it. You'll be breaking some rules over the next seven years, and your near and dear ones will either have to adapt or remove themselves. Again, those who "get" you won't be going anywhere. Let anyone who doesn't back away—and don't try to stop them.

Neptune

The lovely lady Neptune is still moving through Pisces, a water sign like your own, and still making her presence known in your solar fifth house of lovers and playmates, Scorpio. Now, this is a truly romantic energy that's adept at breaking down boundaries and bringing us closer together by subtly reminding us of just how much we two-legged carbon-based units have in common—which will certainly come in handy to us all right about now. In your case, you'll also be ultra-sensitive to the needs of your loved ones, and whether or not they mention their problems, you'll see what's going on and be moved to help. That goes double for children. If you have the feeling that a little one is afraid to mention something they're disturbed about, you'll find a way to tactfully and quietly let them know you're there for them when they're ready—which is really the greatest gift of all.

If you're involved in a creative project—say, art, music, or the theater, for example—you may need to take some time alone every now and then to recharge your batteries and renew your commitment to your cause.

When that happens, don't hesitate to clear your schedule and disappear for a few hours, or however long it takes. Basically, you're channeling a muse now, and she may not show up if you're too distracted by outside activity to pay attention—so make yourself available to her whispers. If you were born between November 2 and 10, your Sun will also be receiving an easy trine aspect from Neptune, so you'll be especially intuitive and creative. Do yourself a favor and don't ignore your instincts. You'll quickly find that your gut feelings are right at least 99 percent of the time.

Pluto

Pluto is set to spend yet another year in sturdy, practical Capricorn and your solar third house of conversations and communications, Scorpio, urging you to come up with rational, practical solutions to any problems that come your way. Now, Pluto is your ruling planet, so you two are tight. Very tight. That means that even if you're not entirely on your game when and if unexpected events come along, you'll still be able to come up with quick-fix solutions. Of course, if you are well prepared—which is what Capricorn planets love most—you probably won't have any problems to deal with in the first place, which of course would be the best of all possible outcomes. Since the third house rules communications, however, and since Pluto is an all-or-nothing kind of energy, it's easy to see how you may have recently developed a talent for intimidating others into agreeing with you—even if you never intended to. You'll need to pay attention to the weight your words are carrying now, and if you notice that others are backing away from you, stop them and ask why—nicely and calmly.

Also, if you get the feeling that you've been able to read the minds of others, don't question your sanity. You're probably right. Just be careful what you do with this newly acquired superpower. If you were born between the 9th and the 16th, Pluto will also be forming an easy, energizing sextile to your Sun this year, the stuff that major, long-term transformations are made of. Are you ready to molt, shed your skin, and become an entirely different person? Bet you are. You're a work in progress right now. Assist that process, even if it's uncomfortable at first and involves giving up a whole lot of situations and people you really weren't ready to say goodbye to. It's all part of the master plan. Let go, let it unfold, and look to the future.

How Will This Year's Eclipses Affect You?

Think of eclipses as celestial exclamation points. They amp up the volume on ordinary life for us all when they occur, but the signs and houses they occupy show where the possibility exists for sudden, intense, and often quite surprising events. Eclipses occur in pairs, six months apart. Solar Eclipses are supercharged New Moons, bringing the Sun and Moon together and marking peak times for planting seeds in any department of life. Lunar Eclipses are high-energy Full Moons, times of dramatic culmination, fulfillment, and often new beginnings as well, provided the slate has been wiped clean.

There will be five eclipses during 2018, making this a memorable year for one and all.

On January 31, the first Solar Eclipse of the year will arrive, all done up in dramatic Leo and set to make its mark in your solar tenth house of career and public reputation. If you've been trying to operate from behind the scenes, prepare to be recognized and don't shy away. No, you're not fond of the spotlight, but it's your turn to shine. Have fun with it.

On February 15, a Solar Eclipse will occur in Aquarius and your solar fourth house of home and family matters, urging you to make some drastic changes based on behaviors you've been noticing for about six months now. If you can't bring yourself to put an end to any unpleasant circumstances just yet, lay down the law at the very least, set up a time frame, and let everyone involved know that you're not in the mood for power struggles. Put them on notice—and be sure you mean it.

The third eclipse of 2018 will arrive on July 12, set and ready to get something started in home-loving Cancer. If you've been trying to get a family member to see the light or simply be respectful because of what you provide for them, it may not be possible just yet, but an event that comes along will most certainly convince them that you won't be playing games with them any longer. Tighten up the rules, if need be. Just make sure you're respected.

The Lunar Eclipse in Aquarius on July 27 is set to finish up something you started back in mid-February, so if you were thinking about moving or making some drastic changes to your domestic situation back then, you'll be ready to finish up those projects now. It might be that you've moved, or you're about to move. It might be that your family size has changed. It doesn't matter. What counts is your willingness to stay the course and keep your nest intact while major changes occur.

The fifth eclipse of the year will arrive on August 11 in Leo, urging you to allow yourself to accept a pat on the back from a coworker, superior, or elder. You've made yourself indispensable to them, and they've come to rely on you. What's the harm in accepting some thanks for it all? Stand there, smile, and enjoy it. You've earned it.

Scorpio | January

Relaxation and Recreation

The Full Moon on the 1st will occur in home- and family-oriented Cancer, a water sign like your own that operates on emotions. Does this mean you'll be wearing your heart on your sleeve? Sure does. Your heart will be quite full, most likely due to the caring gesture of a loved one. This pleasant memory will keep you smiling for a nice long while. Enjoy.

Lovers and Friends

If your sweetheart is acting a bit erratically on the 13th or 14th, try not to take it personally—at least, not until you're absolutely sure you know why. There could be a very good reason for their behavior, and it may actually have little or nothing to do with you. Sit them down for a long, honest heart-to-heart chat.

Money and Success

Conversations concerning finances will go quite well around the 25th, so if you're looking for a raise, bonus, or promotion, this is the time to schedule your meeting with higher-ups. Just be sure you have all your paperwork assembled and ready to be evaluated by them. Don't forget to mention not-so-recent projects you've thoroughly and successfully completed.

Tricky Transits

The Lunar Eclipse on the 31st could make it a tough day to be you, Scorpio, especially if you've been silently feuding with a superior at work or an elderly relative. It would be easy for you to respond quite dramatically to a little thing around this time, but do your best to hold your temper in check. Overreacting won't help.

Rewarding Days

2, 3, 15, 16, 24, 25

Challenging Days

13, 14, 17, 27, 31

Scorpio | February

Relaxation and Recreation

The Sun will tiptoe off into Pisces on the 18th, making it a wonderful Sunday to spend with family members and friends you think of as extended family. You've been working hard trying to impress a higher-up, and that's probably involved a whole lot of overtime. Relax. It's time to kick back and enjoy life. You've certainly earned it.

Lovers and Friends

Around the 25th, someone near and dear to your heart may try to convince you to do something through guilt—and if you don't recognize it for what it is, you'll want to do their bidding just to keep the peace. Don't do that. If someone says "if you loved me, you would" or words to that effect, they're being manipulative—and you know how much you dislike being manipulated.

Money and Success

It will be easy to overspend on the 3rd, no matter where you are or what your financial situation is, so do yourself a favor and don't head out to do any shopping alone. Take along a friend who won't be afraid to talk you out of making a purchase you really can't afford—even if it means actually taking your plastic away until you get home.

Tricky Transits

The Solar Eclipse on the 15th could make your domestic situation difficult for a few days, Scorpio. Sudden events could disrupt your usual schedule, and you may need to reevaluate your position on an important matter. Don't back down once you make your decision. Change isn't always comfortable, but it's often necessary. This is one of those times.

Rewarding Days

5, 6, 7, 14, 21, 27

Challenging Days

2, 3, 10, 15, 17, 28

Scorpio | March

Relaxation and Recreation

The weekend of the 9th looks to be quite fun, Scorpio, especially if you're seeing family and friends—but you'll have to work for it. That may mean organizing a big event or hosting a party, and again, it won't be easy. The good news is that once it's underway and you can see how your efforts have made it all come together, your heart will be quite full.

Lovers and Friends

Loving Venus will set off for red-hot, passionate Aries on the 6th, inspiring you to be especially assertive in the department of romance. Of course, you've never been known to be shy about intimate matters, so this will simply amp up the volume on your sex appeal. Just be sure not to intimidate anyone by coming on too strong. That would defeat the purpose, wouldn't it?

Money and Success

Jupiter will stop in his tracks on the 8th, right there in your very own sign, Scorpio. Now, this can be terrific, especially if you've been waiting for a financial plan to come together. If you're just now trying to get a business off the ground or you're looking for a new position, however, you may need to wait a while before you see any real results.

Tricky Transits

Venus will square off with Saturn on the 13th, Scorpio, and when these two are at odds, disappointment is often on the agenda. Now, that's not a definite outcome of every encounter, but you should prepare yourself, just in case—especially if you've seen this coming for a while. Allow your instincts to guide you and don't let anyone take advantage of you.

Rewarding Days

1, 2, 3, 4, 12, 19, 30

Challenging Days

11, 13, 23, 24, 25

Scorpio | April

Relaxation and Recreation

The Sun and Mercury will get together on the 1st to inspire you to play a serious April Fools' joke on someone near and dear to you. The thing is, you'll need to be careful not to embarrass them in the process. Think of how you'd feel if this happened to you. Make sure it's something funny and not at all mean-spirited.

Lovers and Friends

Stability is the name of the game on the 7th, Scorpio, when Venus and sturdy, responsible Saturn will come together in an easy trine aspect to see to it that promises made will be promises kept. If you've been trying to let someone know just how much you care, there's really no time like the present to sit them down, look into their eyes, and tell them all about it.

Money and Success

On the 19th, the Sun will head off into Taurus, the sign that's best known for its ability to attract success. Since this cosmic changeover will occur in your solar seventh house of relationships, you might want to consider taking on a business partner. If you're happily attached, it might be time to consider combining your resources.

Tricky Transits

The New Moon on the 15th will occur just a little while before Mercury stations to turn direct, Scorpio, creating a rather confusing set of circumstances. This is Aries energy, so you'll be ready to move forward surely and quickly—but you may not be able to just yet, which could be frustrating. Your mission is to do what you can to at least get the project started.

Rewarding Days
1, 7, 12, 16, 17, 30

Challenging Days
3, 4, 5, 11, 22, 25

Scorpio | May

Relaxation and Recreation

You may not have a whole lot of time to relax this month, Scorpio, with so many planets in serious Capricorn and your solar third house of thoughts and communications. Rest assured, however, that when you do settle down, kick back, and resolve to enjoy yourself, you'll be able to do it guilt-free. Aim for the weekend of the 19th.

Lovers and Friends

If you're single and don't want to be, the New Moon of the 15th may be just the ticket for you, Scorpio. It will occur in earthy, sensual Taurus and your solar seventh house of one-to-one relationships, bringing with it the possibility of crossing paths with at least one new person who's just delicious. Your mission is to get out there and mingle.

Money and Success

Talking things over on the 18th or 19th will solve a whole lot of money-oriented issues, Scorpio. Whether the problems are personal or professional doesn't matter. What's really important is that you keep an open mind and allow yourself to examine all possibilities, not just the ones that are currently on the table. Allow yourself to color outside the lines, just this once.

Tricky Transits

Mars and Uranus will square off on the 16th, Scorpio, creating an astrological recipe that's often responsible for sudden events that are quite disruptive. If you're heading out to do some errands, expect your day to be interrupted by totally unforeseen circumstances. Oh, and watch your temper around anyone who had absolutely nothing to do with the situation.

Rewarding Days
10, 11, 14, 15, 18, 19

Challenging Days
1, 5, 9, 12, 13, 16

Scorpio | June

Relaxation and Recreation

The weekend of the 9th looks like fun, Scorpio, especially if you're out and about with one particular person you find absolutely delightful and delicious. If you're single and looking, don't you dare stay home. Head out to meet up with folks who share your ideals and goals for the future, and don't be shy about introducing yourself.

Lovers and Friends

Someone near and dear to you may prove to be a bit problematic around the 14th or 15th, Scorpio—so much so that your feelings toward them will do a major turn-around. If you've had just about all you can take with their erratic or unstable behavior, don't put up with it any longer. Allow yourself to let go of the relationship. Release yourself from any guilt, too. This isn't your fault.

Money and Success

If you're feeling lucky around the 1st—and you really should be—taking a chance on a raffle or investing in a couple of lottery tickets really wouldn't be a bad idea. Just don't go overboard and spend too much. Remember, it only takes one to win, and if it's your time to win, it's your time to win.

Tricky Transits

It may seem that you're a shoo-in for that raise, bonus, or promotion you've been waiting for on the 19th, Scorpio, but just in case, be sure you've covered all your bases when you sit down to have that chat with the higher-up who signs your checks. One tiny detail could throw the process off and you'll have to start all over again. Be thorough.

Rewarding Days

1, 2, 9, 10, 22

Challenging Days

14, 15, 16, 21, 25, 26

Scorpio | July

Relaxation and Recreation

Try something new on the 11th, Scorpio. Experiment with an activity you've always been curious about, for example, or take a friend out for the day to investigate a business that's just opened up. You'll be in the mood to shake things up a little and break up your routine, and you really should do just that. Variety really is the spice of life.

Lovers and Friends

There's just no reason for you to be alone now—not unless you want to be, anyway. You have at least one friend who's been dying to introduce you to someone they feel is just perfect for you. Don't think about all the epic fails these introductions have brought about in the past. Concentrate on how good life will be once you've found the perfect match.

Money and Success

You'll be feeling a bit extravagant around the 22nd, Scorpio, so if you're on vacation and someone tries to sell you something you really don't want, much less need, don't be roped in. Shop, yes, but buy what you know you'll use and, more importantly, what you know you'll enjoy for some time to come.

Tricky Transits

On the 25th, Mercury will stop in his tracks to turn retrograde, just as the Sun and startling Uranus get into a testy, provocative square aspect. Does this mean you should expect the unexpected? Oh, yeah. In fact, if you don't have anywhere to be, staying home and binge-watching something on Netflix wouldn't be a bad idea. No one says you have to stay home alone.

Rewarding Days

5, 8, 11, 20, 21, 22

Challenging Days

9, 10, 12, 24, 25, 26, 27

Scorpio | August

Relaxation and Recreation

If you've made plans for the weekend of the 18th, you may need to adjust them somewhat, Scorpio, as Mercury stations to turn direct in dramatic, fiery Leo. The good news is that no matter where you end up, you'll most definitely be entertained. Take a look around you. What are you seeing that you'd never have seen if you were where you'd planned on being?

Lovers and Friends

Venus will take off for partner-loving Libra and your solar twelfth house of Privacy, Please, on the 6th, Scorpio, marking the beginning of a little over a month of delightful behind-the-scenes encounters with a certain someone you're desperately attracted to. Your mission is to clear your calendar—whenever you can, for as long as you can.

Money and Success

A financial deal you were positive was a sure thing may not turn out to be quite so sturdy around the 7th, Scorpio—but don't give up entirely. You'll probably find that a bit more work is needed to iron out the details—but then, details are one of your specialties, aren't they? Look over the fine print carefully, and update where necessary.

Tricky Transits

A square aspect between Mars and Uranus on the 1st will get your month off to a fiery, unpredictable start, Scorpio, which could be wonderful—or not. If you feel an encounter heating up—in the nicest sense of the word, that is—great. Enjoy it. If what's heating up is tempers, however, excuse yourself. Avoid potentially volatile situations.

Rewarding Days

6, 7, 19, 25

Challenging Days

1, 4, 9, 27, 29

Scorpio | September

Relaxation and Recreation

The New Moon in Virgo on the 9th will join force with Venus in your sign and your solar first house of personality and appearance, urging you to make changes you've been considering—in rapid-fire fashion. Don't hesitate. Get your hair done, join a gym, or invest in a few new items for your wardrobe. Above all else, think about the first impressions you make on others.

Lovers and Friends

If you've been looking to make amends with a dear one, arrange to meet up with them around the 11th. You'll both be willing to compromise a little, and it won't take much for the two of you to make nice. You're good at holding grudges, but it's most definitely time to let this one go and move forward.

Money and Success

Venus will move into your sign on the 9th just as a meticulous, detail-oriented Virgo New Moon arrives. This combination is perfect for financial planning, so if you need capital to put a five-year plan into action, this is the day to start work on it. You'll probably see results as soon as the end of the month.

Tricky Transits

On the 10th, Mars will storm off into startling Aquarius, a volatile energy that will take up residence in your solar fourth house of home and family matters for the next couple of months. Yes, your domestic situation could change, and if so, it will happen suddenly. Just don't worry too much about it. Change is necessary for growth, and you're due for a growth spurt.

Rewarding Days
3, 4, 7, 9, 20

Challenging Days
8, 17, 18, 19, 23, 25

Scorpio | October

Relaxation and Recreation
Getting the whole gang together at your place on the 24th would be a terrific idea, Scorpio, even if it's just for a good, old-fashioned family dinner. The Full Moon in comfort-loving Taurus will be on hand, urging one and all to snuggle up and enjoy the finer things that life has to offer. Good food and good hugs—what could possibly be better? Enjoy!

Lovers and Friends
The one who got away may not have gone all that far, Scorpio. In fact, on the 5th or 6th you may hear from them again—and it won't take long for you to realize that they're looking for another shot at the title. If they hurt you, be sure you're not setting yourself up for the same thing all over again. But if circumstances have changed... well, you might want to consider reconciliation.

Money and Success
Venus will spend most of the month moving retrograde, so it will probably not be possible for you to put off making decisions about money matters you've been ignoring or simply unwilling to deal with. No, it's time to face the facts and figure out what to do about them. Does this mean you'll need an accountant? Not necessarily—but a second pair of eyes wouldn't hurt.

Tricky Transits
The Sun will oppose startling Uranus on the 23rd, Scorpio, creating an atmosphere that's set to bring sudden emotional shifts to just about any of your relationships—even the ones you were sure would never, ever change. Don't jump to conclusions, but do pay attention if someone comes to you with unsettling news about a dear one.

Rewarding Days
4, 6, 12, 22, 24, 27

Challenging Days
1, 2, 10, 11, 17, 31

Scorpio | November

Relaxation and Recreation

From the 5th through the 8th, the Universe will see to it that you have some lucky breaks, Scorpio—the kind that you really need right about now. Does this mean that you'll win the lottery or marry a millionaire you adore? Maybe, but it's far more important for you to focus your energy on doing the right thing, regardless of the rewards. That's when you'll reap the best results.

Lovers and Friends

If you've been at odds with a loved one lately, Scorpio, there's really no reason for that to continue any longer. On the 9th, Venus will see to it that you can easily settle up on an old feud—and maybe even prevent a new one from starting. Your mission is to let go of any negative feelings from the past that are influencing you now. It's time to move on.

Money and Success

Money matters that seemed simple at the onset may not be as easy to handle as you'd originally thought around the 16th, Scorpio—but it's not just you. Venus and Mercury have teamed up to stall, hinder, and delay us all in the department of finances. The best thing you can do right now is to be sure you have absolutely all the information you need before you try to tackle the issue.

Tricky Transits

On the 30th, loving Venus will get into an astrological tug of war with startling Uranus, possibly forcing you to choose between making money and accommodating the emotional needs of your loved ones who've been complaining about not spending enough time with you. Fortunately, you're an expert juggler, and with a little luck, you should be able to do both.

Rewarding Days

5, 6, 7, 8, 27

Challenging Days

3, 15, 16, 28, 30

Scorpio | December

Relaxation and Recreation

If you're planning a pre-holiday get-together and you want to be sure that everyone leaves feeling warm and wonderful, you might want to plan it for the 21st, Scorpio, when a pack of astrological allies will see to it that you're in the mood to forgive, forget, and spread nothing but good feelings to everyone you encounter. There's no use in hanging on to the past—besides, 'tis the season!

Lovers and Friends

Inviting the neighbors over to your place for a cup of cheer around the 15th or 16th would be a terrific idea, Scorpio, especially if you've been meaning to get to know them better. There's something about holidays that brings out the best in everyone. Take advantage of the season—and don't be afraid to pass out some hugs.

Money and Success

You may be broke at the end of the month, but if an opportunity to attend an event or participate in an experience you've always wanted to try presents itself around the 28th, you really should find a way to make it happen. Adventure will be on your agenda, and if you're smart, you'll jump on it. What fun!

Tricky Transits

Fiery Mars will collide with woozy, dreamy Neptune on the 7th, creating a rather confusing set of circumstances. On the one hand, Mars wants to act. On the other hand, Neptune wants to dream. Fortunately, if used right, these two create the perfect astrological recipe for making those dreams come true. Choose a dream, and whether it belongs to you or someone you love, get busy.

Rewarding Days

15, 16, 21, 24, 25, 28

Challenging Days

5, 6, 7, 19, 31

Scorpio Action Table

These dates reflect the best—but not the only—times for success and ease in these activities, according to your Sun sign.

	JAN	FEB	MAR	APR	MAY	JUN	JUL	AUG	SEP	OCT	NOV	DEC
Move					18		5					
Start a class			2		11			25	3	15		
Join a club	2	6		12			11		7		5	28
Ask for a raise	25	21	4	14		19		19				
Get professional advice		14								22		16
Get a loan	24			7		1			9	27		17
New romance			1		15	9					6	
Vacation							22	18			7	

Sagittarius

The Archer
November 22 to December 21

✗

Element: Fire

Quality: Mutable

Polarity: Yang/masculine

Planetary Ruler: Jupiter

Meditation: I can take time to explore my soul

Gemstone: Turquoise

Power Stones: Lapis lazuli, azurite, sodalite

Key Phrase: I understand

Glyph: Archer's arrow

Anatomy: Hips, thighs, sciatic nerve

Colors: Royal blue, purple

Animals: Fleet-footed animals

Myths/Legends: Athena, Chiron

House: Ninth

Opposite Sign: Gemini

Flower: Narcissus

Keyword: Optimism

The Sagittarius Personality

Your Strengths, Gifts, and Challenges

You're a bit of a mystery, Sagittarius—a true hybrid. Your astrological symbol is the centaur, a half-human, half-animal creature, divided at the waist. That said, it's easy to understand how you consider all manner of earthly beings as extended family members, regardless of shape, form, or species. Whether they're bedecked in fur, feathers, scales, or leaves, you think of all living creatures as kindred spirits, and you'll fight for their rights and welfare with all the fiery passion your sign is famous for. Of course, championing causes and espousing at length about the virtues of those causes is what you live for, Sagg. I mean, let's be honest—you're nothing if not opinionated, kids. The good news is that thanks to merry Jupiter, your ruling planet, you're good at it, and you also have one heck of a sense of humor, an extremely entertaining and endearing quality—the likes of which certainly doesn't hurt your chances when you're trying to win others over to your way of thinking.

The best news is that Jupiter has also endowed you with an eleventh-hour lucky streak, so when it seems that you're out of options and you're down to the very last possible second when something positive can happen to turn things around ... well, it's like an action movie—because those things do often actually happen. Don't think of this as blind luck, however. You're a positive, outgoing force to be reckoned with, and when you're sending that much upbeat energy out into the Universe so enthusiastically, the laws of attraction can't help but boomerang those feelings right back in your direction. The thing is, you don't do anything "just a little." Nope. In your mind, it's go big or go home, which means that when you're happy, you're really, really happy—but when you're not, you're really, really not. Your mission is to give moderation a shot every now and then—especially over the next two and a half years. No, don't shake your head. You can do it. And while you're at it, put some elbow grease into championing your personal emotional needs with as much vigor and enthusiasm as you direct toward the groups and institutions you regularly fight for.

Romance and Other Relationships

When it comes to surrounding yourself with people you love, Sagittarius, your motto has always been "the more the merrier." You have a wide circle of interesting, funny friends, most likely from all over the world, and you just love listening to their accents and hearing about their experiences. Your love of new vistas makes you an excellent traveling companion, and you are only too happy to go anywhere and everywhere with equally ardent friends. In friendships and in one-to-one relationships, once you give in, let go of your precious freedom, and sign up for the long haul, you are loyal, trustworthy, and willing to do anything and everything to make your companions happy, from making them laugh at misfortune to buying them whatever their hearts desire.

Obviously, your fortunate partner will enjoy the very best that it's possible for you to give, which, along with your generous spirit, amazing sense of humor, and perpetual optimism, will keep them by your side forever—as long as they don't bore you! You can tolerate just about anything from a partner but tedium, which has ended more than one Sagittarian's relationship. Fortunately, you are more than open to taking them along to meet your friends, whether far or near, and actually prefer it when your sweetheart is part of your closest inner circle. You often have rather odd, long-distance relationships with your family members and tend to think of friends as your "true" family—and those friends often include four-legged, furry critters, whom you consider your children. You lavish love and attention on anyone and anything you are fond of, and are well loved by just about everyone lucky enough to know you.

Career and Work

Whatever professional path you decide to follow in life, Sagittarius, you will follow it with energy and passion, as your fiery disposition dictates. You make an excellent teacher, but tend to teach wherever you go, anyway, whether or not it is your actual job. Many Sagittarians are also comedians and performers, putting Jupiter's gift of laughter to work for them. "Work," however, is not something you are fond of, and you are easily bored. So whatever you choose to do with your life, it absolutely must reflect your beliefs and offer you the daily personal freedom you need to keep your curious soul amused.

Money and Possessions

Now, as to dealing with money—well, let's just say it's not your strong suit. You see money as tokens, exchangeable for amusement, entertainment, and gifts for your lucky loved ones. Telling you to keep a rein on your finances and not overextend is futile, but fortunately, the older you get, the more that lesson will sink in. In the meantime, try not to spend more than you earn!

Your Lighter Side

You have an odd but endless sense of humor, Sagittarius, and your innate optimism and love of new experiences enable you to laugh at whatever the Universe tosses your way. In fact, you love laughter more than anything— other than animals, of course. You often play the clown for others, and are never, ever without a happy, grateful audience. You need travel to keep your mind fresh and your soul at peace, and love nothing more than to hang your hat in interesting new places.

Sagittarius Celebrities

Your Sun sign is famous for being larger than life, Sagittarius, so it's not surprising that many of the celebrities who share it with you can best be described in just that way. To start with, there's Bette Midler, Tina Turner, Frank Sinatra, Samuel L. Jackson, Steven Spielberg, and Walt Disney. Pope Francis took his name from Francis of Assisi, remembered best for his love of animals. Your innate skill for comedy is beautifully exemplified by Jon Stewart, Sarah Silverman, Richard Pryor, and Billy Connolly, all of whom also tend to have rather strong opinions about social and political issues—another quality your sign is famous for.

The Year Ahead for Sagittarius

Your ruling planet, mighty Jupiter himself, will spend most of the year in your solar twelfth house, Sagittarius—a very private spot that's reserved for either alone time or conversations and encounters with those you trust and feel comfortable sharing your secrets with. Now, if you're attached and thinking of getting involved in a secret relationship, spend some time alone and do a bit of reflection. Are you really willing to risk everything you have for what might only be a momentary fling? Think it over carefully. It may be that it's not a person you've become secretly infatuated with, but a cause or an idea. In that case, before you devote yourself unconditionally—which is the only way you'll be willing to do anything right about now—please be sure that you're not reacting to something that happened in the past. Yes, it's good to get rid of old grudges, and yes, it's good to pursue dreams you've recently been thinking of as impossible, and both plans are valid. Just be sure not to let the past invade the present—or the future. In your solitary moments, set aside a bit of time to reflect on what you want. Matter of fact, put together a five-year plan—or a ten-year plan, even.

Don't be surprised if you end up with some rather shocking goals, by the way—and with the fact that you're willing to cut your losses and move forward alone, too. That goes double from May 16 through August 12 and again from September 10 through November 15, when fiery, passionate Mars will be storming through your solar third house of conversations and communications. This unusually long trek will stir up your already rebellious spirit, so heaven help anyone who asks for your opinion—especially if they were thinking you'd smile politely and defer. Nope. Your verbal assertion, shall we say, will be running on high—even if you're not asked for your thoughts on the matter. Oh, and be warned, please. When it comes to polite conversation—chatting nicely about all those causes that are near and dear to your heart, that is—if others don't understand, or worse, if they just don't want to understand, you won't be merciful. When you have an opinion to express, you're always ready to rock, but for the most part, you're good at conveying it to others in a funny, witty, and philosophical way. When assertive, aggressive Mars is on duty in this house, however, it's all too easy to alienate others without meaning to—and one simple sentence might do the job. Does that mean you should keep quiet? Of course not. Just choose your battles—and your words—wisely.

Saturn

Just weeks before 2018 arrived, Saturn marched off into your solar second house, Sagittarius, where he'll remain on duty for the next two and a half years. Since this astrological placement has everything to do with money and possessions—and hence, how you earn your daily bread—and since Saturn has everything to do with earning your keep… well, obviously, it's important that you direct your attention now toward matters concerning the material side of life. No, you're not usually all that interested in managing your finances—unless you're running low on funds, that is—but it's time to account for what you have and what you need to have to continue your lifestyle as you know it. If you're living from paycheck to paycheck, it's time to come up with a long-term plan that will at least give you a safety net when tough times arise. If you're solid and not at all worried about the near future, get thee to a solid, trustworthy accountant and find out how to put aside what you don't really need to spend on a daily basis to ensure that your future will be stress-free and comfortable. Relax, though. No one's saying you can't be extravagant every now and then—just not every day. Putting a bit aside for a rainy day wouldn't hurt, either. Remember, Saturn loves it when we're prepared. If you find yourself on a budget that's tough to keep, don't worry. You may not have everything that you want during this time, but Saturn will provide what you need.

Uranus

Straight through May 15, startling Uranus will remain on duty in your solar fifth house of lovers and friends, Sagittarius. Now, this is nothing new for you—in fact, at this point, you're a bit of an expert when it comes to handling circumstances that change suddenly but often end up quite well. Uranus began influencing you here back in May of 2010, so you've learned to deal with surprises, and since Uranus is known for his unpredictable nature, it's safe to say that a few more are in store for you. If you were born at the tail end of your sign—say, from December 14 through the 21st—all this goes double, as Uranus finishes up passing out trine aspects to your sign. Fortunately, while trines from Uranus are every bit as disruptive as any other aspect he makes, they usually turn out well far more quickly. That means that any and all changes you set into motion now will go along smoothly—as smoothly as possible, that is.

Don't waste any time initiating change when it comes to lovers, playmates, and dealings with kids, though. On May 15, Uranus will move on, set to shake up sturdy, stubborn Taurus and your solar sixth house, where issues of work and health are handled. From that point on, the rhythm of your day will be totally unpredictable—and remember, this transit will last for the next seven years, until 2025. That said, if you're already in the mood to make drastic changes with regard to your profession or the state of your health, this is most definitely the time to get the show on the road.

Neptune

If you were born between December 2 and 9, your Sun will be experiencing a square aspect from Neptune, who just so happens to specialize in fogging up the facts so that we'll pay attention to our intuition. That said, no matter when you were born, keep in mind that squares from transiting planets often bring along circumstances that are frustrating or irritating—and don't get too mad about it, because no one changes or grows without first feeling uncomfortable. In your case, it may be that some of the people closest to you will disappoint you, or that you'll become disheartened or disillusioned with them. In that case, you may feel the need to gradually disappear from their lives—which is exactly what needs to happen.

Think of this time as a shedding or molting period, and if others drift away from you in the meantime, don't try to pursue them or press too hard for answers. Neptune is in the business of making us ultra-sensitive, and in a square to your Sun sign, she'll also make it harder for you to tolerate loud sounds, harsh lights, and threatening situations. Ditch anyone who feels dangerous, even if you initially thought of that as an attractive quality. Matter of fact, ditch anyone or anything that brings you down. You're a sponge right now, so what you need is to surround yourself with positive energies that will lift your spirit and allow you to experience your own particular version of spirituality, no matter what that happens to be.

Pluto

If you haven't already gotten yourself on a strict budget, Sagittarius, it's officially time to get that show on the road. Pluto—who has a reputation for being extremely extreme—has been on duty in your solar second house of personal money matters since 2008, making it essential that you learn to live on what you have, and nothing more. He won't be leaving anytime soon, and he's not famous for going easy on us when we don't cooperate. That said, whatever you can do to make his visit easier is exactly what you'll need to do, ASAP. If that means giving up a thing or two you really don't need and maybe even haven't been paying attention to for a while now, so be it. You're in the process of learning what's truly valuable to you and what's not, and over the past ten years, you've probably already made frugality a way of life—or moderation, at least. The thing is, this year, Saturn—who just loves cutting out frivolities—will team up with Pluto to make sure you pay attention to being economically prudent and oh-so thrifty. Whittle down your budget. Get rid of anything you're paying for but not really enjoying. Most importantly, think about what's important to you on an inner level. What's truly valuable and what's not?

How Will This Year's Eclipses Affect You?

Think of eclipses as celestial exclamation points. They amp up the volume on ordinary life for us all when they occur, but the signs and houses they occupy show where the possibility exists for sudden, intense, and often quite surprising events. Eclipses occur in pairs, six months apart. Solar Eclipses are supercharged New Moons, bringing the Sun and Moon together and marking peak times for planting seeds in any department of life. Lunar Eclipses are high-energy Full Moons, times of dramatic culmination, fulfillment, and often new beginnings as well, provided the slate has been wiped clean.

There will be five eclipses during 2018, marking an extremely unpredictable year for one and all.

The first Lunar Eclipse of 2018 will occur on January 31, all done up in dramatic Leo, set to cause major shifts in your solar ninth house. Now, this is the place where opinions are formed, so don't be surprised if you suddenly change your mind about a political or spiritual cause—in a very big way. Don't beat yourself up about it, either. Just like the rest of us, you have every right to evolve at your own pace.

The Solar Eclipse of February 15 will arrive at 27 degrees of startling Aquarius, in your solar third house of communications and conversations. Now, these lunations tend to bring along sudden change, so you should probably prepare yourself to hear the very last thing on earth you'd ever have expected. Relax, though. This doesn't mean the news will be bad—but it will most certainly be surprising. If you've been looking to get yourself free from a situation that's far too restrictive, don't hesitate. Jump. If you need more freedom, Sagg, it's time to make that happen, even if others don't understand or approve.

On July 12, a Solar Eclipse will occur in home- and family-oriented Cancer and your solar eighth house of loans, inheritances, and shared resources, Sagg. This could mean that a loan will be called in, or that you'll need to take fast action regarding an overdue debt. If it's you who owes, you'll need to figure out how to take care of it. If it's you who's owed, legal counsel may be necessary.

On July 27, a Lunar Eclipse will occur in your solar third house of communications and conversations, helping you to bring closure to a situation that came along quite suddenly back in mid-February—also via an eclipse. Whether it seemed to be for the best or the worst at the time, if you can manage to create something positive now that's a product of what you experienced then, you'll win the game. Go for it!

The last Solar Eclipse of the year on August 11 will be in fiery Leo. It will set up shop in your solar ninth house, once again forcing you to reconsider beliefs you've held dear for a very long time. This time out, however, since it's a supercharged New Moon who's driving, you might just find that someone you've run into recently—who's entirely different from everyone else you know—has inspired you to finally make a break from the past and charge off fearlessly into your future.

Sagittarius | January

Relaxation and Recreation

If your plans for the weekend of the 6th and 7th fall through rather suddenly, Sagittarius, don't get too upset about it. For starters, you're a rather spontaneous soul, so last-minute change doesn't really throw you. Plus, you're a natural-born storyteller, so anyone or anything unusual that comes your way is really just grist for the mill. Still, don't get too attached to your agenda, and have plan B ready to rock.

Lovers and Friends

With startling and often shocking Uranus on duty in your solar fifth house of lovers and playmates for the past seven years, you've become quite used to odd, quirky, and changeable people. Around the 13th and 14th, however, someone new may be along to prove to you that even if you think you've seen it all, the Universe is always full of surprises.

Money and Success

With no less than five planets passing through diligent, hardworking Capricorn and your solar second house this month, Sagittarius, it's easy to see how you might end up putting in a whole lot of overtime for the next several weeks. The good news is that you'll reap the benefits quickly. If you've paid your dues, you should expect a raise, bonus, or promotion shortly. Do yourself a favor, though, and just this once, don't spend it all in one place.

Tricky Transits

A Lunar Eclipse on the 31st will occur in your solar ninth house of far-off loved ones and distant places, Sagittarius—which presents many possible scenarios. For example, you may need to travel suddenly because someone needs you, or you may be visited by someone who senses that you need them now. You might also be bitten by the travel bug and suddenly decide to take off for a place you've always wanted to see. Regardless, keep your schedule as flexible as possible.

Rewarding Days

2, 3, 8, 9, 15, 19

Challenging Days

14, 17, 23, 24, 27

Sagittarius | February

Relaxation and Recreation

With fiery, adventurous Mars on duty in your sign for the entire month, you probably won't be getting much rest, Sagittarius—but you sure will be having some serious fun. If you haven't yet taken some time off, a long weekend is most definitely in order—a long weekend that involves plans that are loose, that is. You're tired of coloring inside the lines. Allow yourself some time to be spontaneous.

Lovers and Friends

If you're single and a family member absolutely insists that you meet up with someone they're sure is just perfect for you, don't resist. If you're skeptical after past major fails, just sign up for coffee and a possible lunch. If you meet up around the 25th or 27th, at the very least you'll drift away from one another peacefully. At best, you could cross paths with a true kindred spirit who'll be around for a very long time.

Money and Success

If you need to refinance your mortgage or consolidate your credit card debt, look into it around the 12th and 13th—but don't sign up for anything permanent until the end of the month. The 27th in particular looks to be a date to shoot for if you've got to sign on the dotted line of any official financial agreement. Your mission is to be sure to read the fine print thoroughly.

Tricky Transits

On the 10th, loving Venus will set off for woozy, dreamy Pisces and your solar fourth house of home and emotions, just as the Sun and excessive Jupiter get into an energetic square aspect. On the one hand, this could be just delightful, especially if you've just changed your domestic situation for the better and are now finally able to enjoy it. On the other hand, you may be a bit befuddled by the recent behavior of a loved one. You absolutely must talk it out.

Rewarding Days

2, 3, 6, 12, 13, 25

Challenging Days

4, 9, 15, 17, 21, 28

Sagittarius | March

Relaxation and Recreation

Loving Venus will set off for your solar fifth house of lovers on the 6th, Sagg, urging you to resume the hunt for the perfect playmate/lover. If you're single, get out there and check out some new peer groups. Keep at it all month, and around the Full Moon on the 31st, you'll likely run into someone who'll pleasantly surprise you with their wit and humor.

Lovers and Friends

On the 22nd, communicative Mercury will station in your solar fifth house of playmates and lovers to begin a three-week retrograde trek. Over the duration, you should probably expect at least one old lover to resurface, possibly because you two simply bump into each other at an odd moment. Your mission is to remember what split you up in the first place before you slip back into comfortable habits from the past.

Money and Success

The Full Moon on the 1st will occur in your solar tenth house of career matters and authority figures, Sagg. Together with a lovely trine aspect between Venus and your Uncle Jupiter that same day, this lunation can illuminate your skills and talents so brightly that a higher-up you've been trying to impress will have absolutely no choice but to notice you. Don't make a scene, though. Let it happen. No need to overdo it.

Tricky Transits

Your ruling planet, Jupiter, will stop in his tracks on the 8th to turn retrograde in your solar twelfth house of secrets—and he'll be wearing sexy Scorpio at the time. Does this mean you're due to become involved in a bit of intrigue that's deliciously mysterious? Possibly. Just be careful what you wish for, and be even more careful about whom you allow to lure you away from your everyday routine.

Rewarding Days

1, 2, 3, 4, 16, 28

Challenging Days

11, 12, 13, 22, 23, 24, 29

Sagittarius | April

Relaxation and Recreation

You're always up for a good joke, Sagg—even if it's on you—and every now and then you've also been known to devise a prank or two. Of course, you mean well and that shows, so not too many people have ever taken offense. That said, if you're in the mood to prank a lover or playmate on the 1st—as per April Fool's Day—be sure they're in the mood for it.

Lovers and Friends

On the 15th, the New Moon in Aries will charge up your solar fifth house of lovers and playmates. If you're happily attached and looking to charge things up a bit, this is the perfect time to plan an adventure—especially if it involves something neither of you have ever done but both of you have always wanted to try. The category is up for grabs. If you're single, prepare to meet someone who'll immediately amuse and entertain you.

Money and Success

If you've got to talk finances, Sagittarius, try to plan it for the 6th or 7th, when Venus and Saturn will make it their business to help you tend to your business. Authorities will be supportive and easy to talk with. Don't hesitate to negotiate now—even if it's totally unplanned. All parties involved will be fair, realistic, and willing to compromise.

Tricky Transits

Loving Venus will take off for your solar seventh house of one-to-one relationships on the 24th, all done up in Gemini—a sign that's almost as famous as yours for its low tolerance for boredom. Someone new and exciting will be along shortly. It's up to you to decide whether to enjoy them on a strictly platonic basis—or otherwise. Careful, though. Their company could be habit-forming.

Rewarding Days

6, 7, 12, 14, 28, 29, 30

Challenging Days

1, 2, 4, 5, 25, 26

⚔ Sagittarius | May

Relaxation and Recreation

With Mars in hardworking Capricorn and your solar second house of financial matters until the 15th, you should probably expect to be putting in a whole lot of overtime to achieve your short-term goals. The good news is that on that very same day, the New Moon in Taurus will provide you with an introduction to someone with experience in the field who'll be able to help you in a very big way.

Lovers and Friends

On the 29th, the Full Moon will shine its bright light on your sign, via your solar first house of personality and appearance. Now, this could mean that a side of you that you've managed to keep hidden until now will suddenly demand to be set free—in which case, please don't argue with the urge, and don't be shy about releasing it, either. Oh, and once you've done it—well, good for you! It's time for a celebration.

Money and Success

Loving Venus in your solar seventh house of one-to-one relationships will get into an uncomfortable aspect with Saturn on the 1st, setting you up for the possibility of a chat about money problems that won't be easy to resolve. Your mission is to keep your mind open to all possibilities, but table any decisions until the 4th, if you're in a hurry, or the 18th, if you have a bit of time to stall.

Tricky Transits

On the 7th, Mercury will square off with Pluto, the stuff that bitter, righteous arguments are made of. That same day, however, Venus and Neptune will be on duty, a pair that's always ready to negotiate a treaty. No matter how mad you are, the possibility remains that you two aren't meant to part ways just yet. If you've been physically or emotionally damaged, however, all bets are off. It's time to make a break for it.

Rewarding Days

6, 8, 11, 22, 23, 24

Challenging Days

1, 5, 9, 12, 26, 28

Sagittarius | June

Relaxation and Recreation

The weekend of the 1st will get your month off to a merry start. It seems that four planets will conspire to put you in the mood for an outing with fun-loving, like-minded friends. The good news is that even if you haven't yet crossed paths with them, circumstances will put you in touch with kindred spirits. All you have to do is clear your schedule, enjoy their company, and pay attention to the messages they've brought along.

Lovers and Friends

You'll be doing a whole lot of chatting with others during the first half of this month, Sagittarius, thanks to communicative Mercury, who'll be making his way through talkative Gemini and your solar seventh house of one-to-one relationships. Your mission, should you choose to accept it, is to lay your cards on the table and let everyone around you know exactly what you expect—and more importantly, what you won't tolerate.

Money and Success

The Sun, Mercury, and Venus will pass through your solar eighth house of shared resources this month, Sagittarius, urging you to sit down with all parties involved and get things settled regarding what's yours and what's theirs. The thing is, you should avoid the 18th and 19th if you've got to sign anything important, especially if you're not quite sure you trust the person who's advising you.

Tricky Transits

Fiery Mars will be in impulsive Aquarius and your solar third house of communications and conversations this month. The good news is that you'll finally be able to let loose with whatever you've been holding back—in a very big, very cleansing way—so you're about to lose some weight, psychically speaking, especially if you don't resist the urge to tell the truth, the whole truth, and nothing but the truth.

Rewarding Days
1, 2, 3, 21, 22

Challenging Days
5, 7, 8, 11

Sagittarius | July

Relaxation and Recreation

With the Sun, Mercury, and loving Venus all passing through your solar ninth house of far-off loved ones and long-distance adventures, it's easy to see how you might just be in the mood to ditch your daily schedule and pursue something a lot more exciting. You'll definitely have a strong taste for the exotic and the unusual this month. Enjoy the veritable buffet of experiences the Universe has in store for you.

Lovers and Friends

Venus will set off for your solar tenth house of authority figures on the 9th, Sagittarius, which definitely bodes well for your relationships with elders and higher-ups—in a business sense. The thing is, you may also suddenly develop a bit of a crush on a superior—or if you're the boss, someone who works for you may make it clear they're interested. What to do? Well, it's up to you, of course, but do consider your paycheck before you dally with someone who signs it.

Money and Success

With Venus in organized Virgo after the 9th, it will be unusually easy for you to keep to your schedule—and maybe even stick to that budget you optimistically put together recently. That said, if you've been good all month and you're thinking you deserve a reward around the 22nd, don't get crazy and blow all the good work you've done. Moderation is the key. Yes, you can.

Tricky Transits

Mercury will turn retrograde on the 25th, just as the Sun gets into it with shocking Uranus and impulsive Mars. Obviously, this could be one of those days for you, Sagittarius, so regardless of what you feel your duties are, if your gut is telling you that making this trip or spending time with this particular someone isn't a good idea, don't go against it. Pay attention to your intuition, and avoid potentially volatile situations.

Rewarding Days
4, 5, 21, 22, 23

Challenging Days
1, 2, 12, 16, 25, 26

Sagittarius | August

Relaxation and Recreation

If you have plans for the 9th or 10th, you may need to scale them back a bit, Sagittarius. A Venus-Saturn square will doubtless make it necessary for you to tighten your belt, at least temporarily. The good news is that since you're not notoriously good with money, the team might just introduce you to a more frugal way of living that will serve you well in the future.

Lovers and Friends

If you have the urge to take a chance on someone new around the 7th, be it a lover or a friend, don't resist. Loving Venus and impulsive Mars will get together in an easy trine aspect on that day, creating the astrological stuff that fortunate encounters are made of. The only caveat is that you two should definitely watch out for being especially extravagant when you're together.

Money and Success

If you can, schedule any business meetings or get-togethers for the 24th or 25th. The heavens will be hosting a Grand Earth Trine, the perfect astrological ingredients for material success. Yes, you'll be able to negotiate, renegotiate, and maybe even be able to advise someone you love based on your recent experiences. It's all good. Just let your intuition be your guide.

Tricky Transits

Bright and early on the 1st, red-hot Mars and startling Uranus will get into a shouting match, a team that's often in the neighborhood when sudden and even shocking events occur. In your case, it may be that you're ready to let someone know that they've deliberately pushed your buttons for the very last time. Go easy on the retaliation, though. You'll want to hold your head up high when you tell others exactly what happened.

Rewarding Days
7, 18, 19, 24, 25

Challenging Days
5, 6, 11, 12, 22, 26, 29

⚹ Sagittarius | September ⚹

Relaxation and Recreation

The 11th and 12th are terrific days for just about any kind of social affairs, Sagittarius, especially if you're trying to keep a low profile. This doesn't mean you won't attract attention—only that when you do, you won't feel the need to go overboard and make a show of yourself or the cause you've been recognized along with. That said, no one's saying you can't take one little discreet bow, if only to thank your supporters.

Lovers and Friends

After the 10th, when fiery Mars sets off for your solar fifth house of play-mates, it will be easy for you to make new friends, get together with loved ones, and bond with younger folks. If you're single and someone from one of those departments surprises you around the 18th, enjoy the moment but take your time deciding whether or not you'd like to make this a per-manent thing.

Money and Success

A wonderfully earthy trine involving the Sun, Jupiter, and Pluto on the 11th will make it possible for you to have positive, successful meetings with authority figures. That said, if you're up for a promotion, pushing for a raise, or hoping for a bonus, this would be the perfect astrological time for you to set up a meeting with the person in charge of those decisions.

Tricky Transits

Fiery Mars will storm off into your communication-oriented solar third house on the 10th, all done up in rebellious, impetuous Aquarius. You were born with the ability to speak your mind without being ashamed, Sagittarius, but this feisty fellow will make it even easier for you to let loose—regardless of whether your opinion has actually been asked for. The good news is that just about everyone in the vicinity will be like-minded and probably agree with you.

Rewarding Days

3, 7, 11, 12, 15, 16, 24

Challenging Days

5, 6, 8, 19, 22, 25, 30

Sagittarius | October

Relaxation and Recreation

The Sun, Venus, and Saturn are making plans that will allow you to enjoy yourself this month—guilt-free, by the way. This means that it's time to work on your wish list. Where do you want to go, and with whom? If you haven't already set a bit of money aside for an adventure, it's definitely time to do it now. If you've got a bit of a stash and no dire debts hanging over you, a long weekend is most definitely in order.

Lovers and Friends

Venus is in charge of not just money but also love, so the fact that she'll be moving retrograde as of the 5th could mean that a relationship matter you thought you'd put to bed—no pun intended—will actually need to be dealt with once again. It's time to tie up all loose ends and to be sure that everyone in your life at the moment is quite aware of their position in your life.

Money and Success

Joint finances and shared resources will be a bit tricky to handle around the 5th, when Venus stops in her tracks to turn retrograde. This could mean that a financial issue you've been trying to dodge suddenly refuses to be ignored any longer—in which case, it might be best for you to face facts and deal with it. If you need to speak with someone who knows their way around money matters like these, set up an appointment on the 12th.

Tricky Transits

Your plans for Halloween could change suddenly due to someone's erratic behavior, so be prepared. This doesn't mean you can't have fun with the kids or take off for a masked party. The important thing is to make it clear to all parties involved in the adventure that from now on, promises made need to be promises kept. Once you've made that point, you can get back to enjoying the holiday.

Rewarding Days

12, 13, 14, 22, 24, 27, 30

Challenging Days

2, 9, 10, 11, 31

⤢ Sagittarius | November ⤢

Relaxation and Recreation

The weekend of the 9th is perfect for enjoying the company of family members and friends you think of as family, Sagittarius. Loving Venus in peace-loving Libra will do her best to inspire everyone in attendance to mind their manners, behave appropriately, and maybe even extend or accept a long overdue apology. Your mission is to keep any sarcastic comments to a minimum—yes, even if they're really funny.

Lovers and Friends

Relationships that aren't currently on solid ground could be problematic around the 30th, when loving Venus faces off with shocking, rebellious Uranus. This pair has been known to break up more than one relationship, so be prepared—but keep in mind that they've also brought more than one couple back together again. Enjoy the reunion, but before you do anything drastic, take some time alone to think about it.

Money and Success

If you've been having money problems and are not quite sure about how to handle them—especially if there's a very old debt involved—you can relax now, Sagg. Well, as of the 16th, anyway, when Venus will station to move direct, that is. It may take a few days to get the show on the road again, but don't be impatient. The trick is to retrace your steps, see what went wrong, and not repeat that mistake.

Tricky Transits

The Full Moon on the 22nd will be in chatty, fun-loving Gemini, a sign you've always been quite fond of, so if you gather together with family and friends, it seems that a good time will be had by all. The thing is, you may also hear a rumor or two, or inadvertently become privy to a bit of gossip—the kind that's not at all well intentioned. Your mission is to shut it down immediately. Don't waste your time on petty speculation.

Rewarding Days

8, 9, 14, 15, 27

Challenging Days

2, 3, 16, 17, 28, 30

✕ Sagittarius | December ✕

Relaxation and Recreation

Bright and early on the 6th, Mercury will turn direct—which sounds like a good thing, and might just be a good thing. The problem is that when Mercury stations, he's basically not moving at all, and since he's in charge of communications and navigations, if you're trying to get from point A to point B, it's imperative that you double-check your facts, directions, and vehicle to ensure it all goes off without a hitch.

Lovers and Friends

If you've been involved in anything you weren't planning to go public with just yet, Sagg, prepare yourself. On the 6th, the New Moon in your sign will combine forces with Mercury to bring all kinds of secrets out of hiding. You've always been a great fan of honesty. Your mission now will be to put your money where your mouth is. Ready or not, here it comes.

Money and Success

You'll be feeling especially generous around the 21st, which, in your case, means you'll be shopping extravagantly—with little or no regard for the future. If you have a last-minute gift to pick up or you spot something a dear one would just adore, wonderful. Just be sure not to make yourself financially vulnerable over the coming months.

Tricky Transits

Everyone loves to have an exciting New Year's Eve, especially you fire signs, Sagittarius. This time around, however, red-hot Mars will be on his way into confrontational, passionate Aries, so do be sure that your holiday plans include others you're sure will be there for you, just in case—the cooperative, cautious, and responsible types.

Rewarding Days
12, 13, 15, 16, 21, 24, 28

Challenging Days
1, 2, 5, 7, 22

Sagittarius Action Table

These dates reflect the best–but not the only–times for success and ease in these activities, according to your Sun sign.

	JAN	FEB	MAR	APR	MAY	JUN	JUL	AUG	SEP	OCT	NOV	DEC
Move					18							
Start a class			4			1	23			15		
Join a club		6				2	21		11		9	21
Ask for a raise	2	27	1	7				24	12			
Get professional advice				29	15				12	24		
Get a loan	3			6	11		8	25	9		11	
New romance	13	25	31					7				16
Vacation						22				26	8	20

Capricorn

The Goat
December 22 to January 19

♑

Element: Earth

Quality: Cardinal

Polarity: Yin/feminine

Planetary Ruler: Saturn

Meditation: I know the strength of my soul

Gemstone: Garnet

Power Stones: Peridot, onyx diamond, quartz, black obsidian

Key Phrase: I use

Glyph: Head of goat

Anatomy: Skeleton, knees, skin

Colors: Black, forest green

Animals: Goats, thick-shelled animals

Myths/Legends: Chronos, Vesta, Pan

House: Tenth

Opposite Sign: Cancer

Flower: Carnation

Keyword: Ambitious

The Capricorn Personality

Your Strengths, Gifts, and Challenges

That whole "cold and emotional" thing ye olde astrology books have too often saddled you with just isn't fair, Capricorn—or even accurate, for that matter. Yes, you're shrewd, especially with regard to career matters and business dealings, but cold? No way—or at least, not without good reason. When you're chilly, it's because a problematic situation has come up, and to solve it, you've removed emotions from the equation—something many of us would dearly love to be able to do every now and then. You then assess the situation, do a feasibility study on all possible outcomes, and finally decide whether it's in everyone's best interests to get involved, versus keeping your distance. Otherwise, you're devoted, uber-reliable, and loyal to a fault, especially when it comes to family members and old, dear friends.

Contrary to other bad press you've had to live with for far too long, you have a terrific sense of humor. The thing is, sarcasm and irony are your chosen styles, each of which can honestly be a bit off-putting. Still, those who know you appreciate your wit, as acerbic as it might be. You're a big fan of penalties and rewards, most often passed out by those in charge, and you have a handle on which is deserved at any given moment. From that point, it's not much of a stretch to imagine you guys constantly ending up in positions of authority, whether or not you applied for the job or even wanted it. Next time you're asked to take over the reins because someone's dropped them, however, do yourself a favor and pause. Take just a moment to think things over. If you want the responsibility and can see yourself fulfilling it well and easily, fine. If you think you might actually enjoy it, even better. If you're overloading yourself because you secretly believe you're responsible for everything, however, do yourself a favor and politely refuse. No fair beating yourself up afterward, either. Even Capricorns have the right to say "sorry, no can do" every now and then.

Romance and Other Relationships

Capricorn planets often feel hungry—starved, in fact. When you're used to getting by with little or none of what you need, you tend to lower your expectations about what to expect from others, and in extreme cases, to wall yourself off from even hoping you might someday feel satisfied, much less content. That's where that whole "cold and unemotional" thing came from to start with. And, like everything else in life, what we do and don't expect from the Universe tends to reveal itself best in our relationships with others, so if you most often end up playing the role of giver, provider, and benefactor, it's not surprising—but it doesn't have to be that way forever. A nice, long look at what you provide to others—perhaps through an honest conversation with a trusted friend or unbiased advisor—may be just the thing to help you realize how much you bring to the table—and how much you fairly deserve in return.

You're the real deal, Capricorn, and anyone who doesn't see that doesn't deserve you. That said, please keep in mind that relationships aren't supposed to be taxing, burdensome, or tiring. If that's what it's come to, no matter how much time you've invested, it might be time to tear up the contract. Of course, the other earth signs, Taurus and Virgo, understand loyalty, reliability, and duty, so if you're in it for the long haul and you want to be half of a couple long enough to see your grandkids at your feet, these signs make excellent choices. You'll find Scorpios to be quite exciting—for all the right reasons—but Cancers will tend the home fires while you're off on your mission to provide for your family.

Career and Work

You're nothing if not driven, Capricorn, often to a fault. The good news is that there's no better or more proven way to ascend the ladder of success than to own that quality, and once you choose your path and you've committed to it, there's very little that can deter you. The best news is that you're definitely not afraid of working hard, no matter what you're doing, even if it's just to earn a paycheck until you decide what you want to be when you grow up. But what will you devote your hardworking hours to, ideally? Well, you're fond of building things, so construction is an option, and since structure is so important to you, being an overseer or inspector comes to you easily. Your respect for authority, however, means that you'll always be in charge, one way or the other.

Money and Possessions

When it comes to money matters, a lot depends on the sign in which your Venus is placed, but for the most part, even if you're uncharacteristically extravagant, you won't spend on anything you deem to be frivolous, and you'll keep your finances in order. If you're living on a shoestring budget, you can handle it, and when you're in the red, you're an extremely careful shopper. Either way, you love nothing better than a deal—and you're not afraid to look around until you find what you're after for the price you're willing to pay.

Your Lighter Side

Since Saturn—Mr. Matter-Of-Fact himself—is your ruling planet, you pride yourself on being realistic and practical, which often means putting your personal likes and dislikes aside to "do the right thing." But let me tell you, kids—when you decide it's time to kick back, nobody does it better. Getting back to that whole "rewards and penalties" thing, once you honestly believe you've racked up enough bonus points on the job to deserve a free-wheeling evening or weekend off—well, there's just no stopping you. Your idea of fun tends to be a tad more strenuous than it is for the rest of us, though. Building something, working on a project, or showing that jigsaw puzzle who's in charge are quite appealing when you have a few hours free, but please do give yourself the gift of laughter by enjoying the company of good friends who'll make you laugh and tempt you to bend the rules—just a little! Go ahead and pack for your vacation a month in advance, if it will make you feel better. That's fine. Just please, please don't be so well prepared for what's coming up next that you forget to relax and enjoy what's happening right now.

Capricorn Celebrities

Regardless of the career you choose, mastering your field is important to you, Capricorn, as this list of highly accomplished members of your sign well proves. Take Nostradamus, whose name and writings are still renowned almost five hundred years after his death. Born in 1892 and no longer with us since 1973, J.R.R. Tolkien's works are still alive and well, and the words of Martin Luther King Jr. "I have a dream"—will never be forgotten. And then, of course, there's the one and only Muhammad Ali. Equally impressive are the achievements of Capricorns who are thankfully still with us: Maggie Smith, Betty White, Diane Keaton, Mary J. Blige, Michelle Obama, Denzel Washington, Stephen Hawking, Tiger Woods, Annie Lennox, Anthony Hopkins, and Joan Baez. Apparently, the old expression "You're not getting older, you're getting better" was written for your timeless sign. Capricorn legends in the making include Kevin Costner, Jude Law, and Lin-Manuel Miranda.

The Year Ahead for Capricorn

Your ruling planet, Saturn, stepped authoritatively into your sign just ten days before the year began, Capricorn, which certainly bodes well for you during 2018—on many fronts—provided you've paid your dues, of course. In particular, with mighty Jupiter in intense, focused Scorpio set to make his way through your solar eleventh house of group affiliations and goals for the future until late November, you're due to see for yourself exactly where your hard work and/or lack thereof have landed you. You may need to pull away from friends who are obviously no longer on the same page, but not to worry. Scorpio planets only tear down what's no longer productive or positive to clear the decks for what's necessary to your personal evolution. Release these relationships, allow yourself to mourn them, and be heartened by the prospect of finding deeper and more meaningful bonds via a whole new social circle. You're a valuable member of any group. It's time to connect with those who'll appreciate you.

Now, let's talk about your finances, possessions, and personal values, all of which will be challenged for more than five months during 2018 thanks to fiery, confrontational Mars in opinionated Aquarius. This assertive, aggressive, and often angry energy will pass through your solar second house from May 16 through August 12 and again from September 10 through November 15. Mars usually spends roughly two months in a sign, stirring the pot in that department of life quite forcefully—so much so that we're forced to defend ourselves on some level. His extended visit in your second house means you'll need to take stock of what matters—and Mars has no patience, so you may need to do it all in a hurry. When it comes to possessions or personal money matters, a personal material inventory may be necessary. Prepare to quickly decide what's got to go and what's worth keeping—and trust your gut. On a deeper level, standing up for your priorities, principles, and ethics with sword drawn will be vital. It's time to champion what you hold dear and unceremoniously toss what's not.

Saturn

At some point this year, those of you born during the first eleven days of your sign—from December 22 through January 2—will receive a visit by a conjunction aspect from Saturn, your planetary patron saint. As I already mentioned, this no-nonsense planet—who, above all else, is famous for delivering unto each of us exactly what we deserve—is a big fan of rewards and penalties. Of course, you folks tend to live your lives acutely aware of that fact, with a strong sense of duty and a formidable work ethic, so advising you to take care of your responsibilities and keep your nose to the grindstone is rarely necessary. That said, even the most benevolent Saturn transit arrives with heavier obligations and additional duties in tow, so don't be surprised if you're handed the reins in some area of life. Keep in mind that this is the beginning of a two-and-a-half-year journey specially designed to show you not just what you're capable of doing but also what you really want to do. Above all else, you'll be asked to do what you do best: prepare, prepare, and prepare some more. Make sure your five- or ten-year plan is practical and realistic. If it's not, go back to the drawing board and stay there until you're sure you're ready, willing, and able to put in the time to make it so.

Uranus

Unpredictable Uranus first set off for your solar fourth house of home, family, and domestic issues back in 2010, Capricorn, all done up in red-hot Aries. Now, lest we forget, Aries was the Greek god of war, astrologically ruled by Mars—his Roman counterpart. Needless to say, with startling Uranus working his way through a sign as fiery and impulsive as Aries, anything is possible, but passionate encounters are guaranteed. Over the past seven years, then, it's a given that your home life and closest personal relationships have been far from boring, to say the least—and quite rocky at times. As of May 15, however, all that is set to change, big time. On that day, Uranus will set off for a seven-year trek through your solar fifth house of lovers, all done up in stubborn, slower-moving Taurus. Does this mean Uranus's energy will be less shocking? Nope—but the consequences of any sudden changes you initiate will most certainly last a heck of a lot longer, so pay attention. Aries energy is warrior energy. It invades, explodes, and moves on to new challenges. Taurus holds on, oftentimes longer than it should. In your case, until mid-May, ongoing drama on the home front will continue—but it will end just as suddenly as it started. From that point on, whether or not you're attached, expect a veritable parade of highly unusual, extremely adamant admirers to cross your path. If you're happily attached, force yourself to just say no. If not—well, hey, why not think of this transit as a buffet?

Neptune

For yet another year, the lovely lady Neptune will continue on her way through her fave sign, Pisces, putting her in your solar third house of conversations, communications, and navigations. This dreamy, woozy energy tends to befuddle even the most practical among us (i.e., you, Capricorn), so even though you're ordinarily quite realistic and not usually inclined to act on feelings rather than facts, consult your intuition before you make any major decisions. It's time to combine the best of what your intellect and your antennae have to offer. If it feels any better, think of this new superpower as "emotional intelligence," a trait so well recognized and highly prized that several books have been devoted to the subject. (Seriously. Google it.) All this goes double if you were born between December 31 and January 9, since Neptune will be forming a stimulating sextile to your Sun. Your creativity will be running on high, so no matter what type of project you've got going, if you start to feel that you're channeling what you need—well, know that you're right. Thank the Universe for the gift, and don't question it. Oh, and expect to "just know" things before you should—including what's around the next corner or what your companion is about to say.

Pluto

Pluto doesn't mess around, Capricorn. He's in charge of birth, death, and rebirth—not to mention the type of concentration that can turn focus into obsession. He's been on duty in your sign and your solar first house of personality and appearance since 2008, and is set to stay there for all of 2018. Needless to say, you won't be shy when it comes to asserting yourself, especially with regard to career and professional matters—but don't be unkind. This relentless energy has probably already put you in the running for at least one position of authority, but more opportunities are set to arrive. Resist the urge to accumulate positions of power simply because you can. If circumstances force you to take charge, use your sharp, business-oriented intuition to delegate. With your ruler, Saturn, also in your sign, this will come to you easily—but you'll still feel guilty for trying to shake off even a bit of the weight that the world has placed upon your shoulders. Don't do that. Allow yourself to do what you can, and pass along what you can't to those who are better-equipped and far more willing to handle the load. If you were born between the 8th and 13th of January, you'll feel all of this far more acutely.

How Will This Year's Eclipses Affect You?

Think of eclipses as celestial exclamation points. They amp up the volume on ordinary life for us all when they occur, but the signs and houses they occupy show where the possibility exists for sudden, intense, and often quite surprising events. Eclipses occur in pairs, six months apart. Solar Eclipses are supercharged New Moons, bringing the Sun and Moon together and marking peak times for planting seeds in any department of life. Lunar Eclipses are high-energy Full Moons, times of dramatic culmination, fulfillment, and often new beginnings as well, provided the slate has been wiped clean.

There will be five eclipses during 2018, marking an extremely unpredictable year.

The first Lunar Eclipse will occur on January 31 in Leo and your solar eighth house of intense change. A crisis is possible, but with this regal sign in charge, you'll handle it with dignity and manage to keep your pride intact. You may need to cut a person or situation out of your life, and you won't hesitate. It may not be the best of times, but once you've adjusted you won't look back, much less feel any regret.

The first Solar Eclipse will arrive on February 15 in your solar second house of finances, all done up in startling Aquarius. A whole new way of making money could be along shortly, or you may be forced to begin the process of liquidating your assets and resources to handle a stressful set of circumstances you never saw coming. If all else fails, turn to a circle of friends for help.

On July 12, expect to feel the effects of a Solar Eclipse in home- and family-oriented Cancer and your solar seventh house of relationships. Someone near and dear to you may move in or announce plans to move out. Either way, be sure to settle all financial matters to the satisfaction of both of you before agreeing to anything permanent. You've been the primary breadwinner for long enough. It's time for compensation.

July 27th will host the arrival of a Lunar Eclipse in Aquarius, signifying the completion and/or culmination of the changes you put into motion during mid-February. Your mission now is to figure out what to do next. Don't be afraid to color outside the lines or raise a few eyebrows if need be. It's important that you greet 2019 with a clean slate and a clear mind. Get the show on the road!

A Solar Eclipse will set you up for yet another brand-new start on August 11. This time around, you'll be asked to make sudden decisions regarding joint finances, shared resources, or intimate relationships that are no longer productive or useful to you. Don't look back and don't dilly-dally around. Eclipses call for determination, willpower, and resolve. Fortunately, if any sign already has a handle on these qualities, it's yours.

Capricorn | January

Relaxation and Recreation

Jupiter and Pluto will get into an exciting sextile on the 15th, activating your curiosity in a very big way—and they'll pretty much influence your entire month. With Jupiter in Scorpio, Pluto's own sign, this double dose of intense energy will urge you to do a bit of detective work. Go ahead, dig—and be prepared for some serious surprises.

Lovers and Friends

The Full Moon on the 1st most definitely won't be boring, Capricorn. You're set up to discover something unbelievable about someone close to you, which could trigger the start or finish of a current relationship— or both! Chances are good that it will be positive—say, if a friend or coworker reveals deeper feelings—but just in case, fasten your seat belt.

Money and Success

The lovely lady Venus will tiptoe into unpredictable Aquarius and your solar second house on the 17th, determined to call your attention to financial issues—even if she has to shock you to do it. You might need to break your piggy bank to help a family member, or an unexpected expense could come along, demanding to be settled immediately. Either way, the point is for you to see how important it is to be financially prepared.

Tricky Transits

The Lunar Eclipse of January 31st will activate your solar eighth house of shared resources and joint finances, so don't expect money matters to calm down just yet. The good news is that even though you may need to put out a bit more than you expected, you might also win something—and it will be a very big something. No fair spending more than you can afford on lottery tickets, though. It only takes one to win.

Rewarding Days

2, 8, 9, 10, 15, 16, 25

Challenging Days

6, 7, 12, 23, 24, 27, 31

Capricorn | February

Relaxation and Recreation

With your ruler, serious Saturn, now in your sign, relaxing might not be all that easy for a while—but make a point of it. This guy's fondness for duties and responsibilities can take all the fun out of life, so your mission is to refuse to let that happen. Put fun time on your agenda, and don't cancel. You'll take care of business better if you give yourself downtime to recharge your batteries.

Lovers and Friends

If a family member has been bugging you to meet someone they're sure is just perfect for you, set it up for the 6th. If you're skeptical, Starbucks is your best bet, but by all means, give them a shot—no matter what happened the last time you agreed to this sort of thing. If you're happily attached, you really should try something new together. What that might be is totally up to you two.

Money and Success

With three planets and an eclipse in unpredictable Aquarius, your financial situation may not exactly be rock-solid this month, Capricorn, but not to worry. Friends and family members will be more than happy to step in and help out. You won't even have to ask—which we know you hate. Just mention your situation and expect an offer to help from someone you've taken care of in the past.

Tricky Transits

Lovely Venus and dreamy Neptune will collide on the 21st, a romantic, nostalgic team that's all about reminiscing about the past. This may not appeal to your no-nonsense nature at first, but if you give in and allow yourself to sit and sigh, you may actually come to terms with something from the past that's been bugging you for some time now.

Rewarding Days

5, 6, 7, 27

Challenging Days

14, 15, 21, 25, 28

Capricorn | March

Relaxation and Recreation

Several planets in fiery Aries will put you in the mood for adventure, Capricorn—to say the very least. Of course, adventures come in all kinds of delightful packages, so whether it's a new person or a new opportunity to try an activity you've always been drawn to—well, be safe, but let it happen. It's important that you allow yourself some playtime.

Lovers and Friends

Loving Venus will charge off into fiery, assertive Aries on the 6th, urging you to stop waiting for the right time and get busy letting a certain someone know you're interested. If a family member seems to be getting in the way, consider that they may simply be afraid of losing you. Sit them down and make sure they know that no matter what, they'll always come first.

Money and Success

Be careful what you do with your checkbook and plastic around the 23rd, Capricorn. Venus and Pluto will square off, a team that can inspire the kind of obsession that causes us to go after what we desire, no matter the cost. Before you plunk down more than you can afford, consider what this could do to your lifestyle. Is it worth it?

Tricky Transits

A pack of planets will get together in your solar third house of navigation and short trips on the 4th, Capricorn, all of them wearing ultra-dreamy Pisces. If you're off on a dream vacation or taking steps to make that happen, this energy is exactly what the astrologer ordered. If you're feeling a bit disoriented, confused, or fuzzy—regardless of why—staying home with a good book or movie might be best.

Rewarding Days

1, 2, 12, 15, 16, 30

Challenging Days

4, 5, 11, 13, 23, 24, 29

Capricorn | April

Relaxation and Recreation

With more than half of the astrological crew passing through hardworking earth signs this month—which, of course, is your element—finding time to relax or play could be tough. No one's saying you should ditch your chores and take off for the weekend if you're not comfortable about it. But please do kick your shoes off every now and then and enjoy the company of your dear ones.

Lovers and Friends

Venus will make her way into your solar sixth house on the 24th, all done up in fun-loving, playful Gemini. Now, this is your house of work and work-oriented relationships, so if you've been trading glances across the workplace with a delicious coworker, there's no time like the present to spend some time with them—as far away from the job as possible.

Money and Success

Financial deals of just about any kind will go along quite smoothly on the 7th, but don't sign anything just yet. Mercury won't turn direct until the 15th, and even then, with Saturn stationing a few days later, you could lock yourself into something you really can't handle. If you must finalize matters relating to money or possessions, be sure to have a trusty professional go over the fine print.

Tricky Transits

From the 15th through the 17th, the Universe will send out some seriously mixed signals. On the one hand, you'll crave something new and exciting—and playmates will abound. On the other, you'll want to be responsible, sensible, and practical. Exercise that famous patience. Put your nose to the grindstone and make plans for the weekend of the 20th.

Rewarding Days

6, 7, 12, 19, 23, 29

Challenging Days

1, 2, 4, 10, 25

Capricorn | May

Relaxation and Recreation

Venus in Gemini is still in the mood to get you out of the office and into your car, en route to a fun destination, which, in extended form, is also known as a vacation. No, you probably haven't had one in a while, and yes, your responsibilities have most definitely increased. Still, a bit of perspective and a break in the action will make you even more productive.

Lovers and Friends

Jupiter's presence in your solar eleventh house of friendships and groups has probably shaken things up in your social life, Capricorn—especially since he's all done up in intense, passionate Scorpio. It wouldn't be surprising to hear that a friend has turned into a lover, or vice versa. If you're contemplating this type of switch, be sure it's not just your libido speaking. Think long-term, big-picture results.

Money and Success

Venus and Uranus will get together on the 19th to set you up for a wonderful financial surprise. It might be that you'll end up with a lottery ticket that pays off, or money you thought you'd never see again may suddenly be returned. Either way, with Mars in Aquarius in your solar second house until mid-September, expect lots of unexpected peaks and valleys.

Tricky Transits

The 12th, 14th, and 16th could be a bit problematic, Capricorn, especially if you've been simmering over an offense for a while now. If you need to clear the air and get something off your chest, the urge to put it all out there now will be overwhelming. Just be careful. Confrontations around these dates could be volatile—and possibly even explosive.

Rewarding Days

4, 6, 8, 18, 19, 25

Challenging Days

7, 12, 13, 14, 16, 28

Capricorn | June

Relaxation and Recreation

The urge to go overboard and make up for lost time—time you haven't been able to spend relaxing, that is—will be quite strong around the 25th, thanks to an excessive Venus-Jupiter square. If you haven't seen much of your friends lately, it's time to put an end to that nonsense. Make it an early night if you must, but do reconnect with them.

Lovers and Friends

The 1st and 2nd look to be quite romantic—and quite spontaneous—times, Capricorn, so if you've been too busy to spend much time with your current sweetheart, here's your opportunity to make things right. It's a weekend, so there's no reason you can't put work aside, even if it's only for a little while. That goes double if you're attached and your partner isn't happy about your schedule.

Money and Success

Mars in unpredictable Aquarius will turn retrograde on the 26th, Capricorn, and from his spot in your solar second house of finances and possessions, this feisty guy could make it necessary for you to put a deal on hold, or even back out completely. Before you do either, be sure you're not acting out of anger or resentment. Table what you can and wait until cooler heads prevail.

Tricky Transits

Neptune will stop in her tracks on the 18th, demanding that you pay attention to a neighbor or sibling who's either in trouble or so lost that they're headed in that direction. Do what you can, but don't damage your finances or your reputation in the process. Offering guidance and helping them come up with a plan may be what's really needed. Use your intuition.

Rewarding Days
1, 2, 3, 13, 19, 20, 22

Challenging Days
5, 6, 12, 18, 23, 30

Capricorn | July

Relaxation and Recreation

This looks to be a rather unsettling month for you, Aquarius, but not to worry. Uranus has just entered your solar fifth house, where recreation and playtime are handled, so even if you can't get away long enough to indulge in your favorite activities, the Universe will toss a few fun-loving, unusual friends your way. Whether you're at work or at play, you definitely won't be bored!

Lovers and Friends

The Solar Eclipse of the 12th could turn your focus toward a relationship that's been fading away or losing its intensity. Yes, it may be time to make a decision. Are you going to put in the time and energy to make it work, or are you willing to let them go? It's up to you. Even if it seems they're initiating these changes, remember—you can change a lot with an honest conversation.

Money and Success

On the 9th, Venus will set off for Virgo, an organized, practical earth sign like your own—and not a moment too soon. Her energy will help you to stabilize your finances—or at least deal with anything unexpected that comes along. Around the 22nd, she'll also arrange for benevolent Jupiter to step in. If you need a loan, now's the time to apply.

Tricky Transits

The Lunar Eclipse on the 27th will occur in unpredictable Aquarius and your solar second house of money matters and possessions, Capricorn. Since assertive Mars will be working with this lunation, the possibility of yet another sudden or startling financial event is on the agenda. If you need advice or you're just craving a talk with someone who'll understand, don't let your pride stop you.

Rewarding Days

4, 5, 8, 11, 13, 21, 22

Challenging Days

1, 2, 12, 25, 26, 27

Capricorn | August

Relaxation and Recreation

There will be a lovely and pleasantly hedonistic assembly of astrological energies on the 25th, making it the perfect Saturday to spend doing absolutely nothing that you don't want to do. Whether that means watching movies with the kids or heading out for some adult beverages with friends doesn't matter. The point is to remove any and all thoughts of responsibilities for a minimum of twenty-four hours. Yes, in a row.

Lovers and Friends

Venus will set off on the 6th for Libra, a peace-loving, cooperative sign she's very fond of. This puts her in a position to help you charm a higher-up, authority figure, or elder who hasn't been especially sympathetic to your needs. Also, if you need to negotiate, mediate, or intercede on behalf of a loved one, this is the time to do it.

Money and Success

When Mercury turns direct on the 18th, it will be in your solar eighth house of shared resources and joint money matters—which could mean you're due for one more bout of financial frustration. Fortunately, however, he'll also be keeping company with Venus—who's in charge of the planetary purse strings. Breathe deeply and try to be patient. Yes, again. It's almost over.

Tricky Transits

On the 1st, Mars and Uranus will get into a testy square aspect, a team that's often in the vicinity when explosions and angry outbursts occur. The more repressed or stifled you feel, the more you'll want to cut someone or something out of your life without much warning. Don't be scared. Just think of how good you'll feel when you've liberated yourself! It's time to get free.

Rewarding Days

6, 7, 12, 19, 25

Challenging Days

8, 9, 10, 11, 18, 26

Capricorn | September

Relaxation and Recreation

The New Moon in Virgo and your solar ninth house will arrive on the 9th, urging you to take your show on the road—literally—and do a bit of traveling. If you can go now, great. If not, make plans—and while you're waiting for the date to arrive, sign up for a class or certificate program that's tailor-made to add another plus to your resume.

Lovers and Friends

On the 12th, excessive Jupiter in passionate, focused Scorpio will make contact with intense Pluto—who happens to own Scorpio, by the way. If you've been flirting heavily with someone but neither of you has made any real moves yet, it won't be long now. Your mission is to be discreet. Yes, sharing your passion has been a long time coming, but please—get a room.

Money and Success

Shopping for a loved one around the 8th could be a costly venture, Capricorn, especially if you're feeling guilty or remorseful. Before you blow off what's really bugging you and opt to soothe your feelings with extravagant, impulsive purchases, think for a second. Wouldn't it be better to have an honest chat and either offer up an apology or, if you're confused, ask them if you should?

Tricky Transits

The Full Moon in assertive Aries on the 24th will arrive just as Saturn forms cranky squares with both Mercury and the Sun, Capricorn—so if you're feeling pretty darn cranky yourself, don't feel too bad about it. If you've been holding back your feelings from one of your nearest and dearests, figure out how to broach the issue before you feel the tension start to crackle in the air.

Rewarding Days
3, 4, 7, 11, 15, 16

Challenging Days
5, 6, 8, 22, 30

Capricorn | October

Relaxation and Recreation

If you're looking for an excuse to take some time off, take a look at what you've accomplished over the past ten months—then give yourself a break. Around the 24th or 27th, your very own ruling planet, Saturn, will be happy to get on board—the astrological equivalent of getting a hall pass from a very strict teacher. Grab it. Who knows when he'll be this benevolent again?

Lovers and Friends

With four planets in Scorpio and your solar eleventh house of groups and friendships, your social life looks pretty darn busy. Of course, Scorpio planets ooze sex appeal without even trying, so don't be surprised if you're propositioned a lot—and I mean a whole heck of a lot. Whether or not you're interested—hey, enjoy it. As hard as you've been working, isn't it time for some physical distraction?

Money and Success

Power struggles with higher-ups and authority figures on the 2nd or 11th could stall or delay that raise, bonus, or promotion you've been waiting for, Capricorn—so if you have interviews or reviews scheduled, rescheduling for the 6th or 12th would be a good idea. Better to wait a little bit than to get caught up in some tough transits and lose your chance altogether, right?

Tricky Transits

Venus, the Goddess of Love, will turn retrograde in Scorpio on the 5th, bringing up intense memories about a certain someone you've never really gotten over. If you're available, reaching out to see if they are too wouldn't be a bad idea. Keep in mind, though, that Scorpio is an all-or-nothing kind of sign, so treading water won't work. Sign up for a second shot at the title, or don't.

Rewarding Days

6, 12, 24, 25, 26, 27

Challenging Days

2, 5, 10, 11, 31

Capricorn | November

Relaxation and Recreation

You've finally gotten used to the new, more rigorous schedule Saturn gave you a year ago, Capricorn—in fact, you're probably doing your chores with time to spare. From the 25th through the 27th, expansive Jupiter will touch base with Mercury and the Sun, urging you to turn off the television, put down the book, open up the drapes, and let the sunshine in.

Lovers and Friends

From the 15th through the 18th, relationships will be extremely tricky, Capricorn. Don't blame yourself. It seems that both Venus and Mercury will stop in their tracks on the 16th—to turn in opposite directions, no less—making intellectual exchanges of the tender kind a whole lot more challenging. No matter what, don't overreact. You may not have all the information just yet.

Money and Success

Venus will form an easy trine aspect with assertive Mars on the 9th, making sure that conversations about money—okay, and love, too—turn out to be polite, affable, and maybe even friendly. If you feel there are apologies out there that need to be extended or accepted, don't just sit there. These two will only be in the neighborhood for a couple of days. Use them.

Tricky Transits

Jupiter will take off for adventurous, curious Sagittarius on the 8th, Capricorn, urging us all to spend the coming year growing, laughing, and learning. He'll be passing through your solar twelfth house of Privacy, Please, so over the coming year, you'll often be in the mood to retreat, regroup, and recharge your batteries. Sure, do some reading or take some online classes. Just don't spend all your downtime alone. Remember that part about laughing.

Rewarding Days

8, 9, 10, 21, 22

Challenging Days

15, 16, 17, 18, 26, 30

Capricorn | December

Relaxation and Recreation

The emotional Moon will be on duty in lavish, showy Leo from the 24th through the 26th, bringing her warm and wonderful energy into all your gatherings. (Oh, and just between you and me, don't be surprised if a few guests you weren't expecting drop by, or if someone has an especially wonderful gift in store for you—say, the opportunity to reconnect with a long-missing loved one?)

Lovers and Friends

Mercury will retrograde back into your solar eleventh house of friendships on the 1st, giving you five more days to mend fences with a dear one you've been at odds with recently. Hey, c'mon—'tis the season, after all. If you're still mad but you can't remember why, it might be time to put an end to this. Do yourself a favor and be the first to reach out.

Money and Success

On the 16th, Venus—Goddess of Love and Money—will make contact with stable, practical Saturn, the ultimate deal maker. Obviously, if you've got last-minute shopping to do, this is the day to do it. You'll get what you want for the right price—after haggling, quibbling, and successfully wrangling—all of which makes the perfect deal even more perfect.

Tricky Transits

Fiery Mars and nostalgic Neptune will get together on the 7th in woozy Pisces and your solar third house of thoughts, turning your thoughts toward the past instead of where they should be—right here in the present. No one's saying you can't honor those emotions and the people associated with them. Just save some sighs for the happy, comfortable feelings the rest of the month will bring.

Rewarding Days
15, 16, 17, 23, 24, 28

Challenging Days
1, 2, 5, 11, 14

Capricorn Action Table

These dates reflect the best—but not the only—times for success and ease in these activities, according to your Sun sign.

	JAN	FEB	MAR	APR	MAY	JUN	JUL	AUG	SEP	OCT	NOV	DEC
Move					18				15			
Start a class	2		19			13	8				8	20
Join a club		21		12			5	19		27		
Ask for a raise		27			14							
Get professional advice			16	29	11			6		25		
Get a loan	15			7			22		11		10	15
New romance	1	6				1			12			
Vacation			1			2		25		26	9	21

Aquarius

The Water Bearer
January 20 to February 19

≈

Element: Air

Quality: Fixed

Polarity: Yang/masculine

Planetary Ruler: Uranus

Meditation: I am a wellspring of creativity

Gemstone: Amethyst

Power Stones: Aquamarine, black pearl, chrysocolla

Key Phrase: I know

Glyph: Currents of energy

Anatomy: Ankles, circulatory system

Colors: Iridescent blues, violet

Animals: Exotic birds

Myths/Legends: Ninhursag, John the Baptist, Deucalion

House: Eleventh

Opposite Sign: Leo

Flower: Orchid

Keyword: Unconventional

The Aquarius Personality

Your Strengths, Gifts, and Challenges

You are a keen observer with a knack for considering unusual alternatives, Aquarius, two qualities that have combined to earn your sign its well-deserved reputation for producing geniuses. "Think outside the box"—which, of course, is where true genius first makes itself known—is your motto. You also know, however, that in order to think outside that box, you've got to become an expert on what's in there. As a result, you have always been a keen and avid observer, both of interesting individuals and of the human condition in general. You watch current trends, but instinctively know where and when those traditions will no longer be applicable to what's really going on with humanity today. You watch a coworker and immediately understand why they are not suited to their work. Either way, you never hesitate to share your findings, and you're definitely not shy about expressing your opinions.

All this makes perfect sense. Your ruling planet is Uranus, the rebellious, radical rule breaker, so whenever you challenge the status quo—especially if you're absolutely sure you have a better idea—you're at your best. "Question authority" is your favorite slogan, as long as you're not the authority being questioned. In that case, the fixed nature of your airy, cerebral sign will work tirelessly to convince any who disagree with you that by not allowing themselves to consider all possibilities, they are limiting possibilities and falling into ruts, which you consider a death sentence.

Romance and Other Relationships

You, Aquarius, are quite aware of how unique each of us truly is—just like snowflakes. You, however, go way, way, way out of your way to make others notice exactly how different your breed of snowflake really is, so when it comes to friends and lovers, "unusual" and "different" are qualities that interest you. That may mean your new flame or BFF came complete with odd piercings, obvious multicolored tattoos, and/or purple hair on the left side of their head, but even if they're wearing pinstripes and sensible shoes, there absolutely has to be something rebellious in their nature. If you're honest about it, you'll admit that's a big part of why you chose them. They're nonconformists, just like you, so you often feel more comfortable around these kindred spirits than you do around your own biological tribe. The good news is that you tend to find "family" wherever you are, and all are welcome. You love socializing with new people from a wide variety of backgrounds. It keeps your spirit alive.

Your unbiased views toward race, creed, and sexuality make you an exciting, open-minded companion, able to remain completely objective about the lifestyles of others—and determined to live your own life exactly as you see fit. Obviously, no one with an ounce of prejudice will gain access to your world, platonically, romantically, or any other kind of way! One whiff of a judgmental attitude is enough to chase you off, and you won't be back. For that reason, fiery, opinionated Sagittarians are often a good match for you, with curious Geminis a close second. Either of these signs will keep your interest, which is quite a feat. Librans are also fun, attentive, and just as sociable as you, but are usually not quite as interested in group activities, a possible problem over the long run.

Career and Work

If it's a vocation that most people haven't ever heard of, Aquarius, your interest in it will be piqued. If the schedule is guaranteed to be erratic and the work itself appeals to the rebel in you, you'll sign up. The deal breaker? The potential for boredom, which you have a very low tolerance for. In your mind, it's like this: if you've got to spend most of your waking hours doing one particular thing, it better be interesting, and it better be flexible, because life changes all the time. Period.

Once you've found that very special little niche, however, you'll be more than willing to put in the time to finish up a project. You're one of the three fixed signs, remember, all of which are notoriously stubborn, albeit in different ways. In your case, once you get an idea in your head, you really can't let it go, so shutting the computer and getting some sleep doesn't come easy. With or without a computer, however, any occupation that raises an eyebrow, like every other aspect of your life, will do just fine.

Money and Possessions

Regarding money, your toys aren't cheap, and they're upgraded all the time, so to support your e-habit, you'll need to earn a tidy sum. Fortunately, you can put your natural affinity for the tech fields to work for you. If you don't write the manuals for a living, you most certainly could. Careful, though. You do have unassuming Pisces on your solar second house, so don't settle for less than you know your skills are worth when you're negotiating salary. You're a valuable commodity. Price yourself accordingly.

Your Lighter Side

You love the group dynamic almost as much as you love change, Aquarius, so when you discover what you deem to be a worthy cause, you set out to share the message, whatever it takes and quite relentlessly. You'll march, protest, man the phones, and plaster bumper stickers on the back of your vehicle. Social networking, e-dating, and tweeting are your guilty pleasures, and anyone who tries to separate you from your phone, computer, and iPad better be ready for a fight. You love to keep abreast of the news, so the Internet often affords you comfort when you're alone—especially since you think of computers as friends. (Yours might even have a name.)

Aquarius Celebrities

You're keeping company with some pretty darn radical, rebellious folks, Aquarius—all of them determined to upset the status quo to ensure that change occurs in positive ways. Take, for example, Abraham Lincoln, who initiated huge social change in his day, plus modern-day rule-breaker Bill Maher and social activists Oprah Winfrey, Ellen DeGeneres, and Yoko Ono. Scientologist John Travolta was born under your sign, as was rebellious John McEnroe and also Kerry Washington, the first woman to headline a network drama since 1968. Free-spirited Alicia Keys and Justin Timberlake are also Aquarius, as is Rosa Parks, the woman who is credited with changing the face of civil rights by being brave enough to break the rules in a quiet but determined way.

The Year Ahead for Aquarius

The really big news for your sign this year involves Mars himself—the ancient God of War, you'll remember, who'll spend no less than five full months in your sign and your solar first house of personality and appearance. He'll be on duty here from May 15 through August 12 and again from September 10 through November 15. Be sure to mark your calendar with those dates—in red, please—so if you begin to wonder why it's suddenly so easy for others to push your buttons, you'll have your answer. Being prepared for the possibility of confrontations when you least expect them will prove valuable on many occasions. Practice counting to ten—or even five, if your impatient little self can't make it that far. Fortunately, you're a cerebral creature, so thinking before you speak or act is something that comes naturally to you—ordinarily, anyway. The thing is, while you can talk yourself into not overreacting when you feel provoked, you can't do much about the behavior of others. If your gut tells you that a situation is escalating into something that could turn quite volatile quite quickly, walk away, right away. Put some distance between you and whoever or whatever is causing your blood pressure to rise—and for heaven's sake, don't get involved in any petty online wars. That goes for Twitter, Facebook, Instagram, and texting as well. Think before you type.

Of course, with Jupiter set to spend most of the year—until November 8, in fact—in intense Scorpio and your solar tenth house of authority figures, it's not hard to imagine you becoming enmeshed in a war of wills with higher-ups, superiors, or elders who you're sure are out to control you. You may be right, but before you cut all ties with them, do your homework. Dig around and try to get to the heart of the matter. What's really going on behind the scenes? Once you figure that out, finding a solution that's comfortable for all parties concerned will come along a whole lot easier.

Finally, check out the upcoming section on eclipses, and circle February 15 and July 27 in red on your calendar, too. Your sign will be influenced by a Solar and a Lunar Eclipse this year, marking a very dramatic end of a certain aspect of your lifestyle—and an equally dramatic beginning. If you've been itching for change but you still haven't done anything about it, know that around these dates, the Universe may make those arrangements for you. Ready or not...

Saturn

Saturn will trudge off into Capricorn—home turf for this diligent, respectable fellow—just days before the year begins, Aquarius. Now, this will put him in your solar twelfth house for the next two and a half years—which could be a tricky situation. To start with, the twelfth house is a very private place, where top-secret emotions are handled. Since Saturn has so much to do with duties and responsibilities, it's not hard to imagine you feeling a bit overwhelmed by obligations you've agreed to take on because no one else would—and pretty darn resentful about those you never agreed to that have been foisted upon your shoulders anyway. In particular, you may end up simmering about someone's lack of concern about carrying their share of the burden—with regard to finances in particular, by the way. This doesn't mean you should walk away from what you know you're rightfully account-able for, but it certainly does mean that you shouldn't allow yourself to be taken advantage of. The problem with twelfth-house transits is that it's easy to become resentful and retreat behind closed doors. Don't do that. Don't turn yourself into a hermit because someone else isn't helping out. Try talking to them, and don't sugarcoat your feelings. If that doesn't work and you need to consult a professional and maybe even file official papers to get a bit of well-deserved relief, don't you dare feel guilty about it. There's absolutely no reason for you to silently assume obligations that rightfully belong to another.

Uranus

This unpredictable guy is your ruling planet, Aquarius—which certainly explains a lot. You're rebellious, unconventional, and quite fond of break-ing the rules. In fact, when someone dares to tell you you're forbidden to do something—well, to your ears, that's an invitation to do just that. This innate quality has been running on high for the past seven-ish years now, ever since Uranus set off for assertive, confrontational Aries—and if you're honest about it, you'll have to admit that you've loved every minute of it. The good news is that Uranus will stay on duty in Aries and your solar third house straight through May 15, so you'll have a few more months to enjoy this energy.

If you were born from February 13 through the 19th, Uranus will also be forming a stimulating sextile aspect to your Sun, urging you to take steps immediately to put an end to any relationship or set of cir-cumstances that are holding you back from being yourself. If that means cutting ties with someone you've suddenly realized has been taking advantage of you, fine. Do it, and don't look back. The best part of sextile aspects from the outer planets is that they set us up for exciting new begin-nings. All you have to do is put together a plan to get yourself free—which won't be hard, given that you folks were born with a wonderful streak of genius, and considering that one of the things you love most about life is personal freedom. (Okay, and your phone. And your computer.) Anyway, it's time to take back your independence. Once Uranus sets off for sturdy, stubborn Taurus on May 15, you'll begin thinking about the ideal living arrangement—once again, with personal freedom in mind. If you've been living with someone and gradually feeling more and more repressed and stifled, you won't put up with it for very much longer. And when you decide to move out or move on, it's going to happen suddenly, so as of mid-May, be sure you have a place to lay your head when you decide you've finally had enough.

Neptune

This woozy, dreamy energy has been making her way through your solar second house since April of 2011, Aquarius, and since this is the place where personal finances are handled, your money matters have probably been a bit difficult to keep track of—even if you've honestly tried. If you've come up against deception—even if you've been deceiving yourself because you simply didn't want to see what someone you cared for was doing to you—well, with the help of Saturn in ultra-practical Capricorn this year, you should be able to catch a glimpse of the reality of the situation, and maybe even take steps to do something about it. The thing is, one of Neptune's talents is to make us believe that everything is already just the way we want it to be. It's time for you to break that spell. On the positive side, Neptune's presence in this house also brings about the possibility of a spiritual awakening of sorts. Take time, whenever you can, to sit quietly and put your priorities squarely in order.

Pluto

Back in 2008, this intense planet set off for your solar twelfth house of secrets and alone time, Aquarius. When he first arrived, you probably spent quite a bit of time behind closed doors, either stewing over a run of unfortunate circumstances or trying to put yourself back together after a major loss. The good news is that with disciplined, practical Saturn set to join him here shortly before 2018 arrives, with just a bit of effort, you'll be able to accept what happened—and, with any luck, to understand why it happened as well. Don't expect too much from yourself at first. If you're still grieving, allow that to happen. Letting go—of anything you cared for, regardless of the reason—is a long, involved, and convoluted journey. Baby steps, kiddo. Baby steps.

How Will This Year's Eclipses Affect You?

Think of eclipses as celestial exclamation points. They amp up the volume on ordinary life for us all when they occur, but the signs and houses they occupy show where the possibility exists for sudden, intense, and often quite surprising events. Eclipses occur in pairs, six months apart. Solar Eclipses are supercharged New Moons, bringing the Sun and Moon together and marking peak times for planting seeds in any department of life. Lunar Eclipses are high-energy Full Moons, times of dramatic culmination, fulfillment, and often new beginnings as well, provided the slate has been wiped clean.

There will be five eclipses during 2018, marking an extremely unpredictable year for one and all.

The first Lunar Eclipse of the year will arrive on January 31, wearing fiery Leo. This dramatic lunation is set to affect your solar seventh house of one-on-one relationships, so preparing yourself for some extremely unexpected news from a dear one is your best bet—and with antennae as keen as yours, you'll most certainly see what's coming well before it occurs. Your mission is to have a strategy in place to cope with it, handle it, and take the best of it.

On February 15, a Solar Eclipse will give you a chance to start over—big time. It will occur in your sign and your solar first house of personality and appearance, urging you to do whatever it takes to ensure that your personal presentation leaves others with the first impression you really want them to have. You might decide to change your wardrobe or your hairstyle—and if so, it will be in a very big way. What you're after is to be more physically authentic to your true self. Go for it!

On July 12, a Solar Eclipse will occur in your solar sixth house, all done up in home- and family-oriented Cancer. You may suddenly find that someone you've trusted for a very long while has been less than honest with you, which will, of course, be quite disappointing. Even if that's not the case, you should expect a major change that strongly affects your daily routine. Don't fight it, even if others aren't happy with your lifestyle choices. After all, whose life is this, anyway?

On July 27, a Lunar Eclipse will occur in your sign, shedding light on a situation that first disrupted your world back in mid-February. You probably made some huge changes back then, and while they seemed drastic at first, an event that comes along now will demonstrate for you just how wise you were to do what you did—and how wonderfully positive the path you chose turned out to be.

The last Solar Eclipse of the year on August 11 will be in fiery Leo and your solar seventh house, showing you how necessary it was for you to let go of a toxic relationship or situation back in January. Give yourself a pat on the back. It hasn't been an easy trip, but you've done it, and you're better for it. A reward is definitely in order.

Aquarius | January

Relaxation and Recreation

If you can make a break for it this month—that is, from work and any other responsibilities—please do so around the weekend of the 19th. You're quite the thoughtful creature, Aquarius, with a brain like a computer. But remember, every now and then computers need to sign off and be restarted. This weekend—or as soon as possible—that will be your mission. Don't think of it as slacking off. Think of it as rebooting.

Lovers and Friends

Loving Venus will contact dreamy, romantic Neptune on the 3rd, setting up the perfect astrological backdrop for romance, Aquarius. Now, you're not much into "the mushy stuff," but every now and then, even a sign as cerebral as yours experiences that certain type of heart thump that makes you smile, sigh, and pretend not to wipe away a tear or two. Don't beat yourself up about it. It's called being human, and it's totally acceptable.

Money and Success

Career-oriented Saturn moved into your solar twelfth house of secrets just a week or so ago, Aquarius. Now, this house has everything to do with working alone and being alone, and Saturn is the primary indicator of how career matters and professional achievements are progressing. That said, if you have the feeling now or over the coming two and a half years—that you'd be better off working solo, check out the possibility.

Tricky Transits

On the 24th, thoughtful Mercury will collide with intense, relentless Pluto, who's famous for hanging on to a grudge. Ordinarily you'd be able to dismiss this feeling, but the two have chosen your solar twelfth house of secret feelings and emotions for their meeting, providing all the necessary astrological ingredients for resentment of the toxic kind. Don't let that happen. If you can't forgive, at least move on without this baggage.

Rewarding Days

2, 3, 17, 18, 19

Challenging Days

7, 13, 14, 24, 27

Aquarius | February

Relaxation and Recreation

On the 6th, an opportunity to try something new and exciting will come along via an interesting, charming, and quite unusual friend or acquaintance. Now, you're fascinated with unusual humans, Aquarius, so you'll definitely be enticed, but that doesn't mean you should get too involved too quickly. Enjoy the adventure, but keep them at arm's length until you know them better.

Lovers and Friends

With Venus in your sign and your solar first house of personality until the 10th, going a bit overboard to make a good impression will be easy to do. That goes double for the 3rd and the 10th, which just so happen to be Saturdays, when all of us feel a bit freer than usual to let go and get a bit crazy. If you can afford it, have fun. If not, do your best to be good.

Money and Success

On the 21st, Venus and Neptune will collide in your solar second house of money matters, Aquarius. They'll both be wearing Pisces—a sign that's adept at erasing boundaries—urging you to forget about your budget and invest in a dream. If there are positive financial facts to back this up, you might just be on the right track. The responsibility falls on you. Be sure you've done your homework.

Tricky Transits

On the 25th, loving Venus and aggressive Mars will get into a square, the stuff that astrological shouting matches are made of. The thing is, these two often inspire "if you loved me, you would" syndrome. Don't be backed up into a corner and feel duty-bound to do something you don't want to out of guilt—and please don't allow yourself to do that to anyone else.

Rewarding Days

2, 14, 21, 26, 27

Challenging Days

3, 10, 13, 17, 25, 28

Aquarius | March

Relaxation and Recreation

If you're out to take some time off to relax, better do it as soon after March begins as possible, Aquarius. Once the 6th arrives, your chances of actually chilling out will steadily decrease. That doesn't mean it won't be possible for you to get away afterward, only that you'll have to jump through a whole lot more hoops to make it happen.

Lovers and Friends

On the 6th, loving Venus will storm off into assertive, aggressive Aries and your solar third house. Now, this is the spot where daily interactions and casual chats are handled, so you might find yourself suddenly attracted to someone you've been crossing paths with for some time now. The good news is that even if you two don't get together forever, you'll exchange important spiritual missives. Don't pass up this chance to receive your celestial message.

Money and Success

On the 1st and 2nd, both Venus and Mercury—who just so happen to be in your solar second house of money matters and possessions, by the way—will form easy trine aspects to extravagant, excessive, and oh-so-generous Jupiter. Yes, if you're going to take a chance on an investment—provided you have absolutely all your facts in order—this is most definitely the time to dive in and trust that the Universe will provide. But seriously—before you do, be sure you're sure.

Tricky Transits

Mercury will turn retrograde on the 22nd in your solar third house of communications, all done up in impatient Aries. You've never been famous for being all that patient yourself, so this combination can produce all kinds of frustrating circumstances—and it's going to last for at least three weeks. Your mission is to find positive distractions, and don't pick on anyone who's not intellectually equipped to fight back.

Rewarding Days

1, 2, 12, 14, 15

Challenging Days

4, 10, 11, 13, 21, 22, 23

Aquarius | April

Relaxation and Recreation

Provided that you're completely and totally caught up with all your work and all your bases are covered with regard to other responsibilities, you may actually be able to get away for an entire day around the 7th—and maybe even two, if you're especially lucky. If you can't make this happen now, make plans for the 21st—even if those plans only include being quietly, blissfully alone for the weekend.

Lovers and Friends

On the 24th, sociable Venus will take off for your solar fifth house, where playmates and lovers are handled. That said, if you've been trying to make time for a romantic evening with absolutely no electronic devices allowed, you'll have three weeks to make it happen. If you've just met someone new, take advantage of every single window the Universe tosses your way to get the show on the road.

Money and Success

Loving Venus, who wrote the book on values, will spend most of the month in quality-conscious Taurus, urging you to make some decisions about what's truly important to you—and what's not. If you've been thinking these things over in private for a month or so, prepare yourself, because very soon, it will be time to step up and make your opinions known. Fortunately, that's your astrological specialty.

Tricky Transits

Your solar twelfth house of alone time will play host to the astrological collision of fiery Mars and serious Saturn on the 2nd, Aquarius—the stuff that depression is often made of. If you're dealing with anxiety or panic attacks, don't keep it to yourself. You're acquainted with all kinds of folks. At least one of them will be willing to listen, and one more will know where to refer you for the answers you need.

Rewarding Days

7, 8, 12, 14, 23

Challenging Days

1, 2, 4, 5, 25, 26

Aquarius | May

Relaxation and Recreation
With Venus in Gemini and your solar fifth house until the 19th, Aquarius, you'll have plenty of opportunities to make up for lost time and do some serious partying. Does that mean you should forget all about your responsibilities and take off without making sure your bases are covered? No, absolutely not. Although, after what you've been through lately, it will be tempting. Handle your absence reliably and sensibly, then take off and have some fun.

Lovers and Friends
Your temper may get away from you around the 16th, when assertive and sometimes angry Mars in your solar first house of personality will square off with startling Uranus in Aries—neither of whom ever knew how to resist the urge to lash out at anyone who's deliberately offensive or aggressive. Just be careful you're reading the situation right before you react. This team plays for keeps.

Money and Success
If a family member offers you financial help around the 22nd, think twice before you let your pride allow you to refuse. You're not known for breaking your promises, so if you say you'll return the favor, you will—and if they've come your way without you asking for a single thing, they already know you're good for it. Be humble. Accept their support graciously.

Tricky Transits
An uncomfortable meeting that takes place between affectionate Venus and strict, uncompromising Saturn on the 1st could get your month off to a rather rocky start, Aquarius. Your mission is to be sure that anyone you're thinking of trusting with a high-priority secret is worthy of the honor. If you're not sure, keep quiet and wait until you know you're not risking too much.

Rewarding Days
11, 18, 19, 22, 23

Challenging Days
1, 5, 7, 16, 26, 27, 28

Aquarius | June

Relaxation and Recreation

The Sun and Mercury will make it easy for you to enjoy yourself during June, Aquarius, since they'll be passing through playful, fun-loving Gemini and your solar fifth house of recreation, playmates, and casual lovers. If you're not attached, your social schedule will fill up in rapid-fire motion bright and early—as soon as the 1st. If you're with someone and happy about it, know that a bit of temptation could be on the way. Nothing you can't handle, of course.

Lovers and Friends

If you feel threatened or intimidated by someone around the weekend of the 8th, Aquarius, don't question your sanity—but do question the motives of whoever it is who's making you uncomfortable. As you know, your antennae have yet to let you down—unless you ignore them, that is. Don't make that mistake now. Let your gut lead the way—and don't hesitate to speak your mind, either.

Money and Success

Over the 5th and 6th, the emotional Moon in Pisces could make it tough for you to see things clearly in the department of finances, Aquarius. If sudden or unexpected expenses come up, don't jump in and commit yourself to a long-term payment plan right away. Take a bit of time with a trusted advisor to figure it out in a rational, practical way.

Tricky Transits

Neptune, the Queen of Illusion, will stop in her tracks on the 18th, set to move retrograde for many, many months in your solar second house of personal money matters. Needless to say, this wouldn't be the best time for you to sign on any dotted lines, especially if you haven't read and understood the fine print. If you're not sure, stall. And keep stalling.

Rewarding Days
1, 2, 13, 22

Challenging Days
5, 6, 8, 11, 21, 25, 30

Aquarius | July

Relaxation and Recreation

On the 5th, a Sun-Jupiter trine aspect will tempt you to start the holiday weekend early—and if you can, you really should. The emotional Moon in Aries will see to it that you're surrounded by fiery, interesting people—so it's a given that you won't be bored, which is what you hate more than anything. Go ahead. Allow yourself a bit of downtime.

Lovers and Friends

Mercury will turn retrograde in your solar seventh house of one-to-one relationships on the 25th, just as shocking Uranus and the Sun get into a testy square. Does this mean you really shouldn't count on any of your plans turning out as expected? Absolutely. The good news is that everyone around you will be dealing with their own mishaps and miscommunications, so if you need to reschedule, no one will mind all that much.

Money and Success

If you've been thinking of changing careers—say, by walking out of your current place of employment the next time you feel you just can't stand it anymore—well, the Solar Eclipse on the 12th could be the straw that breaks the camel's back. Your mission is to be sure you have plan B in place before you decide to ditch it all and declare your independence.

Tricky Transits

If you've been waiting for the right time to tell someone about something you've been hiding, do yourself a favor and avoid the 24th. It may seem like you're doing the right thing—maybe even the compassionate thing—but with Mercury set to turn retrograde, something you're out to clarify will end up being even more confusing. Stall for at least three weeks, and plan your defense.

Rewarding Days

7, 8, 13, 22, 28

Challenging Days

1, 2, 9, 12, 16, 26, 27

Aquarius | August

Relaxation and Recreation

If you have plans for the weekend of the 10th, better be sure they're not set in stone, Aquarius. On the 9th, fun-loving Venus will get into an irritating square aspect with serious Saturn, which means that even if you were set to have some fun, duty may call—no, duty will probably call. You're not unfamiliar with changing horses at the last minute, but this time around, you won't have much notice. Prepare for that eventuality.

Lovers and Friends

Venus will slip into partner-loving Libra on the 6th, where she'll stay for the next five weeks, Aquarius, urging you to find someone to play with on a regular basis. No, this doesn't necessarily mean you'll need to settle down, and no, you most definitely won't have to make any commitments. That said, why not just enjoy the company of a new playmate without worrying about what to do in the future? You might just find that you're enjoying yourself.

Money and Success

The Full Moon in Pisces on the 26th will illuminate your solar second house of personal finances, urging you to take a serious look at a situation you've been entrusting to another person. If anything seems fishy, it could be that you're being deceived. On the other hand, you may not have been properly filled in on all the details. Look things over carefully.

Tricky Transits

On the 18th, Mercury will turn direct, after what probably feels like a very long three-week period. He's been moving in reverse in your solar seventh house of relationships, so misunderstandings—on a major-league level—have probably been the order of the day. Although the details will begin to clear up now, you'll still have some explaining to do. Don't worry. All will be well by the 25th. Be patient.

Rewarding Days

7, 18, 19, 24, 25

Challenging Days

1, 4, 8, 9, 26, 27, 29

Aquarius | September

Relaxation and Recreation

If you receive an invitation around the 3rd to go out and play with a friend—especially if that friend happens to be someone you're wildly attracted to—don't even think about refusing. Take a sick day or a personal day if you have to, but don't let this opportunity go by. At best, you'll find yourself a partner who can keep up. At worst, you'll discover a new friend in that same category.

Lovers and Friends

As of the 10th, when fiery, assertive, and often aggressive Mars sets off for your sign—for the next two months, by the way—you'll probably find that you're a whole heck of a lot more likely to let loose with your feelings than you usually are. That includes anger, however, which you tend to keep in check, so your mission from now on will be to find an appropriate way to blow off some steam without hurting a dear one's feelings.

Money and Success

Venus—who's in charge of money, in addition to love—will set off for intense and often relentless Scorpio on the 9th, which puts her directly in your solar tenth house of authority figures and higher-ups. Does this mean you'll be a bit more adamant about getting what you want from those above you at work? Sure does—but don't worry. With Venus here, they'll be so charmed, they won't realize they're doing your bidding until it's already done.

Tricky Transits

Dutiful, responsible Saturn will stop in his tracks on the 6th in your solar twelfth house, where secret, subconscious feelings are hidden. If you're feeling guilty about something and you haven't yet made amends, you'll need to do that soon—if you want to be able to sleep peacefully, that is. On the other hand, someone who's hurt you may come forward to make their apologies.

Rewarding Days

3, 7, 11, 12, 19, 27

Challenging Days

5, 6, 18, 20, 25, 30

Aquarius | October

Relaxation and Recreation

On the 24th, the Full Moon in Taurus will set up shop in your solar fourth house of home, family, and domestic matters. This comfort-loving lady will inspire you to open your doors to all your dear ones, possibly to put on a huge feast or host an even bigger get-together that's long overdue. If you're game, put those plans in motion at least a week ahead of time.

Lovers and Friends

Fiery, feisty Mars will storm through your sign all this month, Aquarius. Now, you've never needed any help being exactly who you are, so with this assertive energy on duty, your personality might just be cranked up a little bit too much—well, for those who don't understand how important it is to you to be genuine, that is. When it comes to debates, keep your righteous anger under wraps, but don't back down. No way.

Money and Success

Venus will stop in her tracks on the 5th to turn retrograde, Aquarius, and she'll be wearing intense Scorpio at the time and making her way through your solar tenth house of higher-ups and authority figures. Over the next six weeks, you should expect to feel the need to retrace your steps with regard to a recent career decision. It's okay. You're perfectly entitled to change your mind.

Tricky Transits

On the 9th, Mercury will set off for intense Scorpio, a cerebral planet in a sign that's famous for its detective-like qualities. If you're in need of answers and you can't find anyone to help you dig, you'll be more than happy to poke around yourself, just a bit at a time, until you unearth the answers you're after. This may not win you any friends, however, so be warned.

Rewarding Days

6, 12, 13, 22, 24

Challenging Days

5, 10, 11, 23, 31

Aquarius | November

Relaxation and Recreation

The Full Moon in Gemini on the 22nd will make for a merry holiday, and spirits will be running high. You may overdo the celebrating a bit thanks to the influence of the Sun, Mercury, and Jupiter, but as long as you have a designated driver and/or a place to sleep, you may as well go ahead and enjoy yourself. Turn off your phone and ignore the computer—just for a day.

Lovers and Friends

Social outings and gatherings will go along smoothly on the 9th, thanks to an easy, cooperative trine aspect between loving Venus in partner-oriented Libra and energetic Mars in your solar first house of personality. Add in the fiery energy of the Moon in Sagittarius, and you're all set for adventure. Take a chance and try something new, or check out an entirely new peer circle.

Money and Success

With fiery Mars on duty in your sign, there's not much you can't accomplish, Aquarius. Add in a trine aspect between Mars and Venus on the 9th, and it's not hard to imagine you coming across a lucky break—in the department of finances, by the way. Your mission is to pay attention to your gut. When you feel lucky, act on it. Immediately, that is.

Tricky Transits

The 16th looks to be quite a confusing day, Aquarius. If you can manage it, laying low at your place and binge-watching something you've been dying to see wouldn't be a bad idea. The thing is, both Venus and Mercury will be stopped in their tracks to change direction, which usually indicates stalls, delays, and lasting miscommunications. No matter where you are or who you're with, don't say anything you might regret.

Rewarding Days
2, 9, 13, 14, 22, 27

Challenging Days
6, 7, 16, 19, 28

Aquarius | December

Relaxation and Recreation

On the 12th, the emotional Moon in your sign will get together with the Sun and Mercury in fiery Sagittarius to put you in the mood to socialize. Fortunately, you've always had a lively, unusual pack of friends to call when you're in the mood to party or have a spontaneous adventure, so finding someone to share these fun-loving energies with will be easy.

Lovers and Friends

The Universe has seen fit to enlist the fiery, playful energy of the Moon in Leo to make the 24th and 25th pretty darn terrific, Aquarius. This warm and lively lady will turn up the volume on all your encounters, urging you to forget all about work, duties, and anything even remotely resembling responsibilities. It's time to entertain and be entertained. Enjoy!

Money and Success

If you've got last-minute shopping to do and you head out on the 21st, better take a chaperone along, Aquarius. A Venus-Neptune trine will combine talents with Mercury and excessive Jupiter to put you in the mood to set financial concerns aside in favor of making someone smile. Don't get too crazy with your plastic. Remember, when it comes to gifts, thoughtfulness always wins out over extravagance.

Tricky Transits

Mercury will retrograde back into intense Scorpio and your solar tenth house of authority figures on the 1st, Aquarius, possibly bringing along a not-so-pleasant encounter with a higher-up who's unhappy with your performance on a recent project. The good news is that retrogrades are all about second chances. Retrace your steps, figure out what went wrong, and do what you can to make it right.

Rewarding Days

4, 12, 13, 16, 24, 25, 28

Challenging Days

1, 2, 6, 7, 11

Aquarius Action Table

These dates reflect the best—but not the only—times for success and ease in these activities, according to your Sun sign.

	JAN	FEB	MAR	APR	MAY	JUN	JUL	AUG	SEP	OCT	NOV	DEC
Move					11			25				
Start a class	2				18	13		18		15		
Join a club		6				2			3		9	28
Ask for a raise			2						11			16
Get professional advice		21		7			13			24		
Get a loan		27	1	14			7	-				
New romance	3		12					7	3	26	25	
Vacation	19	2		21	19	1	5				27	20

Pisces

The Fish
February 20 to March 20

♓

Element: Water

Quality: Mutable

Polarity: Yin/feminine

Planetary Ruler: Neptune

Meditation: I successfully navigate my emotions

Gemstone: Aquamarine

Power Stones: Amethyst, bloodstone, tourmaline

Key Phrase: I believe

Glyph: Two fish swimming in opposite directions

Anatomy: Feet, lymphatic system

Colors: Sea green, violet

Animals: Fish, sea mammals

Myths/Legends: Aphrodite, Buddha, Jesus of Nazareth

House: Twelfth

Opposite Sign: Virgo

Flower: Water lily

Keyword: Transcendence

The Pisces Personality

Your Strengths, Gifts, and Challenges

Your soul hasn't chosen an easy astrological mission, Pisces—but that's not to say that your work here on our lovely planet won't be greatly rewarding. The thing is, your sign is the personal property of Neptune, and her mission (yes, "her," which we'll discuss later on) is to dissolve boundaries and eliminate barriers. On the plus side, this makes you highly empathetic, so all manner of living beings enjoy the benefits of your kindness, understanding, and compassion. It doesn't matter whether an "other" has two legs or four legs, or whether they're furred or feathered. Matter of fact, leaf creatures also enjoy every bit as much of your compassionate care. In fact, a survey of those of us known as tree huggers would most certainly include an amazing number of folks born under your sign. You feel everything others feel, for better or worse—and whether or not that other is in your physical presence is inconsequential. Even the tears of television or movie characters—regardless of whether they're inspired by joy or sorrow—will bring on your own, just as easily as if you'd known their character personally for decades. Of course, that goes double when it comes to the hopes, dreams, and fears of "real" others.

Naturally, then, when you're around upbeat energy and able to share someone's happiness, you enjoy one of the major perks of your job—basically, to take pleasure in all those warm, fuzzy, happy feelings. Likewise, unfortunately, when you're in the vicinity of negative or hurtful energy, you'll feel that just as keenly—which can take quite a toll on your sensitive little soul. As such, you need to make it your mission to surround yourself only with positive people and to place yourself in equally positive situations. Oh, and one more thing. Neptune's rulership over your sign means that you've been gifted with a superpower: the ability to become pretty much invisible whenever you like. Use this power only for good. No fair infiltrating the ranks in any given situation just because you can.

Romance and Other Relationships

You're an expert at getting to know others, Pisces, thanks to your Neptunian gift for breaking down barriers—and you have a whole lot of tools in your kit to get that job done. Of course, one of the most famous ways to accomplish this task is to share an altered state—Neptune's favorite state of affairs—say, by sharing a glass of wine or enjoying music with a kindred spirit. For that reason, you tend to be drawn to others who also enjoy these pleasant "escape hatches" from reality. That's all well and good, but you'll need to be sure to check in with reality every now and then. In other words, relationships that allow you to avoid reality for more than an evening out or a romantic weekend away should be avoided—big time.

Regardless of whether you're after a friendship or a love relationship, you can avoid negative relationships by listening to your substantial intuition and conducting your initial "interviews" with new acquaintances carefully. Train yourself to recognize pessimists, worrywarts, or dire "doom and gloom" types and steer clear of them at all costs. You tend to have a tendency toward depression, so surrounding yourself with others who have their feet firmly planted here on Planet Number Three will always be your best bet. The earth signs—Taurus, Virgo, and Capricorn—often provide you with the grounding force you need while still being able to share and appreciate the aesthetic side of life you so enjoy. Relationships with the other water signs—Cancer and Scorpio—can also work well for you, since they're every bit as emotional as you are.

Career and Work

When it comes to your career ambitions, Pisces, many of you seem to be drawn toward the helping professions—which only makes sense, given that you have such an empathetic soul. You might work your magic through massage or other Western forms of healing, but just as many of you end up as physical therapists or psychological counselors. Then, too, the metaphysical arts come to you quite naturally, so anything along those lines, from doing psychic readings to leading meditation classes, suits you well. As fond as you are of being around water, you might also enjoy work that involves boating or swimming.

Money and Possessions

With Neptune's magic pink cloud circling you at all times, Pisces, it's easy for you to lose your bearings—not to mention your keys, your wallet, and perhaps even your cash. For that reason, it's important—really important—for you to keep tabs on everything you need, value, and cherish. You're also quite easily parted from the things you love if someone you care for expresses their admiration. Remember, you deserve what you have, so before you gift something you really do need or adore to another, think twice. There are many ways to let someone know you care without taking something away from yourself.

Your Lighter Side

You adore fantasy and romance, Pisces, so when reality becomes a tad too harsh, you often duck away from it, perhaps through music, art, novels, or movies—not to mention substances that take the edge off. Nothing wrong with that, of course—unless it becomes a habit that interferes with your ability to function capably. What you're really after is a break in the action—a distraction from the harsher side of life. Try yoga, metaphysics, or meditation, all of which come to you quite naturally. Of course, the best escape of all, in your book, is water. It doesn't matter whether it's a nice long shower, an even longer bath, or a walk on the beach. Water is your element, and it will always comfort you.

Pisces Celebrities

Your sign's fondness for music, art, photography, and other aesthetic delights shows up quite prominently in the work of fellow Pisceans Michelangelo, Ansel Adams, Andres Segovia, Seal, Queen Latifah, Michael Bolton, Jon Bon Jovi, Rihanna, and Erykah Badu, just to name a few. Your knack for bringing fantasies and dreams to life can be seen in many famous actors and actresses, including William H. Macy, Bruce Willis, Kurt Russell, and Elizabeth Taylor.

The Year Ahead for Pisces

Jupiter will be on duty in sexy, intense Scorpio straight through late November, Pisces, and since this puts the King of the Gods in the mood to do some serious detective work, you can count on your intuitive abilities to be running on high. Now, along with your ruling planet, Neptune, who'll stay in your already uber-intuitive sign all year, it's easy to see how you'll be able to spot a fake, fraud, or con artist a mile away—provided, of course, that your heart isn't involved. You do have a tendency to ignore the facts every now and then, especially when you don't want to see them. But Jupiter insists that we take a look at the big picture, and in such a perceptive frame of mind, chances are good that you'll end up seeing the truth of the matter pretty darn quickly with regard to relationships—yes, even if you don't want to. That goes double for intimate relationships, which just so happen to be Scorpio's specialty. Obviously, since Scorpio belongs to Pluto—who's never been famous for keeping anything around that no longer serves a purpose, by the way—you'll probably find yourself doing quite a bit of "housecleaning" in the Department of Others. Some of those "eliminations" will occur quite quickly and without much warning, by the way, thanks to fiery Mars. This feisty fellow will spend an unusually long amount of time this year in impulsive Aquarius, a sign that tends to inspire sudden action. Think of this planet in this sign as a light switch, and expect to make a whole lot of seemingly abrupt decisions—at least, in the eyes of others. The thing is, he'll be storming through your solar twelfth house of secrets and hidden thoughts, so it's likely that you'll spend quite a bit of time mulling things over in private—or should I say stewing over things in private. The thing is, you can only keep Mars quiet for so long, so once you've reached your breaking point and decided that enough is enough, you'll take swift action. Expect to raise some eyebrows, and don't worry about the reactions of others. When your intuition tells you you're done and you're ready to flip the switch—well, by all means, flip it.

Saturn

Just days before 2018 begins, Saturn will change signs, from outgoing, fun-loving Sagittarius to serious Capricorn—which just so happens to be Saturn's favorite sign. Since he'll be operating on home turf, his energy will be clearer and stronger than usual, so this famously strict taskmaster will be in an even stricter mood than usual (yes, really). Obviously, we all need to be on extra-high red alert, so the area of our charts he'll be inspecting and evaluating is most definitely a place to get it together—and keep it together. Saturn doesn't fool around when it comes to "reminding" us—often not very gently—of our duties, obligations, and responsibilities, both to others and to ourselves. In your case, he'll be starting off on a two-and-a-half-year trek through your solar eleventh house, where group ventures and goals for the future are handled, so if you haven't already realized that the company you keep will end up having an awful lot to do with how quickly—or not—your goals are realized, that's something you need to wrap your mind around right now. You may need to find a whole new peer group that better reflects what you want from your life in the long run. This doesn't mean you'll necessarily need to push away from those who don't share your dreams—although it might—but associating with others who are either on the same path or experienced enough to guide you along the way will become extremely important.

If you're already on the road to realizing your goals, don't get frustrated when—not if—you'll need to jump through hoops, deal with roadblocks, and fight through what may seem to be an unending mountain of red tape. The important thing to consider is the end result. Make a five-year plan—no, matter of fact, make that a ten-year plan—and stick to it. Oh, and if you're already associating with kindred spirts on a similar path, you should expect to be put in charge, so prepare yourself to take over, especially if someone in a position of leadership drops the ball and you're one of the very few folks in the vicinity who know the group's inner workings.

Uranus

Startling Uranus has been on duty in fiery, impulsive Aries for close to seven years now, Pisces, which has put him right smack dab in the middle of your solar second house of personal finances, possessions, and values. Since he's oh-so-fond of electronics, gadgets, and technological toys, you've probably acquired quite a few of those items, many of which are near and dear to your heart—especially because they're not cheap, and you've had to trade many precious hours of your time to earn them. If you've gone a bit overboard in this department, however, it may be time to think about parting with them. Yes, really. Only some of them, though. The good news is that you'll have up until May 16th to decide which to keep, which to gift to a friend or organization, and which to replace, since that's when Uranus will make his way into your solar third house of communications, conversations, and navigations—and that's when you'll want nothing but the best, most innovative tools. After May 16th, however—and this goes double for those of you who were born at the very beginning of your sign—you'll definitely be in the mood to upgrade and update. The third house also has a whole lot to do with your neighborhood and your daily routine, and since Uranus is a rather unpredictable kind of guy, everything from your usual route to work to your vehicle to your neighbors could be set to change—and as per Uranus, it will happen without much, if any, warning. Tell you what, though. It's a terrific time to learn a new language, and an even better time to learn Computerese. This is the start of a seven-year journey of change. It won't be predictable, but if you fasten your seat belt and resolve to cooperate, it will most definitely be exhilarating!

Neptune

Your ruling planet, Neptune, has been on duty in your sign and your solar first house of personality since 2011, Pisces, turning up the volume on your already ultra-sensitive personality. Over the course of these years, you've faced a bit of a challenge. Neptune dissolves boundaries, so you've been even more likely to absorb the energy around you—for better or worse. On the one hand, this means that your instincts and psychic abilities have been running on high, so you've probably amazed even yourself—not to mention others—with just how right on your intuition has been. The thing is, becoming the human equivalent of a sponge means that your vulnerability (and susceptibility to outside influences) is also running on high. What a dilemma! Fortunately, if you haven't already learned how to protect yourself from negative individuals and influences, you'll have another chance during 2018, since Neptune will continue on her journey here all year.

But getting back to instincts, if your antennae don't seem to be working well, take a look at your lifestyle. During Neptune transits, it's easy to become a tad too fond of the escape hatches she encourages us to investigate—including drugs, alcohol, and other addictive habits. Everyone needs a break from reality every now and then—especially you, right about now—but don't overindulge. You stand to learn an awful lot about life now. Resist the urge to run away from it. Oh, and if you're feeling depressed or anxious, get thee to a doctor or therapist and tell them all about it!

Pluto

Pluto has been on duty in hardworking Capricorn and your solar eleventh house of friendships, goals for the future, and group affiliations for years, Pisces, and he won't be going anywhere just yet. His journey here has likely inspired you to become even more intent on finding kindred spirits who share your goals and ambitions for the future, but now that Saturn—who just so happens to own Capricorn—has joined forces with Pluto, that search will become even more important to you. Since Pluto tends to help us clear away the deadwood in our lives, you've likely had to let go of friendships. But if they've been of the shallow or superficial kind, chances are good you haven't looked back or regretted those decisions. Pluto has inspired you to search for depth and intensity in friendships, and now that he's teamed up with Saturn, you'll be even more determined to find your tribe. Of course, Pluto also adores secrets, scandals, and intrigue, so you may have had to deal with some less than savory individuals along the way. But as intuitive as you are, I'll bet they were the first to be dismissed from your life—and if they haven't left yet, they'll be on their way shortly. Pluto also tends to turn us into detectives in the area of the chart he's visiting, so along with your naturally keen intuition, it's going to be next to impossible to pull the wool over your eyes.

How Will This Year's Eclipses Affect You?

Think of eclipses as celestial exclamation points. They amp up the volume on ordinary life for us all when they occur, but the signs and houses they occupy show where the possibility exists for sudden, intense, and often quite surprising events. Eclipses occur in pairs, six months apart. Solar Eclipses are supercharged New Moons, bringing the Sun and Moon together and marking peak times for planting seeds in any department of life. Lunar Eclipses are high-energy Full Moons, times of dramatic culmination, fulfillment, and often new beginnings as well, provided the slate has been wiped clean.

This year, there will actually be five eclipses rather than four. The first Lunar Eclipse will take place on January 31 in proud, fiery Leo and your solar sixth house of work and health. If you've been threatening to diet or ditch a bad habit once and for all, wait no longer. You'll have all the inspiration anyone ever needed to get the job done. Plus, since Leo is one of the fixed signs—all of which are extremely determined energies—you won't want to quit until you've accomplished your aims.

On February 15, the first Solar Eclipse of year will occur in your solar twelfth house of secrets, all done up in startling Aquarius. This could mark the revelation of a secret—for better or worse. If you've been involved with something—or someone—the truth could become known in rather spectacular and quite sudden fashion. Prepare yourself. In the time leading up to this lunation, think about the eventual repercussions this news will have on your own life and those of others.

On July 12, a second Solar Eclipse will arrive, this time announcing that it's time for a change in your solar fifth house of lovers, fun times, and recreational activities. That new hobby you've been thinking about taking up? This is a terrific time to do it. If you're single, don't refuse a family member's offer to introduce you to someone they think would be just perfect for you—no matter what happened last time. Oh, and since this eclipse will occur in home-loving Cancer, you might want to get started on any plans you've been delaying regarding a move, a remodel, or an addition to your nest.

The second Lunar Eclipse of 2018 will occur on July 27, this time in startling Aquarius. Your solar twelfth house will once again play host, and secret activities will once again be the focus. This time around, however, fiery Mars will be in cahoots with the Sun and the Moon, urging you to finish things up with regard to a clandestine situation. If you've been naughty, remember, Christmas is coming, and Santa may be watching!

The last Solar Eclipse of the year will arrive on August 11 in Leo and your sixth house, once again activating your urge to make positive physical changes, most likely to your appearance or your personal presentation. If you haven't yet acted on those New Year's resolutions to change your health or appearance positively, think of this as a second shot at the title—and act on it!

Pisces | January

Relaxation and Recreation

The Full Moon of the 1st will occur in home-loving Cancer. If you've been out playing a tad too much over the past month—and who among us hasn't—it might be time to kick back with the family and enjoy an evening at home. You may also be due for some wonderful news regarding a new home, an opportunity to work from your home, or even a new arrival to your family.

Lovers and Friends

Once again, it's the Full Moon who'll inspire you in this department, Pisces. You single folks could "accidentally" run into someone who's just perfect for you, likely through a neighbor or family member. Hey, just agree to have lunch—or maybe coffee. It can't hurt to smile pretty and say hello, right?

Money and Success

The emotional Moon in fiery Aries will make contact with surprising Uranus on the 23rd, which could mean there's a bonus, promotion, or reward coming your way, quite out of the blue. I might tell you not to spend it all in one place, but you'll be feeling impulsive, so at least be sure you spend it on an experience that will create a lovely memory rather than an object that will tarnish as time goes by.

Tricky Transits

The Lunar Eclipse on January 31st will team up with Mercury's arrival into startling Aquarius, urging you to take stock of just how much time you spend at work. If it's too much and you're exhausted, make it a priority to devote a healthy amount of time to relax and enjoy life! Get a massage, visit a spa, or schedule some time with your funniest, most unconventional friends.

Rewarding Days

1, 5, 8, 15, 16, 19, 28

Challenging Days

7, 9, 13, 14, 24, 27

Pisces | February

Relaxation and Recreation

Whatever new adventure you've been thinking of trying out, you'll have the guts to give it a shot around the time of the Venus-Uranus sextile aspect on the 6th. As long as it won't be harmful to you or anyone else, go for it! Have your bestie or your current flame come along so the memory will remain a permanent part of your emotional scrapbook.

Lovers and Friends

Venus, the Goddess of Love, will set off for your sign and your solar first house of personality on the 10th, Pisces, urging you to strut your stuff and make your presence known—especially around attractive new others. If you're single, this is the perfect time to get out there and mingle. If you're unattached, be on alert that Venus is determined to put an end to all that. Keep your eyes and ears open!

Money and Success

On the 21st, Venus and Neptune will collide in your sign, and since Venus is in charge of not just love but also money, it's easy to understand how keeping track of your finances could be a bit of a challenge around this time, and unrealistic spending could be an issue. If you're out shopping, take a practical friend along who'll wrestle your plastic away before you do any real damage.

Tricky Transits

The Solar Eclipse on the 15th will occur in unpredictable Aquarius and your solar twelfth house of secrets, so if you've been hiding something—well, better prepare for the truth to emerge. If that's what you really want, help the process along. If not, consider whether continuing on your current path is the best course of action.

Rewarding Days

3, 6, 14, 16, 21, 26

Challenging Days

1, 9, 17, 24

Pisces | March

Relaxation and Recreation

With four planets set to pass through your very water-loving sign this month, getting out in nature—especially to sit by a lake, stream, or ocean—would be your best bet when it comes to chilling out. Don't forget about art, music, and metaphysical adventures, though, all of which will feed your soul and make your tender heart happy, too.

Lovers and Friends

The Full Moon of the 1st will illuminate your solar relationship axis, insisting that you open your eyes and deal with reality, for better or worse. It may be time to make a change, but not to worry. That doesn't mean the news will be bad. It might only be that you've finally decided to settle down into a comfortable routine with someone who understands you and shares your goals.

Money and Success

If there's a debt to be paid, Pisces, and you haven't been able to do it just yet—or if you've honestly forgotten about it—look to the Venus-Saturn square on the 13th to remind you. If you can't quite come up with everything you owe, keep in mind that Saturn loves setting up payment plans. The only thing is, once you've given your word, you'll have to stick to it. Don't offer what you can't afford. Be realistic.

Tricky Transits

Mercury will turn retrograde on the 22nd in your solar second house of finances, all done up in impatient Aries. Asking you to wait before you make any major purchases may be out of the question, but do be sure to hold on to your receipts, especially when it comes to electronics or other fun tech toys. Also, be sure to double-check your directions before you take off for parts unknown.

Rewarding Days

1, 2, 4, 15, 16, 18

Challenging Days

10, 11, 13, 23, 24, 29

Pisces | April

Relaxation and Recreation

Around the 14th or 23rd, a charming out-of-towner will catch your attention. Don't resist the urge to get to know them better. Just be sure not to get too used to them being around. The qualities you admire most in them are probably their spontaneity and their willingness to take risks. Enjoy their company whenever possible, but don't get comfortable, much less attached.

Lovers and Friends

On the 7th, a lovely Venus-Saturn trine will see to it that you're nicely grounded and oh-so happy about staying put and putting in your time with a certain person everyone around you was doubtful about from the get-go. See? Once again, it's best to trust those antennae, above all else. Try not to gloat—but if you have to, then just a little.

Money and Success

The Sun and Mercury will take turns dashing through your solar second house of finances this month, all done up in impulsive Aries. It won't be easy to stop yourself from spending—and perhaps overspending—but if you can manage it, your best bet will be to think it over. After all, didn't you just wreak havoc on your credit cards a couple of months ago?

Tricky Transits

The Venus-Saturn trine on the 7th will make you feel warm and safe, Pisces—which might well be true. If that's the case, feel free to lean back, relax, and trust the person you're with. If even one tiny little piece of you has doubts, however, now is the time to address them. Don't be lulled into a false sense of security. Be sure it's all really real.

Rewarding Days

7, 10, 12, 16, 29

Challenging Days

2, 4, 5, 24, 25, 26

Pisces | May

Relaxation and Recreation

With Venus in playful Gemini until the 19th, you'll be easily amused this month, Pisces—and you'll likely also be surrounded by a host of funny, friendly loved ones who laugh as easily and as often as you do. You'll also be easily bored, however, so if the urge for new games and activities arises, be adventurous. Close family members will be more than happy to play along.

Lovers and Friends

The Goddess of Love—yes, Venus herself—will pass into your solar fifth house of lovers on the 19th, Pisces, giving you the opportunity to spend the next several weeks hunting for your soulmate—if you haven't already found them, of course. In that case, stick close to home, do plenty of snuggling, and don't shy away from conversations about home and family matters. Just about anything can be settled amicably now.

Money and Success

If you can avoid buying anything of an electronic nature until after the New Moon on the 15th, Pisces, give it your best shot. Before that time, both Mercury and Uranus—who have equal jurisdiction over gadgets—will be traveling together in fiery Aries, a sign that's better at impulse than the long haul. Force yourself to be patient and wait for the sales!

Tricky Transits

The Full Moon on May 29th will work in cahoots with restless Mercury to activate your solar axis of home and family matters. Expect both sides of life to require your attention in a very big way, and figure out a way to juggle both your responsibilities and your attention. You can do this. You're nothing if not extremely flexible and intuitive.

Rewarding Days
4, 8, 15, 18, 19, 20

Challenging Days
1, 5, 9, 12, 13, 26, 28

Pisces | June

Relaxation and Recreation

The Sun, Mercury, and Venus will take turns passing through Cancer this month, the most home- and family-oriented sign in the heavens. A water sign like your own, this sign inspires tender moments, memorable encounters with loved ones, and a longing to be snuggled up in your nest with your loved ones. Duck out from work whenever you can and spend time with your tribe.

Lovers and Friends

Once loving Venus sets off for showy Leo on the 13th, making a display of your feelings will be important, Pisces—for better or worse. If you need to tell someone how you feel, mention it on that very day. Otherwise, unexpected roadblocks and the negative input of others could stop you from revealing how you truly feel.

Money and Success

Complicated business transactions will become even more challenging around the 19th, when a confusing inconjunct aspect between Venus and Saturn could make it extremely tough to create an environment where all parties concerned may be ready, willing, and able to at least try to understand each other's needs. Whatever you can do to expedite the process before that time will make things a lot easier down the road.

Tricky Transits

Money matters you're trying to straighten out won't be unraveled easily around the 30th. If you can wait a week or so, put the brakes on the plan and give yourself some time to think things over. The worst that can happen is that you may end up short for a while. The good news is that you'll be able to live with the decisions you've made.

Rewarding Days
1, 2, 12, 13, 20, 22

Challenging Days
3, 8, 11, 16, 19, 23

Pisces | July

Relaxation and Recreation
Right up until the 9th, tempting you into playing—even if you should be working—will be all too easy, Pisces. Now, you've been working hard lately, so you probably deserve a few hours—or days—away from the daily grind. Don't feel guilty about taking it, and rest assured that you'll be able to find at least one tried-and-true playmate to keep you company.

Lovers and Friends
Venus, the Goddess of Love herself, will set off for your solar seventh house of one-to-one relationships on the 9th, all done up in practical Virgo. If you've been waiting to announce a decision, wait no longer. It's time to let everyone know exactly how you feel—and more importantly, exactly what you expect from them. If they're not happy with your findings, too bad. It's time to think about your own needs.

Money and Success
Even if you've been spending a tad too much on entertainment and new experiences, Pisces, once Venus sets off for practical Virgo on the 9th, you'll be able not just to curtail your spending but to put yourself on a strict budget. Oh, and it may be time to cut off anyone who isn't carrying their fair share of the weight. No fair feeling guilty!

Tricky Transits
Mars will spend yet another month in often-shocking Aquarius, urging you to take stock of what really matters and unceremoniously ditch what isn't working out, regardless of what others have to say about your choices. Don't back down. This is your chance to make a break for it—and I know you know exactly what I mean. Don't let the moment pass you by.

Rewarding Days
5, 8, 11, 13, 22, 27

Challenging Days
1, 2, 12, 23, 25

Pisces | August

Relaxation and Recreation

The Solar Eclipse on the 11th will make it tough for you to relax, Pisces—even a little bit. On the plus side, your abilities on the job will get you noticed, which will work well for you in the near future, making your career prospects quite rosy. Still, you'll need to download, kick back, and retreat to keep your energy intact. Look to the Grand Earth Trine on the 25th for stability. Announce any permanent decisions then.

Lovers and Friends

The Full Moon on the 26th will arrive with the urge to convince you to make some serious physical changes, Pisces—and after being battered by the past couple of eclipses, you'll probably be quite ready to give in and let those changes happen. The thing is, you'll need to contribute a good amount of energy to making change happen. Are you ready for this? You'd better be!

Money and Success

On the 9th, Venus will square off with Saturn, pitting Ms. Pleasure Seeker against Mr. I Don't Think So. Yes, you'll be struggling with whether or not to indulge, and yes, both indulging and being good will seem to be equally correct choices. Your mission is to juggle. Have some fun, but don't dig yourself into a financial hole to pull it off.

Tricky Transits

After months of being retrograde in Aquarius, red-hot Mars will back up into serious, steady-handed Capricorn on the 12th, fully prepared to take charge of a group situation that's clearly out of hand and in need of competent leadership. Yes, you may be tapped, and no, you may not want to be. Follow your conscience. If you know you're meant to do this, accept the responsibility, even if only temporarily.

Rewarding Days

7, 18, 19, 20, 25

Challenging Days

4, 6, 9, 26, 29

Pisces | September

Relaxation and Recreation

The emotional Moon will contact no less than six planets on the 1st, all of them perfectly ready to provide you with plenty of astrological reasons to kick back and enjoy the company of the ones you love. Since it's the weekend, you really have no choice but to at least try to obey her commands. Resistance is futile—and why would you want to, anyway?

Lovers and Friends

On the 7th, conversational Mercury will get into a Grand Trine with serious Saturn and innovative Uranus—and this, friends, is the stuff that happy new beginnings are made of. Together with the New Moon on the 9th, it's not hard to imagine at least one of those new beginnings arriving as a result of someone new who's entered your life with a message. Whether it's deliberate or not doesn't matter. Your mission is to listen up.

Money and Success

On the 24th, a Full Moon will illuminate your solar second house, Pisces, turning up the volume on your urge to earn your daily bread on your own, without answering to a boss, supervisor, or any other authority figure. If you know you're ready to strike out on your own and an opportunity presents itself, don't be shy. It's time. Go for it!

Tricky Transits

The New Moon on the 9th will plant a seed of new beginnings in your solar seventh house of relationships—but remember, endings often need to come about to make way for beginnings. If you've been trying to cut ties between yourself and a certain someone, wait no longer. You won't be alone for long—unless, of course, you want to be.

Rewarding Days

3, 6, 7, 11, 27

Challenging Days

5, 12, 17, 18, 22, 23, 25

Pisces | October

Relaxation and Recreation

The New Moon on the 8th will occur in sociable Libra, urging you to get out there and have some fun with friends. With four planets in your solar ninth house of long-distance travel and far-off friends, a trip may be on your agenda—possibly because you've found a way to mix business with pleasure. Expect it to be a transformative journey.

Lovers and Friends

Lovely lady Venus will stop in her tracks on the 5th to turn retrograde, bringing the possibility of getting back together with someone from the past. It might be that the one who got away wants another shot at the title. It might also be that you're due to unexpectedly cross paths with a friend you haven't seen in years.

Money and Success

The Full Moon on the 24th will occur in Taurus, a sign that's famous for being a money magnet. If you've been thinking of getting involved with a new business venture, now's the time—especially if you've already done your homework and investigated the situation carefully. This is also a terrific time to approach the boss about that raise, bonus, or promotion.

Tricky Transits

The weekend of the 20th will play host to the emotional Moon in your sign, Pisces—and she'll be making contact with a number of planets. Your feelings will be running on high, and you'll have plenty of opportunities to express them. Just be sure not to let any secrets slip out. This isn't the time to make any announcements that might hurt someone's feelings.

Rewarding Days
4, 5, 6, 12, 22, 24, 27

Challenging Days
2, 9, 10, 11

Pisces | November

Relaxation and Recreation

The Full Moon on Thanksgiving will bring together the Sun in Sagittarius and the Moon in Gemini, two of the most playful signs in the heavens. Whether you're hosting a gathering at your place or you've been invited to feast with family or friends, you can rest assured that a good time will be had by all.

Lovers and Friends

Love and passion will be on the agenda on the 9th, thanks to a fun-loving sextile aspect between loving Venus and fiery Mars. If you're attached, plan something new and exciting with your partner. If you're not and you'd like to be, grab a friend and go somewhere new or try an activity that's recently been piquing your interest. Adventures await!

Money and Success

The New Moon on the 7th will occur in your solar ninth house, urging you to expand your horizons and learn something new. This is a great time to return to school or sign up for a certificate program that will beef up your resume. If you've been thinking about making a long-distance move, a field trip to investigate the area may be in order.

Tricky Transits

Both Venus and Mercury will change direction on the 16th, Pisces, which could make for some confusing and possibly problematic situations. This isn't a good time to make any major decisions or make promises you're not absolutely sure you'll be able to keep.

Rewarding Days

8, 9, 13, 14, 22, 27

Challenging Days

3, 12, 16, 19, 30

Pisces | December

Relaxation and Recreation

The holidays look to be easygoing, comfortable days for you, Pisces, thanks to a playful, affectionate Leo Moon, who'll arrive on the 24th, just in time for gatherings with family and other dear ones. The 21st will also be warm and wonderful, as loving Venus and Neptune come together in a lovely, emotional trine.

Lovers and Friends

Try to avoid getting into arguments or disputes with friends around the 8th or 9th, Pisces, especially if neither of you is willing to compromise. Watch what you say, and be sure not to force anyone to do something they really don't want to do. Consider whether it might be best to just table the matter for a bit.

Money and Success

Venus will set off for shrewd Scorpio on the 2nd, giving you the opportunity to reexamine any business deals you've recently become involved with that aren't exactly working out as planned. The Sun and fiery Mars will square off that day, too, so the urge to cut your losses and wash your hands of the whole situation will be tough to resist.

Tricky Transits

Assertive Mars and Neptune will collide on the 7th in your sign and in your solar first house of personality, Pisces, and you may end up feeling extremely angry without really knowing why. The thing is, if you give yourself some time to think things over in private and you're honest with yourself, you'll figure out where your feelings are coming from.

Rewarding Days

12, 13, 16, 22, 24, 25, 28

Challenging Days

1, 2, 5, 6, 7, 19, 31

Pisces Action Table

These dates reflect the best—but not the only—times for success and ease in these activities, according to your Sun sign.

	JAN	FEB	MAR	APR	MAY	JUN	JUL	AUG	SEP	OCT	NOV	DEC
Move					18			18				
Start a class	5		4			2			7		8	
Join a club		6		12		1			6			22
Ask for a raise	23			7				20		24		
Get professional advice		14		29	11		13		11			
Get a loan			1							27		16
New romance	1	10					8	25			9	20
Vacation			2		19	12	5			26	25